FINAL DRAFT 2

Series Editor: **Jeanne Lambert**
The New School

Jill Bauer
North Seattle College
Mike S. Boyle
Sara Stapleton
North Seattle College

with
Wendy Asplin, University of Washington

CAMBRIDGE
UNIVERSITY PRESS

Shaftesbury Road, Cambridge CB2 8EA, United Kingdom

One Liberty Plaza, 20th Floor, New York, NY 10006, USA

477 Williamstown Road, Port Melbourne, VIC 3207, Australia

314–321, 3rd Floor, Plot 3, Splendor Forum, Jasola District Centre, New Delhi – 110025, India

103 Penang Road, #05-06/07, Visioncrest Commercial, Singapore 238467

Cambridge University Press & Assessment is part of the University of Cambridge.

It furthers the University's mission by disseminating knowledge in the pursuit of education, learning and research at the highest international levels of excellence.

www.cambridge.org
Information on this title: www.cambridge.org/9781009345453

First published 2016
Update published 2022

20 19 18 17 16 15 14 13 12 11 10 9 8 7 6 5 4 3 2 1

Printed in Mexico by Litográfica Ingramex, S.A. de C.V.

A catalog record for this publication is available from the British Library.

Cataloging in Publication data is available at the Library of Congress.

ISBN 978-1-009-34545-3 Student's Book with Writing Skills Interactive Level 2
ISBN 978-1-107-49542-5 Teacher's Manual Level 2

Additional resources for this publication at www.cambridge.org/finaldraft

Cambridge University Press & Assessment has no responsibility for the persistence or accuracy of URLs for external or third-party Internet Web sites referred to in this publication and does not guarantee that any content on such Web sites is, or will remain, accurate or appropriate. Information regarding prices, travel timetables, and other factual information given in this work is correct at the time of first printing but Cambridge University Press & Assessment does not guarantee the accuracy of such information thereafter.

Art direction, book design, and photo research: emc design limited
Layout services: emc design limited

CONTENTS

SCOPE AND SEQUENCE

All academic vocabulary words appear on the Academic Word List (AWL) or the General Service List (GSL). ◉ All academic collocations, academic phrases, and common grammar mistakes are based on the Cambridge Academic Corpus.

WRITING SKILLS	GRAMMAR FOR WRITING	AVOIDING PLAGIARISM
Audience Capitalization and punctuation Titles	Adverb clauses	Recognizing plagiarism
Unity Subject-verb agreement	Quantifiers	Why do students plagiarize?
Vivid language Avoiding sentence fragments, run-ons, and comma splices Correct pronoun use	Adjectives	What is common knowledge?
Distinguishing between fact and opinion Verb tense consistency Coordinating conjunctions	Count and noncount nouns	Finding good sources
Background information The thesis statement	Word forms	Using information without plagiarizing
Sentence variety	Simple present and present progressive tenses	Citing print sources
Clarity Transition words and phrases for sequential order	Phrasal verbs	Citing Internet sources
Hooks	Comparative adjectives	Strategies for paraphrasing

ACADEMIC WRITING AND VOCABULARY

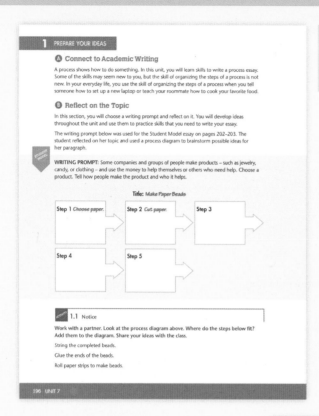

1 PREPARE YOUR IDEAS

A Connect to Academic Writing

A process shows how to do something. In this unit, you will learn skills to write a process essay. Some of the skills may seem new to you, but the skill of organizing the steps of a process is not new. In your everyday life, you use the skill of organizing the steps of a process when you tell someone how to set up a new laptop or teach your roommate how to cook your favorite food.

B Reflect on the Topic

In this section, you will choose a writing prompt and reflect on it. You will develop ideas throughout the unit and use them to practice skills that you need to write your essay.

The writing prompt below was used for the Student Model essay on pages 202–203. The student reflected on her topic and used a process diagram to brainstorm possible ideas for her paragraph.

WRITING PROMPT: Some companies and groups of people make products – such as jewelry, candy, or clothing – and use the money to help themselves or others who need help. Choose a product. Tell how people make the product and who it helps.

Title: *Make Paper Beads*

Step 1 *Choose paper.* → Step 2 *Cut paper.* → Step 3

Step 4 → Step 5

1.1 Notice

Work with a partner. Look at the process diagram above. Where do the steps below fit? Add them to the diagram. Share your ideas with the class.

String the completed beads.

Glue the ends of the beads.

Roll paper strips to make beads.

196 UNIT 7

Students begin to explore a rhetorical mode and connect it to their everyday lives.

B Academic Phrases

Research tells us that the phrases in bold below are commonly used in academic writing.

2.2 Focus on Purpose

Read the paragraph. Then match the phrases in bold to the purpose, or reason why, the writer used them.

Farming in the United States

The United States is a large country with a lot of open land, and as a result, the country has always had many farms. From TV shows and movies, these farms may **appear to be** small, simple places that one family owns. **It is possible** to farm that way today, of course, but more and more farms are actually corporate farms owned by large companies. Overall, there are **a variety of** kinds of farms in the United States, including family farms, corporate farms, and cooperative farms owned by several farmers.

PHRASE	PURPOSE
...... 1 appear to be	a show there is more than one kind
...... 2 It is possible	b show that something seems a certain way
...... 3 a variety of	c show that something can be done

CLASSIFICATION ESSAYS 167

Next, students prepare for their writing by learning corpus-informed academic vocabulary, collocations, and phrases.

The first model shows students how the rhetorical mode is applied in a real-world setting, helping them recognize that academic writing is all around them.

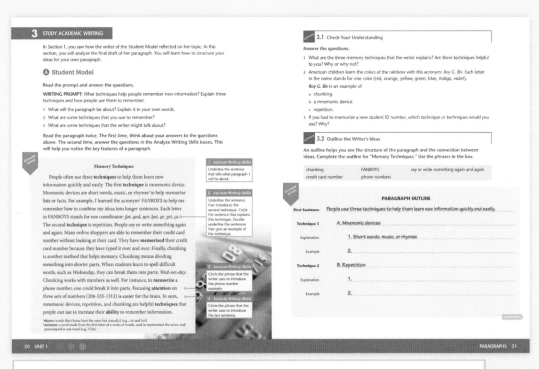

The second model shows a typical assignment from a college writing course. Students analyze this in detail, preparing for their own writing.

4 SHARPEN YOUR SKILLS

In this section, you will learn writing and grammar skills that will help make your writing more academic and accurate.

A Writing Skill 1: Vivid Language

Writers of descriptive paragraphs try to use **vivid language** in their descriptions. Vivid language includes words that help readers imagine they can see or feel the description. Using clear, specific adjectives is one way to make your language more vivid. Avoid unclear, vague adjectives such as *good, bad, nice, happy,* and *fun.*

Here are some vivid adjectives that you can use in descriptions.

VIVID LANGUAGE: SPECIFIC ADJECTIVES	
Size	*average, gigantic, huge, miniature, tiny*
Sound	*high, low, noisy, peaceful, quiet, silent*
Color	*bold, bright, clean, dark, dull, faded, light, multi-colored, red*
Shape	*curvy, round, short, straight, square, triangular*
Texture	*fuzzy, rough, sharp, smooth, soft*
Taste	*delicious, fresh, juicy, salty, sharp, sour, strong, sweet, weak*
Feelings	*content, enjoyable, entertaining, exciting, heartbroken, sorrowful*

4.1 Use Vivid Language

Work with a partner. Look at the photograph and complete the paragraph below. Replace the adjectives in parentheses with specific adjectives from the chart above or other adjectives.

Junkanoo

On the day after Christmas in the Bahamas, people gather for a national celebration called *Junkanoo*. Performers dress in _____ (big) (1) costumes and do African dances. All of the costumes have very _____ (nice) colors and (2) interesting designs. There is drumming and music. The celebration is _____ (loud) (3) and very exciting. Above all, though, it is _____ (fun). Junkanoo makes (4) people in the Bahamas feel _____ (5) (happy). This day celebrates the value of freedom.

Students develop an extensive skill set, preparing them for every aspect of academic writing.

Students study specific applications of grammar for the writing task and learn to avoid common mistakes (informed by the Cambridge Learner Corpus).

Avoiding Common Mistakes 👁

Research tells us that these are the most common mistakes that students make when using quantifiers in academic writing.

1 Use *an amount of* with a noncount noun. Use *a number of* with plural count nouns.

    A number of
A large amount of gestures used in North America are offensive in other parts of the world.

    a small amount
The British will often add *a small number* of milk to their tea.

2 For small amounts that are enough, use *a little* or *a few.*

    a little
It is important to leave little space between you and the person you are talking to.

3 Use *the* or a possessive adjective after a quantifier with *of.*

    the
People in a new culture experience many cultural differences. However, very few of cultural differences are understood quickly.

    my
Very few of friends send letters through the postal service.

4.4 Editing Task

Find and correct five more mistakes in the paragraph below.

Rules of Etiquette on Social Media

    number
A large amount of people around the world are using social media sites like Facebook, Twitter, and Instagram, but few of users know the basic etiquette. The first rule is to avoid sharing all of your thoughts. A few of friends probably share every piece of information from their day, but not everyone wants to hear what they had for lunch. Another rule is to think carefully before adding photos that include other people. Sharing some photos may be embarrassing to others, so it is polite to ask your friends for permission. For example, ask friends before adding any photos of them in swimsuits. An amount of fights between friends happen when they make negative comments on each other's web page. Making positive comments will help avoid problems and show little respect. Finally, an amount of businesses are now searching social media sites before they hire new employees. If they see crazy pictures or a lot of complaints on a person's website, they will not hire that person. In conclusion, it is important to think carefully before sharing any information on the Internet.

E Avoiding Plagiarism

Plagiarism is using someone else's ideas in your writing.

I turned in a draft of a paragraph about the importance of education. My instructor thought that I might be plagiarizing. I used the Internet for ideas, but I don't think I copied anything. What is plagiarism? How do I know if I'm plagiarizing?

Caro

Dear Caro,

The Internet is a wonderful resource, but be careful! Make sure you write the ideas in your own words. Don't cut and paste or copy sentences from the Internet. Instructors in many countries, such as the United States and Canada, value _your_ writing and ideas.

Yours truly,

Professor Wright

RECOGNIZING PLAGIARISM

Read the original paragraph from a text. Then look at the examples of plagiarism in two students' writing.

Original Paragraph

New research shows that exercise helps brain function in older people. Those who take regular walks can pay attention better. According to another study, jogging regularly improves memory. In other studies, mice ran on a small wheel, and they got more blood into their brains. Those mice could learn and remember better than other mice.

The students wrote:	Recognizing plagiarism:
Student A Exercise is good for the brain. <u>New research shows that exercise helps brain function in older people. Those who take regular walks can pay attention better. Jogging regularly improves memory.</u>	This student <u>cut and pasted</u> whole sentences. This is plagiarism.
Student B According to the author, exercise improves <u>brain function in older people.</u> If they walk regularly, they are able to pay attention better. Also, <u>jogging improves memory.</u> Mice who <u>ran on a small wheel</u> received <u>more blood in their brains. Then they could learn and remember better than others.</u>	This student <u>did not use her own words</u>. She only changed a few words. This is plagiarism.

Students learn to acknowledge others' work and ideas and appropriately incorporate them into their writing.

Equipped with the skills and language they have developed throughout the unit, students pull their ideas into the writing process to produce a final draft.

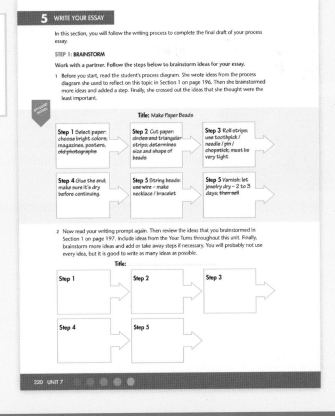

5 WRITE YOUR ESSAY

In this section, you will follow the writing process to complete the final draft of your process essay.

STEP 1: BRAINSTORM

Work with a partner. Follow the steps below to brainstorm ideas for your essay.

1 Before you start, read the student's process diagram. She wrote ideas from the process diagram she used to reflect on this topic in Section 1 on page 196. Then she brainstormed more ideas and added a step. Finally, she crossed out the ideas that she thought were the least important.

Title: *Make Paper Beads*

Step 1 *Select paper: choose bright colors; magazines, posters, old photographs*

Step 2 *Cut paper: circles and triangular strips; determines size and shape of beads*

Step 3 *Roll strips: use toothpick / needle / pin / chopstick; must be very tight*

Step 4 *Glue the end; make sure it's dry before continuing.*

Step 5 *String beads: use wire – make necklace / bracelet*

Step 5 *Varnish: let jewelry dry – 2 to 3 days; then sell*

2 Now read your writing prompt again. Then review the ideas that you brainstormed in Section 1 on page 197. Include ideas from the Your Turns throughout this unit. Finally, brainstorm more ideas and add or take away steps if necessary. You will probably not use every idea, but it is good to write as many ideas as possible.

Title: _____

Step 1

Step 2

Step 3

Step 4

Step 5

THE TEAM BEHIND *FINAL DRAFT*

SERIES EDITOR

Jeanne Lambert brings 20 years of ESL classroom, teacher training, and materials writing experience to her role as series editor of *Final Draft*. Jeanne has taught at Columbia University, City University of New York (CUNY), and The New School, specializing in academic writing and English for Academic Purposes. While at Columbia University, she taught writing courses in both the American Language Program and for the School of International and Public Affairs. At CUNY, she co-designed a faculty development program to help high school teachers align their ESL reading and writing curriculum with college standards. She has worked as an ESL Methods Practicum instructor and currently teaches academic writing at The New School.

AUTHORS

Jill Bauer is an ESL Instructor at North Seattle College and has been teaching ESL for 10 years. She has an MA-TESOL from Seattle Pacific University, where she has also taught teacher training courses. She has worked on curriculum development projects for the Washington State Board of Community & Technical Colleges Basic Education for Adults program.

Mike S. Boyle has been an author, editor, and writer of dozens of English language teaching titles over the last 15 years. He has taught English to learners of all ages in Japan and the United States, and is a graduate of the Iowa Writers' Workshop, where he taught courses in academic and creative writing.

Sara Stapleton is an ESL instructor at North Seattle College and has been teaching ESL for 15 years. She holds an MEd in TESOL from Seattle University and specializes in academic writing, transition to college, study skills, advanced ESL, and Integrated Basic Education and Skills Training.

ACADEMIC WRITING ADVISORY PANEL

The Advisory Panel is comprised of experienced writing instructors who have helped guide the development of this series and have provided invaluable information about the needs of ESL student writers.

Laszlo Arvai, Borough of Manhattan Community College, New York, NY
Leo Kazan, Passaic County Community College, Paterson, NJ
Amy Nunamaker, San Diego State College, San Diego, CA
Amy Renehan, University of Washington, Seattle, WA
Adrianne Thompson, Miami Dade College, Miami, FL

Final Draft was influenced by the opinions and insights of classroom teachers from the following institutions:

UNITED STATES Alabama: Cleburne County High School, Gadsden State Community College, University of Alabama; **Arizona:** Arizona State University, Northern Arizona University, Pima Community College; **Arkansas**: Arkansas State University, University of Arkansas, University of Central Arkansas; **California:** Allan Hancock College, Berkeley High School, California State Polytechnic University, California State University East Bay, California State University Fullerton, California State University Long Beach, California State University Los Angeles, City College of San Francisco, College of San Mateo, De Anza College, Diablo Valley College, East Los Angeles College, El Camino College, The English Center, Evergreen Valley College, Foothill College, Fullerton College, Gavilan College, Glendale Community College, Hollywood High School, Imperial Valley College, Las Positas College, Los Angeles City College, Los Angeles Southwest College, Mendocino College, Mills College, Mission College, Modesto Junior College, Monterey Peninsula College, Palomar College, Pasadena City College, Placer High School, Roybal Learning Center, Sacramento City College, Sacramento State, San Diego Community College District, San Francisco State University, San Jose City College, Santa Ana College, Santa Barbara City College, Santa Monica College, Santa Rosa Junior College, Skyline College, Stanford University, Taft College, University of California Berkeley, University of California Davis, University of California Irvine, University of San Diego, University of San Francisco, University of Southern California, West Valley Community College; **Colorado:** Community College of Aurora, Front Range Community College, Red Rocks Community College, University of Colorado; **Connecticut:** Central Connecticut State University, Enfield High School, Naugatuck Valley Community College, Norwalk Community College, Post University, University of Bridgeport, University of Hartford; **Florida:** Barry University, Florida SouthWestern State College, Florida State University, Hillsborough Community College, Indian River State College, Miami Dade College, Robinson High School, St. Petersburg College, University of Central Florida, University of Florida, University of Miami, University of South Florida; **Georgia:** Augusta State University, Emory University, Georgia Institute of Technology, Georgia Perimeter College, Georgia State University, Interactive College of Technology, Pebblebrook High School, Savannah College of Art and Design, West Hall High School; **Hawaii:** Hawaii Community College, Hawaii Tokai International College, Kapiolani Community College, Mid-Pacific Institute, University of Hawaii; **Idaho:** College of Western Idaho, Northwest Nazarene University; **Illinois:** College of DuPage, College of Lake County, Elgin Community College, English Center USA, Harold Washington College, Harper College, Illinois Institute of Technology, Lake Forest Academy, Moraine Valley Community College, Oakton Community College, Roosevelt University, South Suburban College, Southern Illinois University, Triton College, Truman College, University of Illinois, Waubonsee Community College; **Indiana:** Earlham College, Indiana University, Purdue University; **Iowa:** Divine Word College, Iowa State University, Kirkwood Community College, Mercy College of Health Sciences, University of Northern Iowa; **Kansas:** Donnelly College, Johnson County Community College, Kansas State University, Washburn University; **Kentucky:** Bluegrass Community & Technical College, Georgetown College, Northern Kentucky University, University of Kentucky; **Maryland:** Anne Arundel Community College, Howard Community College, Montgomery College, Johns Hopkins University; **Massachusetts:** Boston University, Mount Ida College, New England Conservatory of Music, North Shore Community College, Phillips Academy, Roxbury Community College, The Winchendon School, Worcester State University; **Michigan:** Central Michigan University, Eastern Michigan University, Grand Rapids Community College, Lansing Community College, Macomb Community College, Michigan State University, Saginaw Valley State University, University of Detroit Mercy, University of Michigan, Wayne State University, Western Michigan University;

Minnesota: Century College, Saint Paul College, University of Minnesota, University of St. Thomas; **Mississippi:** Mississippi College, Mississippi State University; **Missouri:** Missouri State University, St. Louis Community College, Saint Louis University, University of Missouri, Webster University; **Nebraska:** Union College, University of Nebraska; **Nevada:** Truckee Meadows Community College, University of Nevada; **New Jersey:** Bergen Community College, The College of New Jersey, Hudson County Community College, Kean University, Linden High School, Mercer County Community College, Passaic County Community College, Rutgers University, Stockton University, Union County College; **New Mexico:** University of New Mexico; **New York:** Alfred State College, Baruch College, Borough of Manhattan Community College, City University of New York, Columbia University, Fashion Institute of Technology, Hofstra University, Hostos Community College, Hunter College, John Jay College of Criminal Justice, Kingsborough Community College, The Knox School, LaGuardia Community College, LIC/LISMA Language Center, Medgar Evers College, New York University, Queens College, Queensborough Community College, Suffolk Community College, Syracuse University, Zoni Language Centers; **North Carolina:** Central Carolina Community College, Central Piedmont Community College, Duke University, Durham Technical Community College, South Piedmont Community College, University of North Carolina, Wake Technical Community College; **North Dakota:** Woodrow Wilson High School; **Ohio:** Columbus State Community College, Cuyahoga Community College, Kent State University, Miami University Middletown, Ohio Northern University, Ohio State University, Sinclair Community College, University of Cincinnati, University of Dayton, Wright State University, Xavier University; **Oklahoma:** University of Oklahoma; **Oregon:** Chemeketa Community College, Clackamas Community College, Lewis & Clark College, Portland Community College, Portland State University, Westview High School; **Pennsylvania:** Pennsylvania State University, University of Pennsylvania, University of Pittsburgh; **Puerto Rico:** Carlos Albizu University, InterAmerican University of Puerto Rico; **Rhode Island:** Johnson & Wales University, Salve Regina University; **South Carolina:** University of South Carolina; **South Dakota:** Black Hills State University; **Tennessee:** Southern Adventist University, University of Tennessee, Vanderbilt University, Williamson Christian College; **Texas:** Austin Community College, Colleyville Heritage High School, Collin College, Dallas Baptist University, El Paso Community College, Houston Community College, Lone Star College, Northwest Vista College, Richland College, San Jacinto College, Stephen F. Austin State University, Tarrant County College, Texas A&M University, University of Houston, University of North Texas, University of Texas, Victoria College, West Brook High School; **Utah:** Brigham Young University, Davis Applied Technology College, Weber State University; **Vermont:** Green Mountain College; **Virginia:** College of William & Mary, Liberty University, Northern Virginia Community College, Tidewater Community College; **Washington:** Bellevue College, EF International Language Centers, Gonzaga University, The IDEAL School, Mount Rainier High School, North Seattle College, Peninsula College, Seattle Central College, Seattle University, Shoreline Community College, South Puget Sound Community College, Tacoma Community College, University of Washington, Whatcom Community College, Wilson High School; **Washington, DC:** George Washington University, Georgetown University; **West Virginia:** West Virginia University; **Wisconsin:** Beloit College, Edgewood College, Gateway Technical College, Kenosha eSchool, Lawrence University, Marquette University, St. Norbert College, University of Wisconsin, Waukesha County Technical College

CANADA **British Columbia:** Vancouver Island University, VanWest College; **Nova Scotia**: Acadia University; **Ontario**: Centennial College, University of Guelph, York University; **Québec**: Université du Québec

MEXICO **Baja California:** Universidad de Tijuana

TURKEY **Istanbul**: Bilgi University, Özyeğin University

1 PARAGRAPHS

EDUCATION: BRAINPOWER

"People usually forget 90 percent of what they learn in a class within thirty days."

Hermann Ebbinghaus
(1850–1909)

About the Author:

Hermann Ebbinghaus was a German psychologist. He studied memory and learning. He made many discoveries that remain important today.

Work with a partner. Read the quotation about memory. Then answer the questions.

1 Do you agree with Hermann Ebbinghaus? Do you and people you know quickly forget most of what you learn in class?

2 Do you find some things easier to remember than others? Give an example of something that is easy for you to remember.

Ⓐ Connect to Academic Writing

In this unit, you will learn skills to help you write a clear, organized paragraph. Some of the skills may seem new to you, but the skill of explaining your ideas is not new. In your everyday life, you often explain your ideas. For example, you may tell a friend why you like a movie or explain to your teacher why you came late to class.

Ⓑ Reflect on the Topic

In this section, you will be given a writing prompt and reflect on it. You will develop ideas throughout the unit and use them to practice skills you need to write your paragraph.

The writing prompt below was used for the Student Model paragraph on page 20. The student reflected on her topic and used a cluster diagram to brainstorm possible ideas for her paragraph.

WRITING PROMPT: What techniques help people remember new information? Explain three techniques and how people use them to remember.

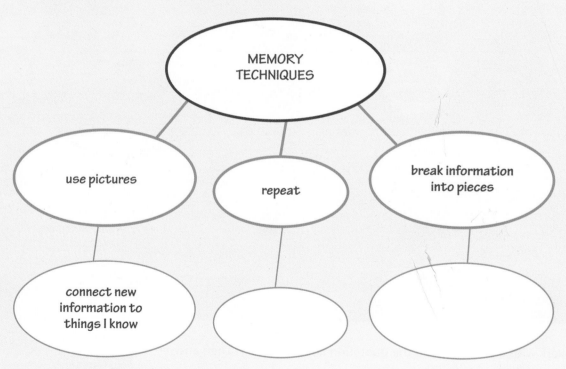

ACTIVITY **1.1** Notice

Work with a partner. Look at the cluster diagram above. Discuss two more techniques the student could write about and add them to the diagram. Share your ideas with the class.

Read the prompt and follow the directions below.

WRITING PROMPT: Choose a skill that you learned, such as riding a bike, cooking, playing a musical instrument, or playing a sport. Describe three ways that you learned the skill.

1 Choose the skill you will describe and write it in the blue circle in the cluster diagram below.

2 Consider all the ways that you learned this skill. Write three of those ways in the other circles.

3 Compare cluster diagrams with a partner.

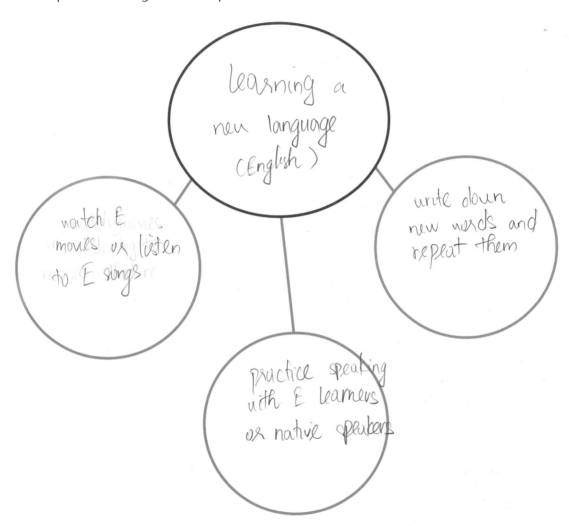

learning a new language (English)

watch E movies or listen to E songs

write down new words and repeat them

practice speaking with E learners or native speakers

In this section, you will learn academic language that you can use in your paragraph. You will also notice how a professional writer uses this language.

Ⓐ Academic Vocabulary

The words below appear throughout the unit. They are from the Academic Word List or the General Service List. Using these words in your writing will make your ideas clearer and your writing more academic.

ability (n)	critical (adj)	memorize (v)	sharpen (v)
attention (n)	master (v)	mental (adj)	technique (n)

 2.1 Focus on Meaning

Work with a partner. Read the sentences. Decide the meaning of the bold words and circle the correct definitions.

1 Sam **memorizes** the spellings of new vocabulary words. He writes them over and over again until he knows them perfectly. **Memorize** means

 a to show a strong interest in something or someone.

 b to learn something so that you will remember it exactly.

2 New mothers often give their newborn baby all of their **attention**. They watch the baby carefully and listen for every cry. **Attention** means

 a focusing all your interest on something.

 b learning a particular job or activity well.

3 Physical health and **mental** health are connected. When you take good care of your body, you also take care of your mind. **Mental** means

 a about the mind or thinking skills.

 b about the body or athletic skills.

4 In sports, coaches teach their players **techniques** that help them improve their skills. Players work on each technique during practice. **Technique** means

    a doing an activity a certain way.   b focusing on an activity.

5 Some people have the **ability** to do complex math problems in their head. They do not need to use a calculator. **Ability** means

    a a skill.   b a job.

6 Lang Lang, a famous young classical pianist, **mastered** the piano by practicing more than six hours a day when he was growing up. **Master** means

    a to make.   b to do something very well.

7 Sleep is **critical** for people's mental and physical health. Getting enough sleep is essential to stay healthy. **Critical** means

    a serious.   b very important.

8 These days some people are using video games to **sharpen** their thinking skills. They want their thinking skills to be better. **Sharpen** means

    a to work.   b to improve.

B Academic Collocations 👁

Collocations are words that are frequently used together. Research tells us that the academic vocabulary in Part A is commonly used in the collocations in bold below.

ACTIVITY 2.2 Focus on Meaning

Work with a partner. Match the collocations in bold to their meanings. Write the letters.

.... 1 Babies have a very short **attention span**. A three-month-old can concentrate on one thing for only about 10 seconds.

    a a way to learn

.... 2 Some **memory loss** happens as people get older. Older people who have serious memory loss may not remember things, such as the names of their children.

    b to watch and listen carefully

.... 3 Good **mental health** helps us in everyday life. We can do better if we have positive feelings about ourselves and our lives.

    c how long someone can focus on one thing

.... 4 When you **pay attention**, you learn new skills more quickly because you keep your focus and therefore notice much more.

    d the problem of forgetting information, people, and experiences

.... 5 There are many **learning techniques** that help us learn new vocabulary. One technique is to create a mental picture of a word.

    e the state of mind that shows if people feel good about themselves and about life

C Writing in the Real World

The author of "Exercise for the Brain" organizes her ideas clearly to make sure that her reader understands them.

Before you read, answer this question: What kind of exercise do you think the brain needs?

Now read the article. Think about your answer to the question as you read.

BY STELLA O'REILLY

EXERCISE
FOR THE
BRAIN

1   Like the body, the brain needs exercise to stay healthy. If we want to have a healthy body, we can go to the gym and work out,[1] but how do we exercise the brain? According to research, brain exercise can be anything that stimulates[2] the brain, for example, working on crossword puzzles or learning a language. However, researchers are finding that some activities stimulate our brains more than others. What activities are the best brain exercises?

2   Being involved in social relationships may be the best kind of brain exercise, according to researchers Melinda Smith and Lawrence Robinson. Relationships with friends and family are **critical** for our **mental health**, but *any* social activity can exercise and benefit the brain. This means interacting[3] at work or at a party is good for the brain. Even hanging out[4] with friends is an excellent brain exercise.

[1]**work out:** do exercises to make the body stronger
[2]**stimulate:** encourage something to grow, develop, or become active
[3]**interact:** communicate or react to each other
[4]**hang out:** spend a lot of free time with a group of people

3 Scientists have also discovered that laughter can exercise many parts of the brain. We hear a joke, we try to figure out what is funny, and then we laugh. Each step of this process makes us use different parts of the brain. Laughter also has the benefit of helping us relax. When we relax our muscles, we feel calm, which is good for the heart. Putting more laughter in our life is easy. One way is to **pay attention** and find the silly moments in life. Another way is to watch a comedy with family or friends.

4 Finally, brain research suggests that people should never stop learning because learning is brain exercise, too. New, challenging, and fun learning is best. Activities such as learning to play an instrument or juggle are especially effective since they require the body and brain to work together in new ways.

5 It is not necessary to **master** any of these activities. However, it is important to do them regularly.

6 All these **techniques** of exercising the brain have multiple benefits. They **sharpen** the brain and slow down **memory loss**. Moreover, with **techniques** like these, exercising our brains can be a lot more fun than going to the gym to exercise our bodies!

 2.3 Check Your Understanding

Answer the questions.

1 The author suggests three ways to exercise your brain. Which of these do you already use? Explain.

2 According to the article, which of these activities would be the best exercise for your brain?

   a watching a scary movie

   b watching a funny movie by yourself

   c watching a funny movie with a group of friends

3 Which social activities does the author recommend to exercise the brain? What other social activities do you think would exercise the brain?

 2.4 Notice the Writing

Answer the questions.

1 Look at the second paragraph. The first sentence tells you the main idea of the paragraph. Which two sentences give examples to help explain the main idea?

2 Look at the fourth paragraph. Which sentence gives the main idea of the paragraph?

In Section 1, you saw how the writer of the Student Model reflected on her topic. In this section, you will analyze the final draft of her paragraph. You will learn how to structure your ideas for your own paragraph.

Ⓐ Student Model

Read the prompt and answer the questions.

WRITING PROMPT: What techniques help people remember new information? Explain three techniques and how people use them to remember.

1 What will the paragraph be about? Explain it in your own words.

2 What are some techniques that you use to remember?

3 What are some techniques that the writer might talk about?

Read the paragraph twice. The first time, think about your answers to the questions above. The second time, answer the questions in the Analyze Writing Skills boxes. This will help you notice the key features of a paragraph.

STUDENT MODEL

Memory Techniques

People often use three **techniques** to help them learn new information quickly and easily. The first **technique** is mnemonic device. Mnemonic devices are short words, music, or rhymes[1] to help memorize lists or facts. For example, I learned the acronym[2] *FANBOYS* to help me remember how to combine my ideas into longer sentences. Each letter in FANBOYS stands for one coordinator: *for, and, nor, but, or, yet, so.* The second **technique** is repetition. People say or write something again and again. Many online shoppers are able to remember their credit card number without looking at their card. They have **memorized** their credit card number because they have typed it over and over. Finally, chunking is another method that helps memory. Chunking means dividing something into shorter parts. When students learn to spell difficult words, such as *Wednesday*, they can break them into parts: *Wed-nes-day*. Chunking works with numbers as well. For instance, to **memorize** a phone number, one could break it into parts. Focusing **attention** on three sets of numbers (206-555-1313) is easier for the brain. In sum, mnemonic devices, repetition, and chunking are helpful **techniques** that people can use to increase their **ability** to remember information.

[1]**rhyme:** words that rhyme have the same last sound(s) (e.g., *cat* and *hat*)
[2]**acronym:** a word made from the first letter of a series of words, used to represented the series, and pronounced as one word (e.g., USA)

1 Analyze Writing Skills
Underline the sentence that tells what paragraph 1 will be about.

2 Analyze Writing Skills
Underline the sentence that introduces the second technique. Circle the sentence that explains this technique. Double underline the sentences that give an example of the technique.

3 Analyze Writing Skills
Circle the phrase that the writer uses to introduce the phone number example.

4 Analyze Writing Skills
Circle the phrase that the writer uses to introduce the last sentence.

3.1 Check Your Understanding

Answer the questions.

1 What are the three memory techniques that the writer explains? Are these techniques helpful to you? Why or why not?

2 American children learn the colors of the rainbow with this acronym: *Roy G. Biv*. Each letter in the name stands for one color (red, orange, yellow, green, blue, indigo, violet).

   Roy G. Biv is an example of

   a chunking.

   b a mnemonic device.

   c repetition.

3 If you had to memorize a new student ID number, which technique or techniques would you use? Why? ~~repetition~~

 3.2 Outline the Writer's Ideas

An outline helps you see the structure of the paragraph and the connection between ideas. Complete the outline for "Memory Techniques." Use the phrases in the box.

chunking	FANBOYS	say or write something again and again
credit card number	phone numbers	

PARAGRAPH OUTLINE

First Sentence — People use three techniques to help them learn new information quickly and easily.

Technique 1 — A. Mnemonic devices

Explanation — 1. Short words, music, or rhymes

Example — 2. ~~remembering acronym holidays in~~

Technique 2 — B. Repetition

Explanation — 1. say or write sth again and again

Example — 2. ~~credit card numbers able to remember their credit card number~~

(CONTINUED)

Technique 3	C.	Chunking
Explanation	1. Break something into shorter parts	
Example	2. Spelling of difficult words, like Wednesday	
Example	3. to memorize a phone numbers	
Last Sentence	In sum, mnemonic devices, repetition, and chunking are useful techniques that people can use to increase their ability to remember information.	

B Paragraphs

A writer uses a paragraph to discuss one **main idea**. Readers expect all the sentences in a paragraph to relate to, or be about, the main idea. To clearly develop a main idea, writers include the following parts in their paragraphs:

- a **topic sentence** to introduce the paragraph's main idea to the reader. The topic sentence is often the first sentence of the paragraph. In the topic sentence, writers tell what they will discuss in the paragraph.

- **supporting sentences** to give specific information about the main idea. Writers also include sentences that offer **details**, or more information about the ideas in the supporting sentences. The information that writers give in their supporting sentences and details includes explanations, examples, and facts.

- a **concluding sentence** to bring the paragraph to a clear and satisfying close. Often writers use this sentence to restate their topic sentence.

An easy way to picture the organization in a paragraph is to think of a sandwich. Look at the sandwich diagram for the Student Model paragraph on page 20.

Topic sentence: People often use three techniques to help them learn new information quickly and easily.

Supporting sentence 1: The first technique is mnemonic device. (+ Details)

Supporting sentence 2: The second technique is repetition. (+ Details)

Supporting sentence 3: Finally, chunking is another method that helps memory. (+ Details)

Concluding sentence: In sum, mnemonic devices, repetition, and chunking are helpful techniques that people can use to increase their ability to remember information.

3.3 Notice

Look at the sandwich diagram on page 22. Read and circle the correct answers.

1 The ideas in the topic sentence and the concluding sentence are **similar / different**.

2 The writer **always / sometimes** added details to the supporting sentences.

3 The order of ideas in the concluding sentence is **the same as / different from** the order of ideas in the three supporting sentences.

 **3.4** Identify the Sentences

Write *TS* for the topic sentence, *SS + D* for supporting sentences plus details, and *CS* for the concluding sentence. Then, on a separate sheet of paper, write the sentences in the correct order to make a well-organized paragraph.

.............1 First, when we laugh, our muscles relax. We feel less stress. This is good for our hearts.

.............2 In conclusion, laughter has important benefits for our bodies, our minds, and our relationships.

.............3 Laughter is good for us because it helps us relax, improves our mood, and strengthens our relationships.

.............4 The second reason is that laughter makes us feel better. When we laugh, we feel less sad. We forget our problems for a while.

.............5 Finally, laughter makes our relationships stronger. People who laugh together feel more connected to each other.

THE TOPIC SENTENCE

The **topic sentence** has two important parts: the topic and the controlling idea.

- The **topic** answers the question: What is this paragraph about?
- The **controlling idea** answers the question: What part of the topic will this paragraph focus on?

Read the topic sentences below and notice the two parts.

TOPIC   CONTROLLING IDEA

People use three techniques to help them learn new information quickly and easily.

CONTROLLING IDEA   TOPIC

There are important benefits to eating well.

 3.5 Recognize Topics and Controlling Ideas

Read the topic sentences. Circle the topics and underline the controlling ideas.

1 My brain helps me memorize facts, take interesting photos, and make important decisions.

2 Eating well can improve a student's attention span.

3 Laughter has many health benefits.

4 Good soccer players use their brains in three essential ways.

CONTROLLING IDEAS

A topic could have many different **controlling ideas**; that is, there are many different ways that a writer could discuss a topic. Think about the topic of the brain. You could write about:

- why the brain is complex
- how the brain changes as we age
- how people can improve the way their brains function
- how children's and adults' brains are different
- how you use your brain at work

The writing prompt will help you determine how to discuss the topic and what your controlling idea will be.

 3.6 Match

The cluster diagram below shows four possible controlling ideas for the topic "eating well." Read the writing prompts and complete the sentences with the appropriate controlling ideas.

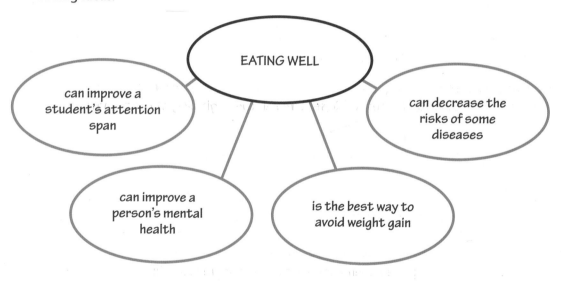

1 **WRITING PROMPT:** Describe the effects of eating well on people's mental health.

Eating well .can improve a person's mental health.

2 **WRITING PROMPT:** Discuss the relationship between diet and disease.

Eating well ..can improve way to person's mental health decrease..

3 **WRITING PROMPT:** Describe the effect of eating well on the behavior of a student with problems paying attention.

Eating well ..can improve a student's attention span

4 **WRITING PROMPT:** Discuss the relationship between the way a person eats and maintaining a healthy weight.

Eating well ..is the best way to avoid

GOOD TOPIC SENTENCES

Because the topic sentence gives readers the main idea, writers need to write topic sentences carefully. They need to make sure the topic sentences are not too general and not too specific for the information in the paragraph.

Suppose you have to write a paragraph for this prompt: *Mastering a new skill can be challenging. What behaviors and attitudes are important for mastering a skill?*

Consider these three possible topic sentences:

It is frustrating to master a new skill.

This sentence is too general. It doesn't mention behaviors or attitudes.

People must have a positive attitude to master the skill.

This sentence is too specific because it focuses on only one specific attitude and skill rather than skills in general, and it doesn't address behaviors.

Certain behaviors and attitudes are important for mastering a new skill: practicing the skill, believing you can master it, and accepting help as you progress.

This sentence is the best because it fully addresses the prompt, mentioning a new skill, behaviors, and attitudes and introducing them.

 3.7 Choose the Topic Sentence

Work with a partner. Read the paragraphs and label the topic sentences *too general, too specific,* or *best*. Then write the best topic sentence at the beginning of the paragraph.

1

Techniques for Studying Creatively

.... One creative technique for studying is to draw new words and ideas. Drawing and coloring help artistic students memorize information. They can remember the word because of the image in their mind. Another creative way to study is to act out the words and information. For example, a student could say the words aloud, like an actor. Some researchers say that when we use our bodies while we are learning, we remember the information more easily. Finally, singing new words and ideas using familiar songs is a fun and effective way to study. Music helps the mind easily remember the information. In conclusion, studying can be much more fun if students use creative techniques.

a There are several techniques for learning.   ....

b Studying can be more effective if students think creatively.   ....

c Music and acting out information are good creative
  techniques.   ....

2

The Amazing Effects of Computer Games

.... First, there are special computer games that people can use. For example, one game trains the brain by having people remember letters that the computer speaks aloud. People have to pay attention and listen carefully. The game slowly increases the number of letters. Another way is to meditate. Scientists say that people who meditate can calm their bodies and their minds more easily than other people. A calm mind can focus better. Also, some people can improve their attention spans by getting more sleep. The amount of sleep people get can affect their ability to pay attention. In sum, today people with short attention spans have different ways to help them develop longer attention spans.

a Games are a good way for people with short attention spans to improve their attention spans. ....

b People with short attention spans can address their problems. ....

c There are several ways that people with short attention spans can improve their attention spans. ....

 3.8 Write Topic Sentences

Work with a partner. Write topic sentences for the paragraphs.

1

Developing the Brain in Children

There are 3 ways to develop the children's brain First, children need loving care. When children feel love, they can develop trust. Trust is important for brain development. Second, children need interaction. Parents should talk and sing to their babies and show them new experiences. This is important to build connections in the brain. Finally, children need healthy food. The brain depends on good food to grow and develop. In conclusion, there are certain things that children must have that are critical for good brain development.

2

My Most Useful Tool – My Brain

The most useful tool to me is my brain First, I use my brain to memorize names. When I see my customers, I say hello and say their names. Repeating like this helps me remember the names. I think this is important for a businessperson. I can see that my customers like it, too. Second, my brain is important when I order merchandise. For example, I have to decide the quantity of the products, like shirts and pants. I have to calculate how much money I have and how much merchandise I can order. Third, I use my brain to study the news. My friends think I have a sharp mind because I like to debate current events. In short, my brain helps me be successful professionally and socially.

6 **UNIT 1**

3.9 Apply It to Your Writing

Look at the cluster diagram you created for your writing prompt in Section 1 on page 15. Write a topic sentence. Share your topic sentence with a partner. What information do you think your partner will include in the paragraph?

....

....

SUPPORTING SENTENCES AND DETAILS

Writers use **supporting sentences** to make the main ideas of their paragraphs clear and convincing to readers. In the supporting sentences, writers give readers the important points about the main idea. These important points often include facts, examples, and explanations.

Read the supporting sentences for the topic sentence below. All of these sentences support the main idea in the topic sentence.

Topic sentence: *Sleep is critical to mental and physical health in many important ways.*

Supporting sentences:

Most adults need seven to eight hours of sleep each night. (This sentence gives a fact – a statistic or number.)

When people do not sleep well, they cannot concentrate or remember things. (This sentence gives an example of why sleep is critical.)

Sleep gives the body time to clean itself of chemicals that are bad for the brain. (This sentence gives an explanation of why sleep is critical.)

Many times writers include one or two **details** – facts, examples, and explanations – for each supporting sentence. Details strengthen the main idea and make the paragraph more interesting.

 3.10 Recognize Supporting Sentences and Details

Work with a partner. Circle the supporting sentences and underline the details.

How the Brain Helps Reduce Stress

Starting a new job is a stressful experience that makes the brain work its hardest. First, there are many things to learn about the job. When I started my first full-time job, I had to have four hours of training. I took notes, but the manager spoke very fast and explained things very quickly. My brain had to work hard, but I finally learned. Also, there were so many new names to remember. I used fun techniques like matching a word with the person's name. For example, I memorized Harry's name because he always wore a hat. In sum, with a new job there is a lot to remember, but the brain can do it.

ACTIVITY **3.11** Write Supporting Sentences

Write two supporting sentences for each topic sentence. Discuss your sentences with a partner.

1 **Topic sentence:** Starting a new school is a stressful experience for many students.

_____

_____

2 **Topic sentence:** Learning a new language is a challenging experience that makes the brain work hard.

_____

_____

ACTIVITY **3.12** Write Details

Choose one topic sentence from Activity 3.11 and write it below. Copy the first supporting sentence and add a detail. Then copy the second supporting sentence and add a detail.

_____

_____

_____

_____

_____

_____

ACTIVITY **3.13** Apply It to Your Writing

YOUR TURN

Think about the ideas you wrote for your writing prompt in Activity 1.2 on page 15 and your topic sentence in Activity 3.9 on page 27. Choose one way that you learned a skill and use it to write your first supporting sentence below. Add details.

_____

_____

_____

_____

CONCLUDING SENTENCES

Writers use **concluding sentences** to end their paragraphs. A concluding sentence reminds the reader of the main idea of the paragraph. The concluding sentence:

* restates the topic sentence in a new way. It does not simply repeat the words in the topic sentence.

  Topic sentence: *People can use **memory techniques** to help them **remember** something better and longer.*

  Concluding sentence: *In sum, there are **techniques** that people can use so that they **do not forget** information.*

* may summarize the main points from the supporting sentences that were in the paragraph.

  Topic sentence: *People need to practice **healthy habits** for **better mental health**.*

  Concluding sentence: *In conclusion, **good sleep, healthy eating, and regular exercise** can help people feel good about themselves and their lives.*

* does *not* add new information. The sentence below would *not* be a good concluding sentence because it adds *also good for the body*. The body is not part of the main idea in the topic sentence.

  Topic sentence: *People need to practice **healthy habits** for **better mental health**.*

  Concluding sentence: *In conclusion, **good sleep, healthy eating, and regular exercise** can keep the brain healthy. ~~Those things are also good for the body.~~*

* often begins with a transition phrase, such as *in sum, in short,* or *in conclusion*.

 3.14 Choose Concluding Sentences

Work with a partner. Read the topic sentences. Circle the best concluding sentence. Explain your answers.

1 **Topic sentence:** People can use various techniques to prevent stress.

   a In short, people today live very stressful lifestyles.

   b In conclusion, exercising and having hobbies are two ways that help people avoid stress.

   c In short, people can use various techniques to prevent stress.

2 **Topic sentence:** Creative study habits can help students learn better.

   a In conclusion, students can improve their learning by making the way they study more creative.

   b In sum, when students use different ways of studying, they can be better students, and there are many ideas on the Internet to help them.

   c In sum, there are many ideas on the Internet to help students learn more.

3 **Topic sentence:** There are three practical ways to improve attention span.

   a In conclusion, these three simple techniques can help people increase their attention spans.

   b In sum, many people have difficulty improving their attention spans.

   c In short, there are only three ways to improve your attention span.

Work with a partner. Write concluding sentences for the paragraphs below.

1

Techniques for Learning to Dance

I learned how to dance using three techniques that my dance instructor taught me. I practiced steps over and over. While waiting for the bus, I pretended I was a ballerina, and I jumped and moved my arms. I also watched other dancers perform. I noticed how they moved, and I thought about how I could move like that. I listened to music when I was doing other things. My dance instructor wanted us to know the music really well. As I did my chores, I listened and imagined myself dancing. *In short, my dance instructor taught me three ways to dance*

2

Negative Behaviors of Teenagers

Teenagers have certain negative behaviors. Part of the reason is that the frontal areas of their brains are still developing. These areas are involved in planning, thinking about consequences, and controlling behavior. That is why teenagers often do not think about consequences. When they want to do something, they do it. They don't realize until afterward that it was a bad idea. Also, they can be rude. For example, they ignore their parents and yell and get mad when someone criticizes them. Finally, they are moody. They are often very happy one moment and then very sad the next. Their moods can make them difficult to live with. *In conclusion there are some negative behavior the youth have nowadays*

Ⓐ Writing Skill 1: Audience

Before writing, writers ask: Who is going to read my writing? The answer is the writer's **audience**. In school, you will usually write for your instructor and classmates, an academic audience. The following guidelines can help you write appropriately for an academic audience.

1 Do not use abbreviations, contractions, or informal language.

                            because
People should reduce their stress ~~b/c~~ high stress can cause memory loss.

         cannot
The brain ~~can't~~ work well without nutritious food.

                     instructions
The writer includes tips and ~~stuff~~ for exercising.

2 Use the appropriate person, or pronoun, in your writing. Academic writing usually uses third person (*he, she, it, they*) rather than first person singular (*I*) or second person (*you*). The writing prompt will help you determine what is appropriate.

WRITING PROMPT: What learning techniques should students use to increase memory?

Students   *they*
~~You~~ *should use learning techniques to remember more, and ~~you~~ should use these techniques consistently.*

If the writing prompt asks for a personal response, it is acceptable to use first person (*I*).

WRITING PROMPT: What learning techniques do you use to increase memory?

*There are three main learning techniques that **I** use to increase my memory.*

 4.1 Correct Mistakes

Find and correct five more examples of inappropriate language.

WRITING PROMPT: Sometimes students have study habits that are not helpful. Discuss three common study mistakes that students make. How can they change these unhelpful study habits?

The Negative Study Habits of Students

Students can change unhelpful study habits. One unhealthy habit is that many students

stay awake all night to study before a test. This means that they are tired on test day and

     cannot
usually ~~can't~~ pay attention. They can change this habit by studying the week before the test.

Then they can get enough sleep the night before the test b/c they are already prepared. Next,

it is common for students to procrastinate. They wait until the last minute to do homework

and writing assignments. As a result, they don't have time to ask the teacher questions or do research. You need to start assignments early. Finally, many students wanna study at home, but there are too many distractions there. For example, they may fall asleep, watch TV, or check Facebook. They could go to the library to study in a quiet place. In short, if you have any of these unhelpful habits, they can change by planning a better study schedule, not procrastinating, and finding a less distracting place to study.

B Writing Skill 2: Capitalization and Punctuation

Writers usually follow these **capitalization rules**.

RULES FOR CAPITALIZATION	
1 Always capitalize the pronoun *I*. (Writers do not use this pronoun frequently in academic writing.)	**I** *I use certain techniques when **i** study.*
2 Begin each word of a new sentence with a capital letter.	*Remember that the brain is a muscle. It has to be exercised.*
3 Capitalize proper nouns. Proper nouns are the names of specific people, places, or things: *Alice Quinn, Boston, Google.* Capitalize titles of people (*Mr., Mrs., Ms., Dr., Professor*) used before the person's name. Do not capitalize common nouns. Common nouns are general names of people, places, and things (*professor, city, computer*).	PROPER NOUN PROPER NOUN ***Dr. Thomas Crook*** *from **England** says to laugh more every day.* COMMON NOUN COMMON NOUN *Many **researchers** have studied the **effects*** COMMON NOUN *of **video games**.*

 4.2 Correct Capitalization

Read the sentences. If the capitalization is correct, write *correct*. If it is wrong, rewrite the sentence with the correct capitalization.

1 I remember information best when I write it down.
   correct

2 professor smith encourages students to read their notes after class.
   Professor Smith encourages students to read their notes after class.

3 For example, listening to classical music can increase concentration.

4 some researchers in the united states are creating a map of the brain.

5 Many Doctors recommend eating a small meal before studying.

Writers usually follow these **punctuation rules.**

RULES FOR PUNCTUATION

1 Always end sentences with a period, a question mark, or an exclamation point. Do *not* use a comma.	*People also need to eat well for good brain health.* *When is the best time of day to study?* *A child's brain is not fully developed, it is still changing.* (. It) *Food is the fuel for the brain!* (.)
Writers usually do not use exclamation points in academic writing.	
2 Use commas in a list of three or more words, phrases, or clauses.	*Brain development is quite different in children, teenagers, and adults.* *People can sharpen their minds by going for a walk, playing their favorite sport, or going to the gym regularly.*
3 Use commas before words like *and* and *but* when they connect two independent clauses.	INDEPENDENT CLAUSE *Many people believe video games are harmful,* INDEPENDENT CLAUSE *but researchers disagree.*
4 Use commas after dependent clauses that start with words such as *if, when,* and *although* when they begin a sentence.	*When people sleep well, they feel mentally sharper.*
5 Use commas after transition words and phrases such as *first, also, finally, for example, however,* and *in addition.*	*For example, small children have very short attention spans.*

 4.3 Correct Punctuation

Rewrite the paragraph with correct punctuation on a separate sheet of paper.

Healthy Habits for Good Mental Health

People need to practice healthy habits for better mental health First a good night's sleep is critical to brain health, Adults need seven to eight hours of sleep each night When people do not sleep well they cannot concentrate or remember things well Also people need to eat well, Unhealthy foods do not provide the brain with enough energy to work efficiently Finally people need to exercise to keep their brains sharp. The brain needs a lot of oxygen to stay healthy and exercise brings oxygen to the brain In sum good sleep healthy eating and regular exercise can keep the brain healthy.

C Writing Skill 3: Titles

The **title** of a paragraph gets the reader's attention **and** tells the reader what the paragraph will be about. Here are some ways to write good titles.

TITLES	
1 Choose a title that is not too specific and not too general. A title that is too specific or too general will not give your readers a clear idea of what the paragraph is about.	GOOD TITLE: *Memory Techniques* TOO SPECIFIC: *Memorizing Phone Numbers, Addresses, and Dates* TOO GENERAL: *Memory*
2 Use a phrase. Do not use a complete sentence. Do not put a period at the end of a title.	~~*Healthy Habits Are Good for the Brain.*~~ GOOD TITLE: *Healthy Habits for a Healthy Brain*
3 Center titles over the paragraph.	***Memory Techniques*** *People can use memory techniques to help them remember things better and longer. …*
4 Capitalize nouns, verbs, adjectives, and adverbs. Do not capitalize prepositions, conjunctions (*and, but*), or articles (*a/an, the*) unless they are the first word in the title.	ADJ NOUN PREP ADJ NOUN *Mental Benefits of Video Games* ART ADJ NOUN PREP ADJ NOUN *The Best Exercises for Mental Health*

 4.4 Choose Titles

Work with a partner. Read the paragraph writing prompts and three possible titles. Check (✓) the best title for the paragraph. Discuss why the other two choices are not good titles for the paragraph.

1 **WRITING PROMPT:** What are three ways people can stay mentally sharp when they get older? Give examples to support your ideas.

    Title A: Growing Older and Staying Mentally Sharp

    Title B: Older Adults Should Play Video Games

    Title C: Growing Older and Staying Mentally Sharp by Playing Video Games

2 **WRITING PROMPT:** These days very young children use technology like smartphones and computers. Do you think that this is harmful or helpful to them?

    Title A: Smartphones and Computers Are Harmful to Children

    Title B: Technology and Children

    Title C: The Effects of Technology on Young Children

3 **WRITING PROMPT:** Medical students have to memorize thousands of medical vocabulary terms. What learning techniques could help these students master this vocabulary?

☐ Title A: Learning Techniques

☐ Title B: Memorizing Medical Vocabulary

☐ Title C: Medical Students Can Use Games to Learn Vocabulary

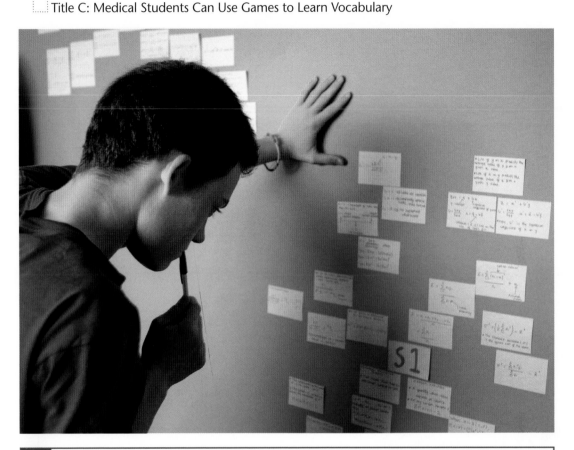

 4.5 Capitalize Titles

Rewrite the titles with correct capitalization.

1 how positive thinking Helps The Brain   ....

2 linking Smell and Memory   ....

3 Mastering A language   ....

4 Teaching others improves memory   ....

Ⓓ Grammar for Writing: Adverb Clauses

Adverb clauses begin with **subordinators** (or **subordinating conjunctions**) such as *when, since, while, although, even though,* and *because*. An adverb clause has a subject and verb, but it is not a sentence by itself; it is a dependent clause. This means that it must always be joined to a main clause (or an independent clause). Writers use adverb clauses and subordinators to show readers the relationship between ideas. They put the important idea in the main clause and a related idea in the subordinate clause; the subordinator shows how the two ideas relate.

Follow these rules when using adverb clauses.

ADVERB CLAUSES

1	An adverb clause can come before or after the main clause.	**SUBORDINATOR** **ADVERB CLAUSE** *Since my grandmother wants to stay mentally sharp,* **MAIN CLAUSE** *she is studying Arabic.* **MAIN CLAUSE** *My grandmother is studying Arabic* **SUBORDINATOR** **ADVERB CLAUSE** *since she wants to stay mentally sharp.*
2	Use a comma when the adverb clause comes before the main clause, but not if it follows the main clause. For subordinators that express contrast, such as *while* and *although*, use a comma when the subordinator starts or ends a sentence.	*Because stress harms the brain, people should learn to relax.* *People should learn to relax because stress harms the brain.* *Video games can benefit the brain, although many people believe they are harmful.* *Although many people believe they are harmful, video games can benefit the brain.*
3	Use *because* and *since* to give a reason.	*Because/Since stress harms the brain, people should learn to relax.*
4	Use *although* and *even though* to show a strong contrast or unexpected idea. Use *while* to show a contrast that is not as strong.	*Although/Even though many people believe video games are harmful, they can benefit the brain.* *While stress is usually bad for the brain, it is impossible to avoid.*

 4.6 Choose Subordinators

A Circle the correct subordinator.

1 Some people meditate every morning **because /, although** they say it helps them focus during the day.

2 Exercise helps the brain **because / , while** being inactive hurts the brain.

3 **Since / Even though** students know that they should get more rest before a test, they do not get it.

4 **Because / Although** jokes exercise our brain, listening to jokes is good for us.

5 My mother prepares healthy foods for our family **because / , even though** these foods are often more expensive.

B Look at A. Underline the main clauses and circle the adverb clauses. Notice the order and punctuation of the clauses.

ACTIVITY **4.7** Connect Ideas

Choose an appropriate subordinator to connect the ideas. Then write a sentence with an adverb clause that comes before the main clause.

1 teenagers have trouble thinking about consequences / the brain is still growing during adolescence

Because the brain is still growing during adolescence, teenagers have trouble

thinking about consequences.

2 listening to music as I write helps me focus / I know my parents do not believe it

....

....

3 relationships with family and friends are important for mental health / all social connections are good for the brain

....

....

4 people should try to get enough sleep / sleep helps people to function well

....

....

Avoiding Common Mistakes

Research tells us that these are the most common mistakes students make when using adverb clauses in academic writing.

> 1. When the clause refers to the previous sentence, do not start a new sentence with subordinators such as *because*.
>
>   People enjoy telling ~~jokes. Because~~ ^jokes because^ it feels good to laugh.
>
> 2. Do not use *although* and *but* in the same sentence.
>
>   *Although people know that eating well can prevent disease, ~~but~~ many continue to eat unhealthy food.*
>
> 3. Make sure to spell *although* correctly.
>
>   ^Although^ ~~Althought~~ he studied every day, he did not master the vocabulary.

 **4.8** Editing Task

Find and correct four more mistakes in the paragraph below.

Cooking for Your Brain

Although cooking does not seem like an intellectual activity to some, ~~but~~ it can provide some benefits to the brain. First of all, it can be a way for people to learn new skills. If people try making new recipes from different cultures, for example, the brain has to learn skills and ideas. Learning is good for the brain. Because it makes the brain work hard. Also, cooking can be a physical activity. Although cooking is not as physical as jogging or playing soccer, but it still requires effort. This effort brings oxygen to the brain. The brain needs oxygen to work well. Finally, cooking can provide social interaction. Althought cooking does not have to be social, it can be. People join cooking classes or cook with friends at home. Social activities like these are beneficial for the brain. Because building relationships makes people feel closer and less stressed. This is good for the brain. In short, cooking is a necessity, but it can also help the brain function better.

E Avoiding Plagiarism

Plagiarism is using someone else's ideas in your writing.

I turned in a draft of a paragraph about the importance of education. My instructor thought that I might be plagiarizing. I used the Internet for ideas, but I don't think I copied anything. What is plagiarism? How do I know if I'm plagiarizing?

Caro

Dear Caro,

The Internet is a wonderful resource, but be careful! Make sure you write the ideas in your own words. Don't cut and paste or copy sentences from the Internet. Instructors in many countries, such as the United States and Canada, value <u>your</u> writing and ideas.

Yours truly,

Professor Wright

RECOGNIZING PLAGIARISM

Read the original paragraph from a text. Then look at the examples of plagiarism in two students' writing.

Original Paragraph

New research shows that exercise helps brain function in older people. Those who take regular walks can pay attention better. According to another study, jogging regularly improves memory. In other studies, mice ran on a small wheel, and they got more blood into their brains. Those mice could learn and remember better than other mice.

The students wrote:	Recognizing plagiarism:
Student A Exercise is good for the brain. <u>New research shows that exercise helps brain function in older people. Those who take regular walks can pay attention better. Jogging regularly improves memory.</u>	This student <u>cut and pasted</u> whole sentences. This is plagiarism.
Student B According to the author, exercise improves <u>brain function in older people.</u> If they walk regularly, they are able to pay attention better. Also, <u>jogging improves memory.</u> Mice who <u>ran on a small wheel</u> received <u>more blood in their brains.</u> Then they <u>could learn and remember better than others.</u>	This student <u>did not use her own words</u>. She only changed a few words. This is plagiarism.

4.9 Practice

Read the original paragraph on page 39 again. Then read the two students' paragraphs below. Underline the sentences or phrases that are plagiarized.

Student C

Several studies show that exercise is good for the brain. For example, older people who take regular walks can pay attention better. Also, jogging regularly can improve memory. Exercise is even good for mice. When they ran, they could learn and remember better than other mice.

Student D

Exercise leads to good brain health. Exercise improves brain function in older people. People who go for regular walks pay attention better. Jogging is also a good exercise. It leads to better memory. In other research, when mice ran on a small wheel, they got more blood into their brains. This led to better learning and remembering for the mice.

In this section, you will follow the **writing process** to complete the final draft of your paragraph. The writing process helps writers think about, organize, and write their ideas.

STEP 1: BRAINSTORM

Work with a partner. Follow the steps below to brainstorm ideas for your paragraph.

1 Before you start, read the student's brainstorm chart. She wrote ideas from the cluster diagram she used to reflect on this topic in Section 1 on page 14. Then, she brainstormed and wrote down more ideas as she thought about the topic. Finally, she underlined the three ideas that she thought were the strongest.

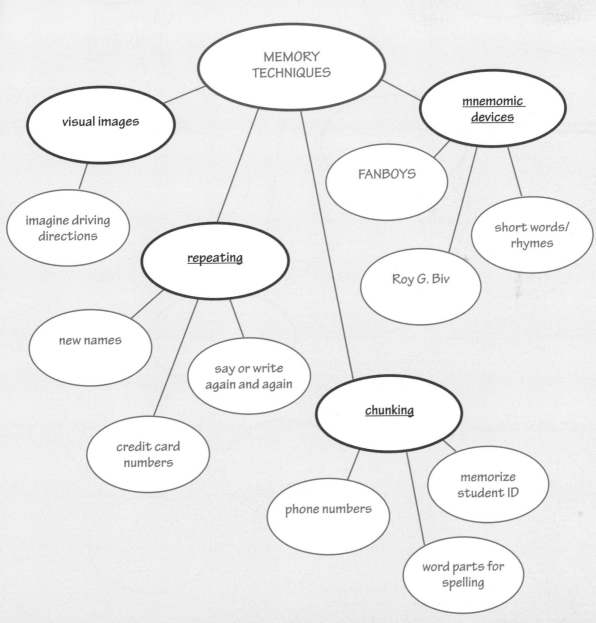

2 Now read your writing prompt again. Then review the ideas that you brainstormed in Section 1 on page 15. Write the best ones in the cluster diagram below. Include ideas from the Your Turns throughout the unit. Finally, brainstorm more ideas. You will probably not use every idea, but it is good to write as many ideas as possible.

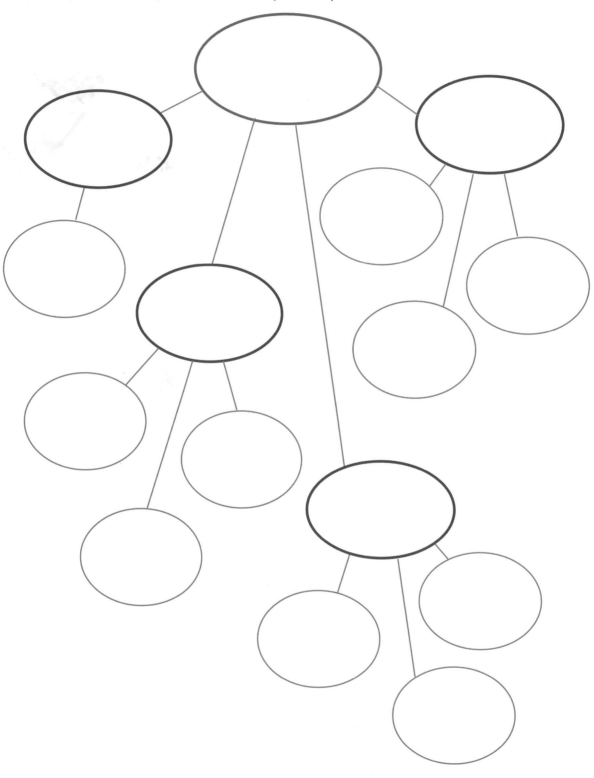

STEP 2: MAKE AN OUTLINE

Making an outline helps you organize ideas. Complete the outline below with ideas for your paragraph from Step 1 on page 42.

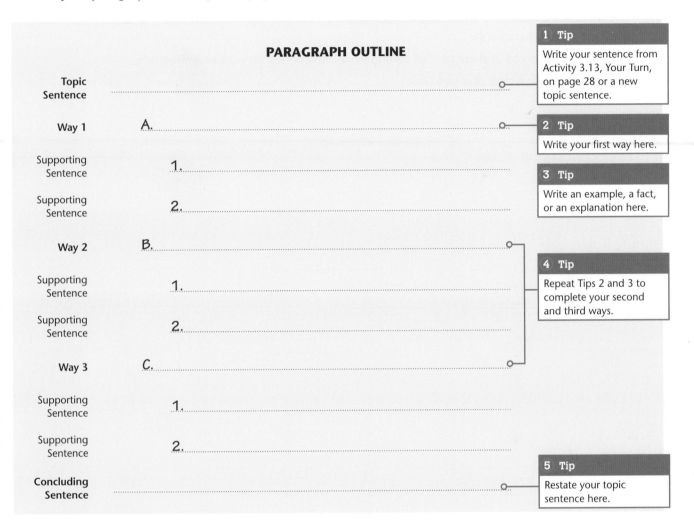

PARAGRAPH OUTLINE

Topic Sentence	....
Way 1	A. ....
Supporting Sentence	1. ....
Supporting Sentence	2. ....
Way 2	B. ....
Supporting Sentence	1. ....
Supporting Sentence	2. ....
Way 3	C. ....
Supporting Sentence	1. ....
Supporting Sentence	2. ....
Concluding Sentence	....

1 Tip
Write your sentence from Activity 3.13, Your Turn, on page 28 or a new topic sentence.

2 Tip
Write your first way here.

3 Tip
Write an example, a fact, or an explanation here.

4 Tip
Repeat Tips 2 and 3 to complete your second and third ways.

5 Tip
Restate your topic sentence here.

STEP 3: WRITE YOUR FIRST DRAFT

Now it is time to write your first draft. Here are some suggestions on how to get started.

1 Use your outline, notes, and the sentences you wrote in the Your Turns in this unit and in Step 2 above.

2 Focus on making your ideas as clear as possible.

3 Add a title.

After you finish, read your paragraph and check for basic errors.

1 Check that all sentences have subjects and verbs.

2 Look at every comma. Is it correct? Should it be a period?

3 Check that you have used commas after adverb clauses when they start sentences.

4 Check that your topic sentence and supporting sentences are clear.

STEP 4: WRITE YOUR FINAL DRAFT

1 After you receive feedback on your first draft, review it carefully. Fix any errors.

2 Make a note of errors that were most frequent. Try to avoid them as you write.

3 Review the Academic Words and Collocations from this unit. Are there any that you can add to your paragraph?

4 Turn to page 255 and use the Self-Editing Review to check your work one more time.

5 Write your final draft and hand it in.

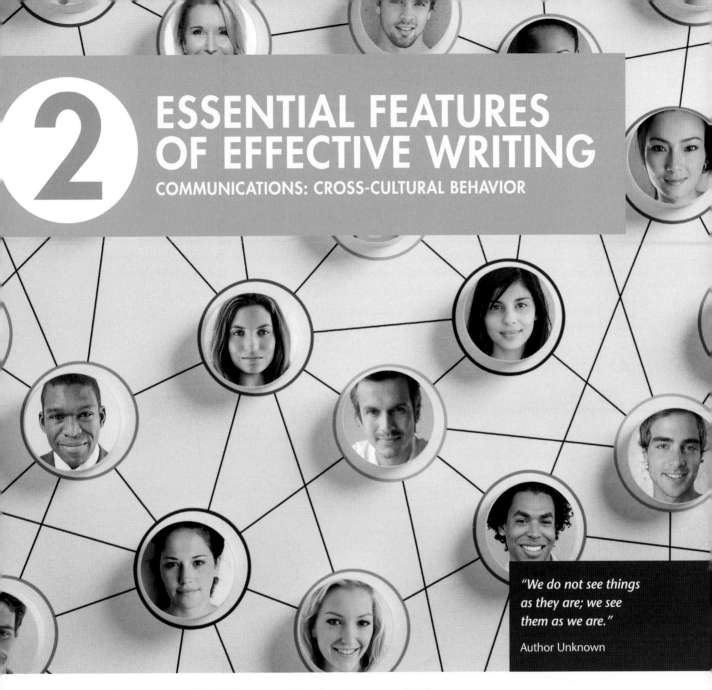

② ESSENTIAL FEATURES OF EFFECTIVE WRITING
COMMUNICATIONS: CROSS-CULTURAL BEHAVIOR

"We do not see things as they are; we see them as we are."

Author Unknown

Work with a partner. Read the quotation about communication.
Then answer the questions.

1 The quotation is about how we understand the world around us. What does it mean to see things as *we* are? How is that different from seeing things as *they* are?

2 Our culture influences how we see and experience the world. For example, it shapes how we behave and how we view the behavior of others. What are some behaviors that you view as polite? What are some behaviors that you view as impolite?

3 Have you ever changed your mind about someone's behavior? What made you see their behavior differently?

Ⓐ Connect to Academic Writing

In everyday conversation, people sometimes give information out of order. As a result, it may be confusing to follow their thoughts. When this happens, you can ask them questions to help make things clearer. Here is an example.

TOM: My grade on that last paper was really low. And I can't figure out why. But Mr. Tavela has office hours today at 1:00. Oh, and I'm meeting Matt at 2:00 – I almost forgot. I really have to talk with him.

SAMANTHA: With who? With Matt?

TOM: No. With Mr. Tavela, to ask him about my grade.

In academic writing, however, the reader cannot ask questions, so each paragraph must be clear and organized. Putting your ideas in a clear order is an important part of writing effectively. In this unit, you will learn skills that will help you write a paragraph in a logical and coherent order.

Ⓑ Reflect on the Topic

In this section, you will be given a writing prompt and reflect on it. You will develop ideas throughout the unit and use them to practice skills you need to write your paragraph.

The writing prompt below was used for the Student Model paragraph on page 52. The student reflected on his topic and used a cluster diagram to brainstorm ideas for his paragraph.

STUDENT MODEL

WRITING PROMPT: Describe the behavior and dress of people at a large celebration or event, such as an outdoor concert, a sports event, or a parade.

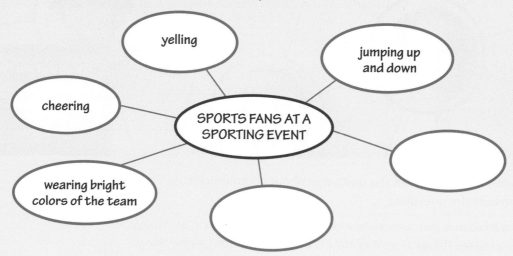

ACTIVITY **1.1** Notice

Work with a partner. Look at the cluster diagram above. What is the topic? Discuss two more ideas the student could write about and add them to the diagram. Share your ideas with the class.

Read the prompt below and follow the directions.

WRITING PROMPT: Choose a country and a common social situation. For example, you might choose dinner at a friend's home; a birthday, graduation, wedding, or other celebration; a college classroom or a workplace, or any other situation with rules for behavior. Describe the etiquette – or the appropriate behavior – for that situation.

1 Write the social situation in the blue circle in the cluster diagram.

2 Write three examples of etiquette for that situation in the other circles.

3 Compare cluster diagrams with a partner.

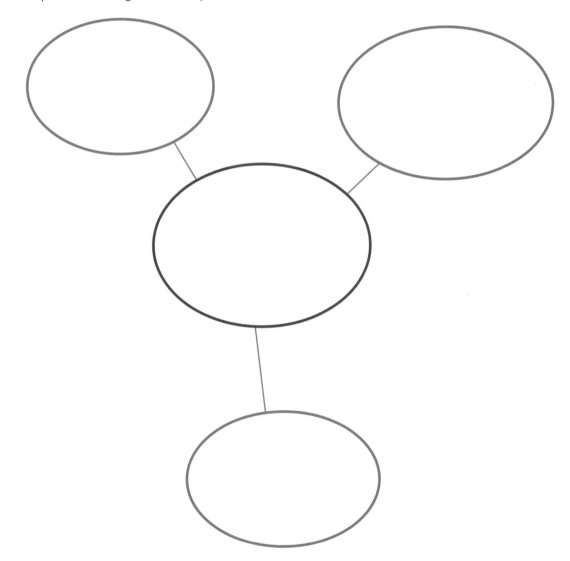

In this section, you will learn academic language that you can use in your paragraph. You will also notice how a professional writer uses this language.

Ⓐ Academic Vocabulary

The words below appear throughout the unit. They are from the Academic Word List or the General Service List. Using these words in your writing will make your ideas clearer and your writing more academic.

avoid (v)	communicate (v)	custom (n)	regard (v)
brief (adj)	culture (n)	interpret (v)	respectful (adj)

 2.1 Focus on Meaning

Work with a partner. Read the sentences. Decide the meaning of the bold words and circle the correct definitions.

1 In the Philippines, the **custom** is to wear slippers in the house. **Custom** means

    a usual behavior or tradition.   b clothing for special occasions.

2 We can **interpret** a smile in many different ways. For example, a smile can mean "thank you," "hello," or "I'm happy to see you." **Interpret** means

    a to confuse something.   b to describe or give a meaning to something.

3 When Americans say "How are you?" they wait a **brief** moment for an answer. **Brief** means

    a including much information.   b lasting only a short time.

4 People **communicate** many emotions with their face. **Communicate** means

    a to give information to others through speech, writing, or body movements.

    b to have something in common with other people.

5 Calling an older person *Sir* or *Madam* is **respectful**. **Respectful** means

    a polite to someone, especially someone older or more important.

    b not attentive to someone, especially someone older or more important.

6 In the United States, people look each other in the eye when they talk. It is rude to **avoid** looking into someone's eyes. **Avoid** means

    a to focus on.   b to not do something.

7 In some parts of the world, people **regard** showing the bottom of a shoe as very rude. **Regard** means

    a to have an opinion about someone or something.

    b to like someone or something.

8 In American **culture**, it is polite to shake hands when you meet someone. **Culture** means

    a cities and towns of a country.   b habits, traditions, and beliefs of a country or group.

B Academic Phrases

Research tells us that the phrases in bold below are commonly used in academic writing.

 2.2 Focus on Purpose

Read the paragraph. Then match the phrases in bold to the purpose, or reason why, the writer used them.

Nonverbal Behavior and What It Can Say about You

A number of nonverbal behaviors **can** communicate the relationship between two Americans in conversation. Personal space **is one of the** clearest signs. Friends and family usually stand or sit much closer to each other than strangers. **Another** sign that shows people's relationships **is** their eye contact. Two strangers will avoid looking each other in the eye for too long. They will make only brief eye contact. On the other hand, close friends will make eye contact for much longer periods. In brief, people can interpret a lot about relationships by watching nonverbal behaviors.

PHRASE	PURPOSE
.... 1 **A number of** nonverbal behaviors **can** …	a introduce a supporting sentence
.... 2 … **is one of the** clearest signs.	b add a supporting sentence
.... 3 **Another** sign that shows people's relationship **is** …	c introduce the main idea of the paragraph

C Writing in the Real World

The author of "Body Language in Translation" uses paragraphs to organize his ideas logically and connect them smoothly so that the reader is not confused.

Before you read, answer these questions: What is body language? Is body language different in different cultures?

Now read the article. Think about your answers to the questions above as you read.

BODY LANGUAGE IN TRANSLATION
By Pietro Laporta

1 What is your body language **communicating?** You need to think about more than just your verbal language when you are living in a new **culture.** Your body language, too, can show respect or disrespect.

2 The "OK" sign is **one of the** most common gestures in the United States. To make an OK sign, the thumb and first finger form a circle, and the other three fingers are upright and relaxed. Many Americans use this gesture to show approval.[1] However, in quite a few **cultures,** for example, in Greece and Brazil, this gesture is considered to be very rude.

3 **Another** gesture that Americans use to show approval **is** the "thumbs up" sign. To make a thumbs up, the thumb stands up straight and the other fingers curl into the palm. Americans need to **avoid** using this gesture in the Middle East or Australia because people there will **interpret** the thumbs up as an insult.

4 Do you look people in the eye when you are talking to them? In Japan, holding eye contact for too long is not **respectful.**

[1]**approval:** thinking that something or someone is good or right

However, Canadians show respect by looking people in the eye with only **brief** breaks to look away. If there is little eye contact, Canadians may feel that the other person is bored. The amount of eye contact that another **culture** expects is often a difficult thing for people to get used to.[2]

5 Greeting **customs** are also a very important part of body language, but there are many different ways to greet people. The French kiss each other on the cheek. Argentines often hug. Canadians shake hands. In some **cultures**, men and women do not touch each other at all when they greet. The rules for touching are very different from **culture** to **culture**. Therefore, **one of the** best ways to say hello may be to smile and nod only.

[2]**get used to:** to become familiar with something or someone

6 If you want to respect others, it is important to understand and use appropriate etiquette and body language. But what happens when you start using another **culture's** body language? Ann Cuddy, social psychologist and professor at Harvard Business School says, "Your body language shapes who you are." Does this mean that if you come to the United States from another country, for example, and you use American body language, you will become more American? It is something to think about.

2.3 Check Your Understanding

Answer the questions.

1 The article mentions ways you might not show respect in different cultures. Give three examples.

2 Ann Cuddy suggests that changing your body language can change you. Do you agree? Why or why not?

3 What are some common gestures in your culture? Have you learned any gestures from other cultures? If so, what are they?

2.4 Notice the Writing

Answer the questions.

1 Look at the second, third, fourth, and fifth paragraphs. How many types of body language does the article talk about?

2 Look at the paragraphs again. What are the different types of body language in each paragraph? Why do you think the author organized the paragraphs this way?

In Section 1 on page 46, you saw how the writer of the Student Model reflected on his topic. In this section, you will analyze the final draft of his paragraph. You will learn how to organize your ideas for your own paragraph.

Ⓐ Student Model

Read the prompt and answer the questions.

WRITING PROMPT: Describe the behavior and dress of people at a large celebration or event, such as an outdoor concert, a sports event, or a parade.

1 What will the paragraph be about? Explain in your own words.

2 What kinds of behavior could the writer include in his paragraph?

Read the paragraph twice. The first time, think about your answers to the questions above. The second time, answer the questions in the Analyze Writing Skills boxes. This will help you notice the key features of the paragraph.

STUDENT MODEL

The Behavior of Sports Fans

In many **cultures**, people's behavior at sports events is very different from their everyday behavior. One of these differences is in the clothing they wear. Many of the fans at a football game will wear clothes such as hats, shirts, or jackets in their team's colors. Some people **regard** colors like orange and gold as being too bold for their normal clothes. However, many sports fans wear bright colors like these to a game. A few fans even paint their faces in the team colors. Furthermore, sports fans often yell encouragement to their team or insults to the opposite team. If somebody does this at a restaurant, people may **interpret** the behavior as mental illness. However, it is the **custom** to yell and scream at a sports event. Lastly, physical contact is very common between strangers at important games. This is the strangest behavior because on a normal day, there is little physical contact between strangers. Usually strangers **avoid** touching each other. In contrast, quite a few strangers celebrate with each other if a team does something well. They "high-five" each other or give each other **brief** hugs. In short, people at sports events show unusual behavior that is different from their behavior in their everyday lives.

1 Analyze Writing Skills

Underline the topic sentence. Circle the controlling idea.

2 Analyze Writing Skills

How many supporting sentences did the writer include? ....

3 Analyze Writing Skills

Circle the words that show the author is adding another supporting sentence.

4 Analyze Writing Skills

Do all of the supporting sentences help explain the controlling idea? Circle *Yes* or *No*.

5 Analyze Writing Skills

Underline the concluding sentence.

3.1 Check Your Understanding

Answer the questions.

1 The writer talks about three differences between sports fan behavior and everyday behavior. What are they?

2 Is sports fan behavior similar in your culture? Share some examples of how it is the same or different.

3 What other social rules and behavior have you noticed at sports events?

 3.2 Outline the Writer's Ideas

Complete the outline for "The Behavior of Sports Fans." Use the phrases in the box.

hats, shirts, jackets	insulting the opposite team	yelling and screaming
hugging	physical contact with strangers	

PARAGRAPH OUTLINE

Topic Sentence   In many cultures, people's behavior at sports events is very different from their everyday behavior.

Behavior 1   A. Wearing team colors

     Detail   1.

     Detail   2. Bright colors

Behavior 2   B.

     Detail   1. Encouragement to own team

     Detail   2.

Behavior 3   C.

     Detail   1. High-fives

     Detail   2.

Concluding Sentence   In short, people at sports events show unusual behavior that is different from their behavior in their everyday lives.

B Coherence

Coherence is an important feature of effective writing. A paragraph has coherence if it is logically organized in a way that will be clear to readers. Writers put their ideas in an order that makes sense. This is called **logical order**.

Here are three common kinds of logical order:

- **chronological (time) order:** ideas organized in the order they happen or happened
- **spatial (location) order:** ideas organized by position of things in space
- **rank (importance) order:** ideas organized in the order of importance

Writers use chronological order to show the sequence of events or processes.

> *When people meet for the first time, they often follow specific etiquette. **First,** they smile and nod. **After that,** they say hello and introduce themselves. **Then** they shake hands using their right hands.*

Writers use spatial order to describe a physical space or object. They might describe what they see from left to right, top to bottom, or front to back.

> *In the United States, the table setting is always the same for a meal. The fork is **on the left side** on top of the napkin. The plate is **in the middle** of the place setting. **On the right side,** the knife and spoon are placed next to each other.*

Writers use rank order to show which ideas are most important. They might rank the ideas from most to least important or least to most important. In this example, the ranking is from least to most important.

> *Americans show their appreciation for music at a concert in three ways. **One** behavior is clapping. When a band is **good,** the audience claps at the end of it. **Another** behavior is clapping and cheering. When a band is **really good,** the audience claps and cheers. **Finally,** when a band is **amazing,** the audience stands up and claps and cheers.*

Work with a partner. Read the paragraphs below and write the type of order they use: *chronological*, *spatial*, **or** *rank*. **Underline the words or phrases that show that order.**

1

Unofficial Rules for Classroom Seating

In my experience, students in a classroom follow certain rules about where they sit and how they act. In the front are the smart students. These students want to see the board and take notes. They participate and ask questions. They are usually respectful to the instructor and do not speak when she speaks. In the back are the students who are tired or bored. They think class is boring. Breaks are too brief for them. They usually have their phones on their lap and look at them often. One custom that they have is avoiding questions. In the middle are students like me. We want to learn, but we do not want to participate too much. We are happy that the smart students talk. We do not act disrespectfully like the students in the back. In sum, I think that there are some rules in classrooms that students all know, and we sit where we feel comfortable.

The paragraph above uses .... order.

2

How Nurses Use Nonverbal Clues

Nurses can learn a lot about how their patients feel by looking for nonverbal clues. One method that is often useful is to look at patients' physical behaviors. For example, if a patient is feeling pain in the right arm, he or she will use the left arm more often. Another very useful method is to listen to how the patients' voices sound. If a patient is in pain, he or she will often speak more quietly and with less energy. Finally, and most importantly, nurses can watch the patients' facial expressions. Even if a patient is trying to hide pain, a nurse can sometimes see the pain in the patient's eyes. In short, patients may not explain how they feel, but good nurses will figure out how to take good care of them.

The paragraph above uses .... order.

3

Steps for Online Dating

There are certain steps that people follow to meet people online. First, the online dater creates a profile that describes his or her personality. The profile includes hobbies, interests, and career. After that, the online dater contacts people that he or she is interested in meeting. If the person responds, the two people will exchange a few messages. Finally, they will decide to meet face-to-face for the first time.

The paragraph above uses .... order.

3.4 Choose an Organization Pattern

With a partner, read the following writing prompts. Discuss which type of order you would use: chronological, spatial, or rank. There may be more than one correct answer.

1 Describe the etiquette for visiting an elderly relative.

2 What movements do babies make before they begin to walk?

3 Describe the traditional clothes for a bride in your culture.

3.5 Apply It to Your Writing

Look at the cluster diagram you created for your writing prompt in Section 1 on page 47. What is the best way to organize your paragraph – chronological, spatial, or rank order? Write sentences that show this organizational order.

....

....

....

TRANSITIONS

Another way to build coherence is by using **transitions** to connect your ideas. Transitions are words that show the way the ideas in the sentences of a paragraph are connected. Transitions help your reader follow your organization. The chart below gives examples of transitions for different paragraphs on small talk (casual conversation) in the United States.

CHRONOLOGICAL/SEQUENTIAL ORDER	
first, second, after that, then, next, finally, lastly	*First, strangers might smile at each other. Then one stranger asks a question.*
ADDITIONAL INFORMATION	
in addition, furthermore, also, too	*In addition, body language matters because strangers interpret body language. The distance between the two people is important, too.*
EXAMPLES	
for example, for instance	*Good topics are topics that others are likely to enjoy. For instance, many Americans enjoy discussing sports.*
DIFFERENCES	
however, on the other hand, in contrast	*Soccer is not a popular topic of conversation in Texas. In contrast, it is very popular in Seattle.*
CONCLUSIONS	
in conclusion, in short, in summary	*In short, topics of conversation, body language, and physical distance are all important parts of speaking with a stranger.*

3.6 Choose Transitions

Work with a partner. Read the paragraph and circle the appropriate transition.

Nonverbal Behavior in American Women and Men

In everyday situations in America, women and men act differently. They have different nonverbal behavior. **First, / In addition,** many women take turns when speaking. They wait
(1)
for the other person to finish before they talk. **Furthermore, / However,** women often nod or
(2)
offer other encouragement when they are listening to someone talk. **In short, / For example,**
(3)
they might say "uh-huh" or "really." Men do not do this as often. **In addition, / In short,** men
(4)
tend to make fewer gestures with their hands while they are talking. **After that, / In conclusion,**
(5)
American men and women both use nonverbal behavior but with some differences.

 3.7 Use Transitions

Read each sentence. Use the transition in parentheses to add another sentence.

1 Weddings have some very important traditions. (too)
   Holiday celebrations have important traditions, too.
2 When visitors arrive at a friend's house, they knock on the door. (after that)

3 Many people say thank you by sending a note. (in addition)

4 Men usually wear pants and a shirt to work. (on the other hand)

5 Etiquette includes many different kinds of behavior. (for instance)

6 Hosts will invite guests into their home. (then)

 3.8 Apply It to Your Writing

Look at your cluster diagram in Section 1 on page 47 and think about your writing prompt. Write two supporting sentences about your topic. Add a sentence with details to each sentence. Use transitions to connect the ideas.

1 Supporting sentence: ....
   Sentence with detail: ....
2 Supporting sentence: ....
   Sentence with detail: ....

In this section, you will learn writing and grammar skills that will help make your writing more academic and accurate.

Ⓐ Writing Skill 1: Unity

As you have already learned, a paragraph is about one topic. This serves several important purposes:

- to clearly explain your ideas about the topic

- to keep the readers' attention on your ideas

- to make your ideas easy to follow

When a paragraph stays on topic, or is about one topic, we say that it has **unity**. To achieve unity, all the sentences in a paragraph need to support the controlling idea in the topic sentence. If some sentences do not support the controlling idea, we say these sentences are off topic, or irrelevant. Effective writing avoids sentences that are off topic. Notice the crossed-out sentence in the following paragraph. Why is it off topic?

Behavior on the Baseball Field

Baseball players have different rules of behavior during a game than they have in their normal lives. One example is that they spit during a game. Many players chew sunflower seeds and spit the shells on the ground. ~~You might expect a lot of sunflowers to grow on the field, but I have never heard of this happening.~~ Another difference is in arguing. You can often see players argue with each other or the officials during the game. They stand chest to chest and yell in each other's face. They will get in trouble if they do this for too long during a game, but doing this at all is very bad behavior in normal life.

The crossed-out sentence is irrelevant because it does not add information about behavior. Instead, it introduces a new idea about sunflowers growing on the field. This idea does not belong in the paragraph. It makes the paragraph lose unity.

ACTIVITY **4.1** **Establish Unity in a Paragraph**

Read the paragraph. Find and cross out the two sentences that are off topic.

Gift Giving in the United States

In the United States, gift giving is a large part of the culture, and there are different rules for different occasions. One example of a celebration that involves gift giving is a child's birthday party. At these parties, close friends and relatives often give gifts to the birthday boy or girl. After all of the guests arrive, the birthday boy or girl opens the gifts in front of all of the guests. A child's first birthday is one year after the birth. In addition, people buy gifts for baby showers and weddings. For these parties, the celebrant often creates a gift registry, or list of the gifts that he or she wants. The guests then choose a gift from the list and buy it. I have never been to a baby shower, but I would like to go to one. Finally, for most occasions, people wrap gifts in colorful paper or bags and ribbons. However, gifts for some occasions, such as thank-you presents, do not need to be wrapped. In conclusion, knowing the rules for each occasion will make giving a gift much easier.

B Writing Skill 2: Subject-Verb Agreement

In English, subjects and verbs can be singular or plural. If you use a singular subject, you need a singular verb:

A child is playing.

If you use a plural subject, you need a plural verb:

Children are playing.

Here are some more specific rules that can help with subject–verb agreement.

RULES FOR SUBJECT-VERB AGREEMENT	
1 Ignore prepositional phrases when you are looking for the subject.	SUBJECT PREPOSITIONAL PHRASE VERB *Women in this country often work outside the home.*
2 Noncount nouns are singular.	NONCOUNT NOUN VERB *Coffee is a very popular beverage.*
3 A gerund phrase is singular.	GERUND PHRASE VERB *Shaking hands is very important in American culture.*
4 Most indefinite pronouns are singular. These pronouns include *everyone, everybody, someone, somebody, anyone, anybody, no one, nobody,* and *each.*	INDEFINITE PRONOUN VERB *Everybody takes a number from the machine.*

4.2 Use Subject-Verb Agreement

Read the paragraph. Use the simple present tense for the verbs in parentheses. Use the correct singular or plural verb form.

Active Listeners Make Good Listeners

A good listener _____(1)_____ (be) someone who pays attention to the speaker. A good listener _____(2)_____ (show) that he or she is actively listening. One method _____(3)_____ (be) to nod while the other person _____(4)_____ (talk). Speakers in a conversation _____(5)_____ (do not) always interpret a nod to mean agreement. Nodding also _____(6)_____ (show) that somebody _____(7)_____ (be) paying attention. Second, a good listener _____(8)_____ (give) the speaker other kinds of encouragement. For example, listeners _____(9)_____ (say) "uh-huh" or "OK." Finally, speakers _____(10)_____ (know) that the listeners _____(11)_____ (be) interested when listeners _____(12)_____ (ask) questions. Questions from a listener _____(13)_____ (help) continue the conversation. In short, communication _____(14)_____ (be) much better when the speaker and listener are both active.

ⓒ Grammar for Writing: Quantifiers

Quantifiers are words or phrases that show the number or amount of something. They describe how much or how many. Quantifiers are often used in academic writing to help writers avoid overgeneralizing. For example, think about the sentence *Men have short hair*. This sentence is an overgeneralization. It is false because it suggests that all men have short hair. To make it true, you can add a quantifier: *Some men have short hair*.

Here are some common quantifiers.

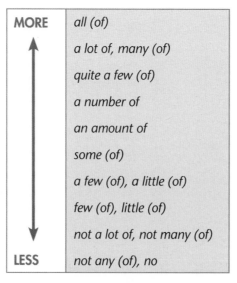

MORE	*all (of)*
	a lot of, many (of)
	quite a few (of)
	a number of
	an amount of
	some (of)
	a few (of), a little (of)
	few (of), little (of)
	not a lot of, not many (of)
LESS	*not any (of), no*

Follow these rules when using quantifiers.

QUANTIFIERS	
1 Use these quantifiers before plural count nouns only: *many, quite a few, a number of, a few, few, not many (of)*	COUNT NOUN *Many <u>children</u> learn etiquette quickly.* COUNT NOUN *There are **a number** of <u>ways</u> to show respect.*
2 Use these quantifiers before noncount nouns only: *an amount of, a little, little*	NONCOUNT NOUN *Talking loudly shows **little** <u>respect.</u>* NONCOUNT NOUN *People spend a large **amount of** <u>money</u> on gifts.*
3 Use these quantifiers before both count and noncount nouns: *all (of), a lot of, some (of), any (of), no*	NONCOUNT NOUN *Children always show **some** <u>respect</u> to adults.* COUNT NOUN ***Some** <u>friends</u> give gifts to each other on their birthdays.*
4 Use these quantifiers to show a small amount that is not enough: *few, little*	*I made **few** <u>friends</u> when I first arrived in this country. (not enough friends)* *During the holiday, people have **little** <u>time</u> to be alone.*
5 Use *of* to describe a specific noun or pronoun that has already been introduced.	*Americans have many **occasions** for giving gifts.* ***Quite a few of** <u>these occasions</u> involve parties or other gatherings.*

 ACTIVITY **4.3** Use Quantifiers

The following sentences are overgeneralizations. Use the quantifiers above to correct them. There may be more than one correct answer.

1 Women talk more than men do.

2 Teenagers do not know social rules.

3 Teenagers know the etiquette for social situations.

4 Children do not stay quiet while adults are talking.

5 Children kiss their older relatives to say hello.

Avoiding Common Mistakes

Research tells us that these are the most common mistakes that students make when using quantifiers in academic writing.

> 1 Use *an amount of* with a noncount noun. Use *a number of* with plural count nouns.
>
>   **A number of**
> ~~A large amount of~~ gestures used in North America are offensive in other parts of the world.
>
>   **a small amount**
> The British will often add ~~a small number~~ of milk to their tea.
>
> 2 For small amounts that are enough, use *a little* or *a few*.
>
>   **a little**
> It is important to leave ~~little~~ space between you and the person you are talking to.
>
> 3 Use *the* or a possessive adjective after a quantifier with *of*.
>
>   **the**
> People in a new culture experience many cultural differences. However, very few of ∧cultural differences are understood quickly.
>
>   **my**
> Very few of ∧friends send letters through the postal service.

 4.4 Editing Task

Find and correct five more mistakes in the paragraph below.

Rules of Etiquette on Social Media

              number
A large ~~amount~~ of people around the world are using social media sites like Facebook, Twitter, and Instagram, but few of users know the basic etiquette. The first rule is to avoid sharing all of your thoughts. A few of friends probably share every piece of information from their day, but not everyone wants to hear what they had for lunch. Another rule is to think carefully before adding photos that include other people. Sharing some photos may be embarrassing to others, so it is polite to ask your friends for permission. For example, ask friends before adding any photos of them in swimsuits. An amount of fights between friends happen when they make negative comments on each other's web page. Making positive comments will help avoid problems and show little respect. Finally, an amount of businesses are now searching social media sites before they hire new employees. If they see crazy pictures or a lot of complaints on a person's website, they will not hire that person. In conclusion, it is important to think carefully before sharing any information on the Internet.

D Avoiding Plagiarism

There are many reasons that students plagiarize. Plagiarizing may seem difficult to avoid, but there are strategies to help.

Q I'm studying in the United States instead of in my county. If I get bad grades, my parents will make me return home. I'm worried because I'm not a good writer. I know copying ideas is wrong, but the experts write better than I do! What can I do? I want to stay and study here.

Wendi

A Dear Wendi,

I'm glad you know that copying is wrong. If you copy someone else's work, you won't get a better grade. Your teacher will know if the writing isn't yours. Your teacher wants to see <u>your</u> work. She wants <u>you</u> to think for <u>yourself</u>, and she values <u>your</u> ideas. Also, your school probably has an academic integrity policy. It says you will be honest in your academic work. That also means you won't plagiarize. If you do, you could fail the course. Talk to your teacher about ways to avoid plagiarizing.

Good luck,

Professor Wright

WHY DO STUDENTS PLAGIARIZE?

Student's Reason	Strategy to Use
I waited until the last minute to write my paper.	**Organize your time.** Start early. Do a little bit every day.
I don't know the words in English to write about my topic.	**Ask for help.** You can ask your teacher, a librarian, or a classmate.
Everybody copies from the Internet, so I can, too.	**Don't be like everybody else.** Copying is always wrong. It is also against your school's academic integrity policy.

 4.5 Practice

Work with a partner. Read the situation below. Write two strategies to help Maria avoid plagiarizing.

Maria has a writing assignment that is due in a week. She cannot think of any ideas. Someone told her about a website with ideas on her topic, and she can copy them from the website.

Strategy 1: ....

Strategy 2: ....

5   WRITE YOUR PARAGRAPH

In this section, you will follow the writing process to complete the final draft of your paragraph.

STEP 1: BRAINSTORM

Work with a partner. Follow the steps below to brainstorm more ideas for your topic.

1 First, read the student's brainstorm chart below. He wrote ideas from the cluster diagram he used to reflect on this topic in Section 1 on page 46. Then he brainstormed and wrote down all the things people wear and the things they do during a sports event. Finally, he underlined the items that he thought were the strongest.

SOCIAL SITUATION: A SPORTS EVENT	
WHAT PEOPLE WEAR: wearing team colors painting faces wearing bright colors	**PEOPLE'S BEHAVIOR:** standing for exciting parts parties, including before and after OK to arrive early don't do anything dangerous cheering whole crowd dancing (the wave) hugging strangers yelling and screaming jumping up and down

2 Now read your writing prompt again. Then review the ideas that you brainstormed in Section 1 on page 47. Write the best ones in the chart below. Include ideas from the Your Turns throughout the unit. Finally, brainstorm more ideas. You will probably not use every idea, but it is good to write as many ideas as possible.

SOCIAL SITUATION:	
RULES FOR BEHAVIOR:	**EXAMPLES:**

STEP 2: MAKE AN OUTLINE

Complete the outline below with ideas for your paragraph from Step 1.

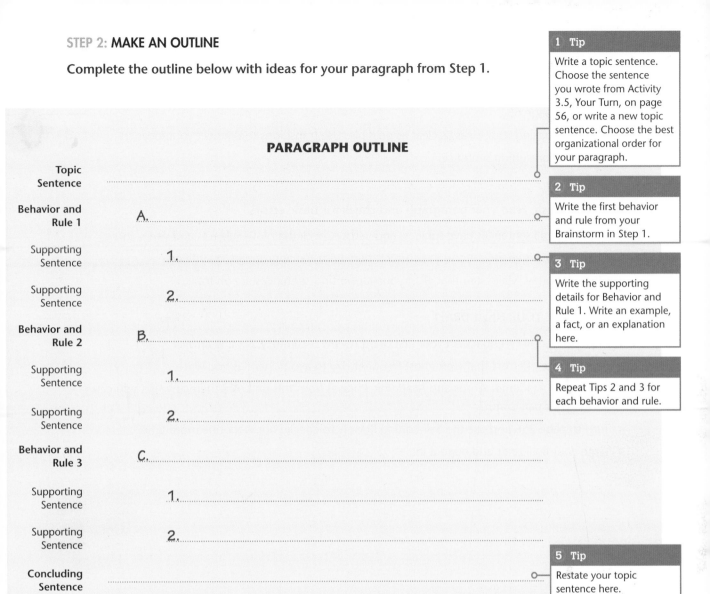

PARAGRAPH OUTLINE

Topic Sentence	....
Behavior and Rule 1	A. ....
Supporting Sentence	1. ....
Supporting Sentence	2. ....
Behavior and Rule 2	B. ....
Supporting Sentence	1. ....
Supporting Sentence	2. ....
Behavior and Rule 3	C. ....
Supporting Sentence	1. ....
Supporting Sentence	2. ....
Concluding Sentence	....

1 Tip
Write a topic sentence. Choose the sentence you wrote from Activity 3.5, Your Turn, on page 56, or write a new topic sentence. Choose the best organizational order for your paragraph.

2 Tip
Write the first behavior and rule from your Brainstorm in Step 1.

3 Tip
Write the supporting details for Behavior and Rule 1. Write an example, a fact, or an explanation here.

4 Tip
Repeat Tips 2 and 3 for each behavior and rule.

5 Tip
Restate your topic sentence here.

STEP 3: WRITE YOUR FIRST DRAFT

Now it is time to write your first draft. Here are some suggestions on how to get started.

1 Use your outline, notes, and the sentences you wrote in the Your Turns in this unit and in Step 2 on page 65.

2 Focus on making your ideas as clear as possible. Use transitions to connect your ideas.

3 Include a concluding sentence.

4 Add a title.

After you finish, read your paragraph and check for basic errors.

1 Check that all sentences have subjects and verbs. Check that your subjects and verbs agree.

2 Check for overgeneralizations and correct them with the appropriate quantifiers.

3 Check for unity. Make sure that all of your supporting sentences are on topic.

STEP 4: WRITE YOUR FINAL DRAFT

1 After you receive feedback on your first draft, review it carefully. Fix any errors.

2 Make a note of errors that were most frequent. Try to avoid them as you write.

3 Review the Academic Words and Academic Phrases from this unit. Are there any that you can add to your paragraph?

4 Turn to page 256 and use the Self-Editing Review to check your work one more time.

5 Write your final draft and hand it in.

3 DESCRIPTIVE PARAGRAPHS

GLOBAL STUDIES: NATIONAL IDENTITIES

"National identity is not something governments can invent. It is more a feeling than an opinion … ."

Robert Colls (1949–)

About the Author:

Robert Colls is a writer and professor. He writes about history, culture, and identity.

Work with a partner. Read the quotation about national identity. Then answer the questions.

1 *Cambridge Academic Content Dictionary* defines *identity* as "who a person is, or the qualities of a person or group that make them different from others." What do you think *national identity* means?

2 Colls describes national identity as a feeling. For example, many people feel that peace and unity are two qualities that describe Switzerland's national identity. What do you feel are two qualities of your country's national identity?

3 Colls says that governments cannot invent national identity. Where do you think national identity comes from?

Ⓐ Connect to Academic Writing

In this unit, you will learn skills to write a descriptive paragraph. Some of the skills may seem new to you, but the skill of describing is not new. In your everyday life, you use the skill of describing when you tell a friend about the date that you had last weekend, or when you tell your family about a restaurant that you went to. When you describe someone or something, you introduce the subject and help the listener or reader experience, feel, and understand the subject.

Ⓑ Reflect on the Topic

In this section, you will be given a writing prompt and reflect on it. You will develop ideas throughout the unit and use them to practice skills that are necessary to write your paragraph.

The writing prompt below was used for the Student Model paragraph on page 74. The student reflected on her topic and used a chart to brainstorm ideas for her paragraph.

WRITING PROMPT: Describe a national celebration and its significance to a culture.

Subject: El Grito (Mexico's Independence Day)		
What can you observe or experience?	**How does it make you feel?**	**What do you know about it?**
- Mexico flag and colors - Mexican music - fireworks	- excited - happy - proud to be Mexican	- independence from Spain - "el grito" = "the shout" - September 16 - 1810: Father Hidalgo rang church bell

 1.1 Notice

Work with a partner. Look at the chart above. Do these ideas give you a sense of El Grito? What more do you want the writer to tell you? Share your ideas with the class.

1.2 Apply It to Your Writing

Read the prompt and follow the directions below.

WRITING PROMPT: In every country, people's sense of national identity is connected with certain objects and events. Choose one object or event from a country that you know. Describe the object or event and tell why it is important to the national identity of people from that country.

1 Choose a country that you are familiar with. Make a list of some important objects and events that represent that country.

2 Decide which object or event will be the subject of your descriptive paragraph. Then fill in the chart below about that object or event. Write three examples for each question.

3 Compare charts with a partner.

Subject:		
What can you observe or experience?	**How does it make you feel?**	**What do you know about it?**

2 EXPAND YOUR KNOWLEDGE

In this section, you will learn academic language that you can use in your descriptive paragraph. You will also notice how a professional writer uses this language and the features of descriptive writing.

Ⓐ Academic Vocabulary

The words below appear throughout the unit. They are from the Academic Word List or the General Service List. Using these words in your writing will make your ideas clearer and your writing more academic.

acceptable (adj)	ethnic (adj)	reveal (v)	struggle (v)
concern (n)	identity (n)	social (adj)	values (n)

 2.1 Focus on Meaning

Work with a partner. Read these sentences about Canada's national identity. Match the words in bold to the letters of their meanings.

A

.... 1 Peace and respect for cultural differences are **values** that most Canadians share.

.... 2 Many countries have one official language. Canada has two: English and French. Bilingualism is an important part of Canadian **identity**.

.... 3 Many Canadians feel that health care is an important **social** issue. They are proud to have a national health-care system to provide care for all people in the society.

.... 4 Canada's population includes people from more than 200 **ethnic** groups. Some of the largest groups are French, Chinese, and North American Indian.

a about society and the way people live together

b relating to a group of people who share the same national, cultural, or racial backgrounds

c beliefs people have about what is right and important in life

d the quality that makes a person or group think of themselves as unique and different from others

B

.... 1 The red maple leaf appears on Canada's flag, money, and coat of arms. This fact **reveals** the leaf's importance as a symbol of Canada.

.... 2 Canadians sometimes **struggle** to find one national identity because many different groups are important in their culture and history.

.... 3 **Concern** about the environment is especially strong among young Canadians.

.... 4 Multiculturalism is an important part of Canada's identity. Most Canadians think it is **acceptable** for immigrants to keep their own traditions.

a to show something or make something known

b allowed, and not considered wrong

c something that worries you because it is important to you

d to try very hard to do something difficult

B Academic Collocations

Collocations are words that are frequently used together. Research tells us that the academic vocabulary in Part A is commonly used in the collocations in bold below.

ACTIVITY **2.2** Focus on Meaning

Work with a partner. Match the collocations in bold to their meanings. Write the letters.

.... 1 One major **ethnic group** in Canada is French Canadian. The ancestors of the French Canadians came from France.

.... 2 In the United States today, people are concerned about how the economy affects **social class**. More Americans are poor and fewer Americans are in the middle class.

.... 3 Respect for the elderly is a common **social value** in Vietnam. Many families live together with grandparents in order to show respect by caring for them.

.... 4 Many Americans are proud of their diverse **ethnic backgrounds.** For example, one American family has members from Trinidad, Ecuador, and the United States.

.... 5 Bastille Day is an important national celebration in France. French people celebrate the history of their nation on this day. The holiday is part of France's **national identity**.

a a group of people who share a culture and language

b the nationalities that make up a person's history

c a feeling that is shared by people from the same country that is based on shared traditions, culture, and language(s)

d a group of people who earn a similar amount of money and share a similar social status in a society

e ideas and principles that a society believes in, such as peace, justice, respect for others

C Writing in the Real World

The author of "Melting Pot or Salad Bowl … or Chocolate Fondue?" uses descriptive writing to create word pictures that make her ideas clear.

Before you read, answer these questions: What is a melting pot? What does the writer mean by melting pot?

Now read the article. Think about your answers to the questions above as you read.

MELTING POT
OR **SALAD BOWL …** OR
CHOCOLATE FONDUE?
— by Sofia Perez

1   As an immigrant to the United States, I have **struggled** with the question of how I fit in and what it means to be an American. This may seem like an old question, but it is one that is new for each generation of immigrants. Everyone knows that America consists of many different cultures and **ethnic groups**. And most people agree that immigrants are an important part of America's **identity**. But exactly how do immigrants fit in and affect America? There are two common symbols that suggest very different answers– the melting pot and the salad bowl. I've never found either very **acceptable**. Apparently, economist Timothy Taylor, of Macalester College, doesn't either. He suggests a different image – chocolate fondue.[1] It's much better, I think. So let's look at all three symbols.

[1]**chocolate fondue:** a dessert of melted chocolate in which people dip pieces of fruit, cake, etc.

2 Imagine a small porcelain[2] bowl on a table in a laboratory. A scientist places two balls in it. Each ball is a different kind of metal. Next, he places the bowl on a special burner[3] and turns on the flame. The flame grows taller and taller. It turns different colors – orange, red, blue, white. The balls begin to melt. They become liquid and mix together. The scientist removes the bowl from the flame. As the metal mixture cools, there is one metal – not two. For some, America is like this melting pot: Many immigrants come to the United States and mix to become one. The melting pot is about assimilation. Some people believe that there is a basic American culture and set of **values**. They believe that all the different immigrant groups should assimilate, or melt, into that one American culture and set of **values**.

[2]**porcelain:** a hard, shiny, white material used to make cups and plates
[3]**burner:** an instrument that produces a controlled flame

3 Next, picture a big bowl of salad. The salad has leafy, green lettuce; round, red tomatoes; skinny, orange carrots; and many other ingredients. The ingredients are all combined, but each is separate. Carrots are still carrots. Tomatoes are still tomatoes. The salad bowl is about diversity. This is the idea that immigrants all contribute to America and all are free to keep their way of life in America. People with this view think that diversity makes America better. It is like a good salad with many separate flavors and textures. They are not **concerned** about having one **identity**.

4 Now what about the chocolate fondue? Here's how Taylor describes it: "Our different cultural and **ethnic backgrounds** are the strawberries, pineapple, and cherries…. Then we are dipped in America. We swim in America." Yes—that's it! I'm neither an American (in the melting pot) nor an Argentinian (in the salad bowl). Instead, I'm an Argentinian grape swimming in chocolate. The chocolate fondue idea combines the melting pot and salad bowls into a much better, more appropriate symbol (and I confess: I'm a chocolate lover).

2.3 Check Your Understanding

Answer the questions.

1 The article mentions three symbols that represent American national identity. What are they?

2 There is a debate about language in the United States. Some Americans want to make English the official language of the United States. Does this opinion support assimilation or diversity? Why?

3 Based on your experience, do you think America is more like a melting pot, a salad bowl, or chocolate fondue? Why?

2.4 Notice the Features of Descriptive Writing

Work with a partner. Notice how the writer organized ideas in the paragraphs. Answer the questions.

1 Look at the second paragraph. What words help you see what the scientist is doing with the melting pot?

2 Look at the third paragraph. What words help you see the salad?

In Section 1 you saw how the writer of the Student Model reflected on her topic. In this section, you will analyze the final draft of her paragraph. You will learn how to organize your ideas for your own paragraph.

Ⓐ Student Model

Read the prompt and answer the questions.

WRITING PROMPT: Describe a national celebration and its significance to a culture.

1 What will the paragraph be about? Explain in your own words.

2 What are some important parts, or features, that you think the writer will include in her description?

Read the paragraph twice. The first time, think about your answers to the questions above. The second time, answer the questions in the Analyze Writing Skills boxes. This will help you notice the key features of the paragraph.

STUDENT MODEL

The Importance of El Grito de Dolores

El Grito de Dolores is an important national celebration in Mexico and an important part of Mexico's **national identity**. Many people think that Cinco de Mayo is Mexico's Independence Day, but El Grito de Dolores, on September 16, is Mexican Independence Day. Each year before the 16th of September, decorations **reveal** that a great celebration, or *fiesta*, is coming. People hang the Mexican flag from their houses and cars. They put lights, balloons, and pinwheels[1] in the streets and on the buildings. Everything is red, white, and green because these are the national colors. On the evening of September 15, everyone starts to gather for an exciting **social** event. Families and friends go to the center of town. They eat traditional Mexican foods and dress in traditional Mexican clothes. The sound of mariachi music is everywhere. The largest gathering in the nation is in Mexico City in *el Zócalo*, which is the public square in the center of the city. Almost half a million people go there. If Mexicans live in another country, they might even watch this on TV. People shout and make noise with musical instruments. The square becomes more and more crowded. People are excited. They are waiting to watch the reenactment[2] of El Grito. This is the most important and interesting part of the celebration. *El Grito* means "the cry." In the 1800s, the Mexican people had many **concerns** about

1 Analyze Writing Skills

Underline the topic sentence. Circle the national celebration the writer will describe.

2 Analyze Writing Skills

Underline the phrases in lines 5–8 that the writer uses to help you see the decorations.

3 Analyze Writing Skills

Circle the word in this line that describes people's feelings.

[1]**pinwheel:** a colorful decoration or toy that children can spin
[2]**reenactment:** a performance in which people repeat the actions of a historical event

their Spanish rulers, and they wanted freedom. Father Hidalgo was one of those **concerned** leaders. In 1810, he rang the bell in his small church and called the people to fight for liberty. This started a 10-year **struggle** for independence. Now, every September 15 at 11:00 p.m., a government leader acts like Father Hidalgo. He rings a bell and cries, "My fellow Mexicans, long live Mexico!" The people continue celebrating into September 16 by watching fireworks, singing the national anthem, and shouting *"Viva Mexico!"* El Grito de Dolores is a special and important celebration for the people of Mexico.

4 Analyze Writing Skills

Do all of the supporting sentences in the paragraph help you see, hear, feel, and learn about the celebration? Circle *Yes* or *No*.

 ACTIVITY **3.1 Check Your Understanding**

Answer the questions.

1 The writer says that El Grito is a special and important celebration for the people of Mexico. What three parts, or features, of the celebration did she write about?

2 If you were in Mexico in the second week of September, what would you expect to see?

3 How do you think Mexican people feel about Father Hidalgo? Why do you think they feel that way?

3.2 Outline the Writer's Ideas

Complete the outline for "The Importance of El Grito de Dolores." Use the phrases in the box.

crowded and excited   red, white, and green colors

leader rings a bell and cries out

PARAGRAPH OUTLINE

Topic Sentence El Grito de Dolores is an important national celebration in Mexico and an important part of Mexico's national identity.

Feature 1 A. The decorations

Detail 1. Flags

Detail 2. Lights, balloons, and pinwheels

Detail 3.

Feature 2 B. The gathering

Detail 1. Traditional clothing, music, and food

Detail 2. Locations: in town centers, at el Zócalo, on TV

Detail 3.

Feature 3 C. The reenactment

Detail 1. Important history

Detail 2.

Detail 3. Fireworks, national anthem, "Viva Mexico!"

Concluding Sentence El Grito de Dolores is a special and important celebration for the people of Mexico.

B Descriptive Paragraphs

Descriptive paragraphs describe a subject – a person, place, thing, or idea – in a way that creates a clear picture of it in the reader's mind. Writers create this picture by describing the subject's main features with clear details. Features are important parts or characteristics. For example, in the Student Model paragraph, the writer focuses on three main features of El Grito: the decorations, the people, and the reenactment. To make her description clear and vivid, she combines several types of details.

TYPES OF DESCRIPTIVE DETAILS	
• **Spatial location** (prepositional phrases) helps show the location of physical features and their details so that the readers can clearly imagine the subject.	*People hang the Mexican flag **from their houses and cars**.* *They put lights, balloons, and pinwheels **in the streets** and **on the buildings**.*
• **Sensory details** help the reader see, touch, smell, hear, or taste the subject.	*The **sound of mariachi music** is everywhere.* *Everything is **red, white, and green** because these are the national colors.*
• **Feelings** create an impression about the subject.	*People are **excited**.* *In the early 1800s, the Mexican people had many **concerns** about their life under Spanish rule.*
• **Relevant information** often includes facts that the reader must know to understand the subject. It can also include examples and explanations.	***Almost half a million** people go there.* *Now, **every September 15 at 11:00 p.m.**, a government leader reenacts El Grito de Dolores.*

Work with a partner. Read the paragraph. Then answer the questions on page 79.

Symbols of Freedom

The Statue of Liberty is one of America's best-loved monuments, perhaps because it symbolizes freedom. The statue itself has symbols. One of the most important symbols on the statue is the golden torch in the statue's right hand. The torch is easy to see because the statue raises her right arm high. The torch means a light in the darkness. With this light, the Statue of Liberty is like a guide to people. She is boldly showing the way to freedom. When immigrants see the torch, they feel hopeful about their future. Another symbol on the statue is the seven-point crown on her head. The points make the crown look like the shining sun. The crown also means light. The statue is providing the light of freedom. It creates a sense of optimism and confidence for the future. Many people do not know about one of the most powerful symbols of freedom. At the bottom of the statue, there are broken chains around her feet. One can only see these chains from the air, but the creator of the statue put them there for a special purpose. They show that the Statue of Liberty was chained. However, now the chains are broken, and she is free. The detailed symbols of the Statue of Liberty make this monument one of the main symbols of freedom in the United States.

1 The writer focuses on three features of the Statue of Liberty. What are they?

2 Why do you think the writer chose these features? What does the writer want you to experience, feel, or understand about the Statue of Liberty?

3 The writer describes these features of the statue with different types of details. Complete the chart with information from the paragraph.

FEATURES	SPATIAL LOCATION	SENSORY DETAILS	FEELINGS	FACTS AND RELEVANT INFORMATION
The torch	in the statue's right hand – raises right arm high		feel hopeful	a guide showing the way to freedom
The crown		looks like the sun shining	optimism and confidence	
The chains		broken		can only see them from the air

 3.4 Apply It to Your Writing

Think about the ideas you wrote for your writing prompt in Section 1 on page 69. What do you want the reader to experience, feel, or understand about this subject? List three features that you might describe in your paragraph.

....

....

....

SPATIAL LOCATION

Writers often describe the location of physical features to help readers create pictures in their minds. To do this, writers use prepositional phrases, as prepositional phrases express spatial location. Prepositional phrases include phrases such as *at the top, in the center, at the bottom, on the left,* and *in the middle.* Notice the prepositional phrases used to describe Argentina's coat of arms. The coat of arms is an image that symbolizes the country's national values.

PREPOSITIONAL PHRASES

At the top of Argentina's coat of arms, there is a bright yellow sun. It symbolizes Argentina as a shining new nation.

In the center, there is a red hat on top of a stick. It symbolizes liberty.

At the bottom of the design, two hands are clasped together. They symbolize unity.

ACTIVITY 3.5 Identify Spatial Location

Work with a partner. Describe the back of the one-dollar bill from the United States. Complete the sentences with the prepositional phrases from the box.

at the bottom	in the center	on the right
in front	on the left	

1 ...., there is a pyramid. It represents the strong foundation of the United States.

2 .... of the pyramid, there are the Roman numerals MDCCLXXVI (1776). They represent the year the United States became an independent country.

3 The word "one" appears in large letters .... of the bill.

4 ...., there is an eagle. The eagle is the national bird of the United States and a symbol of the country.

5 There is a shield with thirteen stripes .... of the eagle. The stripes symbolize the thirteen original colonies.

ACTIVITY 3.6 Write Spatial Locations

Choose a bill or coin. Write three sentences to describe the pictures, images, or designs on the money. Use prepositional phrases.

1 ....

....

2 ....

....

3 ....

....

SENSORY DETAILS

Writers of descriptions include **sensory details** – details that appeal to the five senses – to help readers experience their subjects. To add sensory details, writers study their subjects carefully and ask:

- **Sight:** What do I see? What does it look like?
- **Sound:** Can I hear anything? How does it sound?
- **Smell:** Can I smell anything? How does it smell?
- **Taste:** What can I taste? How does it taste?
- **Touch:** What can I touch? How does it feel?

Writers may use all or some of these senses in their descriptions. For example, here are some sensory details that the writer of "The Importance of El Grito de Dolores" brainstormed before writing her paragraph, even though she did not use all of these ideas in her description.

SIGHT	SOUND	SMELL	TASTE	TOUCH
- flags everywhere - red, white, and green - people in traditional clothes - colorful fireworks - people dancing - parades	- mariachi music - people shouting - the bell & the grito - people singing national anthem	- great Mexican food smells good	- spicy, delicious food, traditional food - feasts	- traditional clothes feel heavy

 3.7 Identify Sensory Details

Read the paragraph. Underline the sensory details that help you see, hear, touch, taste, or smell the çay. Then write the underlined words or phrases in the chart at the top of page 82.

Turkish Hospitality Served with Çay

An important part of any national identity is the food or drinks that are traditional in the country, such as çay in Turkey. Çay, or Turkish tea, is central to Turkish hospitality. The most popular çay is a special black tea from the coast of the Black Sea. It has a strong taste, and some say it has a slight orange flavor. Çay is traditionally served in a small tulip-shaped clear glass. This allows people to see its dark brown color. Many tea drinkers add water to make the tea lighter in color and less strong in taste. The glass does not have handles. Therefore, servers cannot fill it to the top. People need a place to hold the cup without burning their fingers on the hot glass. The tea is always served with one or two white sugar cubes. Many add this sugar to make the tea very sweet. It is common for Turkish people to gather together in cafés to drink çay with friends and family, and this tea is almost always served to guests in Turkish homes.

SIGHT	SOUND	SMELL	TASTE	TOUCH

 3.8 Write Sensory Details

Choose a food or drink that is important in your culture. Brainstorm ideas for sensory details to describe and complete the chart below. Then use the information in the chart to write sentences describing the food or drink with sensory details.

SIGHT	SOUND	SMELL	TASTE	TOUCH

....

....

....

....

....

....

....

FEELINGS

Writers use adjectives to add **feelings** to their descriptions. Feelings help the reader experience the importance of the event or object. Here are some examples you have already seen in this unit:

*People are **excited**. They are waiting to watch the reenactment of El Grito.*

*When immigrants see the torch, they feel **hopeful** about their future.*

Adjectives to describe feelings often include:

concerned	hopeful	peaceful	sorry
excited	hopeless	proud	surprised
glad	inspired	sad	thankful
grateful	joyful	shocked	upset
homesick			

 3.9 **Review Adjectives to Describe Feelings**

Work with a partner. Take turns reading the adjectives in the list above. Circle the ones you do not know. Help each other understand the words.

 3.10 **Write about Feelings**

Choose four adjectives. Use each one in a sentence about your writing topic.

....

....

....

....

RELEVANT INFORMATION

Writers may add **relevant information** – examples, explanations, and facts – to their descriptions to help their readers understand the subject. Here is a fact, an example, and an explanation from the description of the Canadian National Vimy Memorial, a monument that reveals important characteristics about Canada's national identity:

- **Example:** *At the entrance to the memorial are memorial plaques to many ethnic groups, **such as Greeks, Moroccans, and Armenians** who fought at Vimy.*

- **Explanation:** *Canadians are proud of the monument **because it shows important Canadian values.***

- **Fact:** *On the monument are the names of **11,285 Canadians.***

3.11 Add Relevant Information

Complete the description of Argentina's coat of arms. Write the letters of the correct information on the lines.

a   When two people reach an agreement, they often shake hands. (example)

b   In ancient times, freed slaves used to wear red hats like this one. (explanation)

c   In May 1810, the May Revolution began in Argentina. It was the beginning of Argentina's struggle for independence from Spain. (fact)

Argentina's Coat of Arms

Argentina's coat of arms has many interesting images. The yellow sun at the top is called the *Sun of May*. It is an important symbol in Argentina because it symbolizes Argentina as a shining new nation. .... In the center of the coat of arms, there is a red hat on a stick. People are
(1)
often confused about this image. However, the red hat is an old symbol of freedom because

.... The stick, or *pike*, represents a willingness to struggle for freedom. The handshake at the
(2)
bottom of the coat of arms is a common symbol of unity. For example, ... Altogether, the
(3)
images on Argentina's coat of arms reveal the country's values of freedom and unity.

3.12 Apply It to Your Writing

YOUR TURN

Think about the subject that you are going to describe in your paragraph. Look at your chart in Section 1 on page 69. Review the features that you plan to describe. Write three sentences to describe one or more of these features. Use sensory details, spatial location, feelings, and/or relevant information.

1   ....

....

....

2   ....

....

....

3   ....

....

....

In this section, you will learn writing and grammar skills that will help make your writing more academic and accurate.

A Writing Skill 1: Vivid Language

Writers of descriptive paragraphs try to use **vivid language** in their descriptions. Vivid language includes words that help readers imagine they can see or feel the description. Using clear, specific adjectives is one way to make your language more vivid. Avoid unclear, vague adjectives such as *good*, *bad*, *nice*, *happy*, and *fun*.

Here are some vivid adjectives that you can use in descriptions.

VIVID LANGUAGE: SPECIFIC ADJECTIVES	
Size	*average, gigantic, huge, miniature, tiny*
Sound	*high, low, noisy, peaceful, quiet, silent*
Color	*bold, bright, clean, dark, dull, faded, light, multi-colored, red*
Shape	*curvy, round, short, straight, square, triangular*
Texture	*fuzzy, rough, sharp, smooth, soft*
Taste	*delicious, fresh, juicy, salty, sharp, sour, strong, sweet, weak*
Feelings	*content, enjoyable, entertaining, exciting, heartbroken, sorrowful*

4.1 Use Vivid Language

Work with a partner. Look at the photograph and complete the paragraph below. Replace the adjectives in parentheses with specific adjectives from the chart above or other adjectives.

Junkanoo

On the day after Christmas in the Bahamas, people gather for a national celebration called *Junkanoo*. Performers dress in .... (big)
(1)
costumes and do African dances. All of the costumes have very .... (nice) colors and
(2)
interesting designs. There is drumming and music. The celebration is .... (loud)
(3)
and very exciting. Above all, though, it is
.... (fun). Junkanoo makes
(4)
people in the Bahamas feel ....
(5)
(happy). This day celebrates the value of freedom.

B Writing Skill 2: Avoiding Sentence Fragments, Run-ons, and Comma Splices

Writers must use correct sentences in academic writing. That means they must avoid these common sentence errors.

FRAGMENTS, RUN-ONS, AND COMMA SPLICES

1 A **fragment** is an incomplete sentence. The sentence is missing a subject and/or a verb. To fix a fragment, add the missing subject or verb.	Fragment (missing verb): This **nation** ^{has} many different religions, languages, and values. Fragment (missing subject): The United States has many cultures. <s>Is</s> ^{It is} a large country, too.
2 **Run-ons** are two sentences (independent clauses) that are joined together without punctuation or a conjunction. To fix a run-on: Join the independent clauses with a comma and a conjunction such as *and* or *but*. OR Separate the independent clauses with a period. You can introduce the second sentence with a transition word.	Add a comma and *and*: The Statue of Liberty is holding a torch ^{, and} she has a tablet. Add a period: The Statue of Liberty is holding a torch ^{. Also,} she has a tablet.
3 **Comma splices** are two sentences (independent clauses) that are joined only with a comma. Commas cannot connect sentences without a conjunction. To fix a comma splice: Add an appropriate conjunction after the comma. OR Separate the independent clauses with a period.	Add a conjunction: The melting pot represents assimilation, ^{but} the salad bowl represents diversity. Add a period: The melting pot represents assimilation<s>,</s> ^{. The} the salad bowl represents diversity.

4.2 Identify Sentence Errors

Each item below has one error. Write *F* (fragment), *R* (run-on), or *C* (comma splice) on the line.

.... 1 Americans celebrate their struggle for independence on the Fourth of July, this day is a national holiday.

.... 2 A country's money often has interesting images and designs they reveal important social values or history.

.... 3 New York City is a diverse city. For example, neighborhoods with many different ethnic restaurants and stores.

.... 4 Ecuador has amazing natural resources, many Ecuadorians are concerned about protecting their wild animals, plants, and lands.

.... 5 A lot of Canadian families have a Chinese background. Therefore, many Canadians celebrate Chinese holidays. Like Chinese New Year.

4.3 Correct Sentence Errors

Rewrite the items from Activity 4.2 as correct sentences on a separate sheet of paper.

ⓒ Writing Skill 3: Correct Pronoun Use

Pronouns replace or refer to nouns. Writers use pronouns in paragraphs to avoid repeating the name of a person, place, thing, or idea.

NOUN   PRONOUN

*Americans value independence. Therefore, **they** teach their children to be independent.*

Review the different types of pronouns in the chart.

PRONOUNS				
Subject	**Object**	**Possessive Determiner + Noun**	**Possessive**	**Reflexive**
I	*me*	*my* + noun	*mine*	*myself*
you	*you*	*your* + noun	*yours*	*yourself*
he	*him*	*his* + noun	*his*	*himself*
she	*her*	*her* + noun	*hers*	*herself*
it	*it*	*its* + noun	—	*itself*
we	*us*	*our* + noun	*ours*	*ourselves*
they	*them*	*their* + noun	*theirs*	*themselves*

ACTIVITY 4.4 Choose Correct Pronouns

Read the paragraph. Replace the words in parentheses with the correct pronouns or determiners from the chart on page 87.

The Meaning of the American Penny

An American penny has many details, and the details are there for a reason.

_____ (These details) represent American values and history. Abraham
(1)

Lincoln is on the face of the penny. _____ (Abraham Lincoln) was the
(2)

sixteenth president of the United States. Most Americans accept that Lincoln is one of the

most important people in American history. _____ (These Americans)
(3)

consider _____ (Lincoln) a hero because he saved the country during
(4)

a difficult civil war. On the back of the penny, there is a picture of the Lincoln Memorial in

Washington, D.C. This monument is designed in a Greek style. A statue of Abraham Lincoln

is in _____ (the monument). If you look very closely at a penny, you can
(5)

see _____ (Lincoln's) statue. Also on the back of the penny is the Latin
(6)

phrase *E Pluribus Unum*. It means "Out of the many, one." Americans adopted this phrase as

_____ (Americans') motto. In particular, Americans use *E Pluribus Unum*
(7)

to describe _____ (Americans) as one people from many different ethnic
(8)

backgrounds.

D Grammar for Writing: Adjectives

As you have seen, writers use adjectives to help them describe their subjects. Some adjectives can be confusing to use. They look similar, but they are used differently. See the examples in the chart below.

-ING AND *-ED* ADJECTIVES	
1 Use an *-ed* adjective to describe how a person feels: *amazed, bored, confused, disappointed, excited, interested, relaxed, shocked, surprised*	*-ED* ADJECTIVE *People are usually **excited** when they visit a famous place for the first time.*
2 Use an *-ing* adjective to describe what a person, place, thing, or idea is like: *amazing, boring, confusing, disappointing, exciting, interesting, relaxing, shocking, surprising*	*-ING* ADJECTIVE *It is **exciting** to visit famous places for the first time.*

PROPER ADJECTIVES FOR NATIONALITIES AND LANGUAGES	
1 Use correct proper adjectives to describe people, places, or things from a specific nation. Notice that proper adjectives begin with a capital letter. 2 Many words for nationalities and languages can be used as adjectives or nouns.	ADJECTIVE ADJECTIVE ADJECTIVE ***Chinese** dumplings, **Italian** ravioli, and **Polish** pierogi are similar in many ways.* ADJECTIVE NOUN *The **French language** is important to the **French**.*

4.5 Write *-ed* and *-ing* Adjectives

Work with a partner. Read the paragraph and complete the adjectives with *-ed* or *-ing* endings.

Christmas Celebrations

Christmas celebrations are a part of many cultures. However, some countries have unique Christmas traditions. In the Philippines, for example, some people are so excit‿‿‿ about (1) Christmas that they begin hanging lights and decorations in September. The Christmas light displays are amaz‿‿‿. (2) People cover houses, buildings, and even parks with special lights. In Sweden, there is another interest‿‿‿ (3) tradition. People from other cultures are surpris‿‿‿ (4) to learn that a goat is a popular Swedish Christmas decoration. Before Christmas, people build gigantic straw goats called *Yule Goats.* They put the goats in their towns or cities. The Gälve goat, in the city of Gälve, is the most popular. Unfortunately, it is common for criminals to set fire to the Gälve goat and destroy it. Many Swedes are disappoint‿‿‿ (5) because the Gälve goat usually does not survive until Christmas. These two Christmas traditions are examples of how some cultures celebrate Christmas in unique ways.

4.6 Write Proper Forms for Languages and Nationalities

Look at the underlined words. Complete the sentences with the correct form of the related language or nationality.

1 Soccer is one of the most popular sports around the world, but in the United States many people prefer .... football.

2 .... is spoken in South America. It is different from the version spoken in Spain.

3 In Jamaica, the food has had many cultural influences, including African, Spanish, British, Chinese, and Indian. As a result, ... food has a unique, spicy flavor.

4 In Canada, many people play hockey. This sport is a popular .... pastime.

5 Some common cooking ingredients in Korea include garlic, ginger, and red pepper. Consequently, ... food is often very hot and spicy.

Avoiding Common Mistakes

Research tells us that these are the most common mistakes that students make when using adjectives in academic writing.

1. Do not confuse *-ed* and *-ing* adjectives. Remember that *-ed* adjectives describe how someone feels, and *-ing* adjectives describe what someone or something is like.

   The United States has an ~~interested~~ **interesting** national identity.

2. Do not confuse the following verbs and adjectives:

   | VERB | ADJECTIVE |
   to interest ≠ interested

   | VERB | ADJECTIVE |
   to relax ≠ relaxed

   | VERB | ADJECTIVE |
   to worry ≠ worried

   Other cultures ~~are interested~~ **interest** him.

   He is ~~interest~~ **interested** in other cultures.

3. Remember to capitalize proper adjectives.

   Many Canadians can speak both the ~~english~~ **E** and the ~~french~~ **F** languages.

 4.7 Editing Task

Find and correct six more mistakes in the paragraph below.

Soccer – The National Sport of Brazil

Soccer is not just a sport in Brazil. Some ~~brazilians~~ **Brazilians** consider soccer to be like a religion. Most people agree that soccer is a national passion. As in many nations, the people of brazil are very diverse. There are many different social classes and ethnic groups. However, almost everyone in Brazil is interest in the Brazilian national soccer team. When the national team is playing, most Brazilian citizens are worry. Will they win or will they lose? Brazilians are united in their concern for their country's team. Thousands of brazilian fans go to the soccer games. The fans are exciting. They cheer or sing loudly in portugese. They wear their team's colors: blue, green, and yellow. They wave huge Brazilian flags. These soccer games bring the people together to cheer for their team. Soccer is an important part of Brazil's national identity.

E Avoiding Plagiarism

In most academic writing, you should state where you find the information for your writing. However, sometimes it is not necessary.

I wrote about how the culture of the United States comes from many places. I included statistics to support my paragraph. My instructor said I have to say where I got my information. I also wrote that Ellis Island was one of the biggest immigration centers. My instructor said I did not need to say where I found this information. When do I have to say where I get my information?

Nattapong

Dear Nattapong,

There is some information that many people know. We call that "common knowledge." For example, most people in the United States know about Ellis Island. You can find information about it in many different places. You don't need to say where you find that kind of information. However, statistics are different. They are from someone's research. Most people don't know that information, so it is not common knowledge. You should always state where you learned it. I hope that helps!

Sincerely,

Professor Wright

WHAT IS COMMON KNOWLEDGE?

Common knowledge is information that many people, or a community of people, know. You don't have to say where you found this information. However, information from research or government reports is not common knowledge. You should state where you found that kind of information.

Read this chart for information about common knowledge.

Common knowledge is:	Common knowledge is not:
Facts accepted by most people *Mosquitos carry malaria.*	Data or information that comes from research *In 2010, there were 219 million cases of malaria worldwide.* From http://kff.org/global-health-policy/fact-sheet/the-global-malaria-epidemic-4/
Common sense knowledge *If you cough, you should cover your mouth.*	Opinions or theories of others *If you are planning to travel, the Center for Disease Control advises getting a flu shot two weeks before the trip.* From http://www.hopkinsmedicine.org/healthlibrary/conditions/infectious_diseases/influenza_flu_85,PO0625/

ACTIVITY **4.8** Practice

Work with a partner. Write *CK* for the sentences that are common knowledge. Write *NCK* for the sentences that are not common knowledge. Explain your answers.

.... 1 Cooks should prepare fish within two or three days because it can spoil very quickly.

.... 2 Oceans cover most of the Earth's surface.

.... 3 Japanese businesspeople often exchange gifts; in contrast, this is not common in Germany.

.... 4 People with professional degrees earned the highest weekly salaries, at over $1,300 per week.

.... 5 Ellis Island treated poorer immigrants to the United States differently from first-class passengers.

.... 6 According to a recent survey, many Americans below the age of 35 think there is no national identity in the United States.

.... 7 Some political leaders believe that the United States needs significant immigration reform.

In this section, you will follow the writing process to complete the final draft of your paragraph.

STEP 1: BRAINSTORM

Work with a partner. Follow the steps below to brainstorm more ideas for your paragraph.

1 Before you start, read the Student Model writer's freewriting. After setting a specific amount of time to write, she wrote about everything that came to mind about her topic. She didn't worry about spelling, grammar, or punctuation. She just wrote and wrote. That's called freewriting.

Student Model Freewriting
WRITING PROMPT: Describe a national celebration and its significance to a culture.
Do I really want to write about el Grito? … I gotta take a step back & think about this. The most popular celebrations in my country: 5 de Mayo, Christmas, el Grito. OK. Many countries celebrate Christmas. 5 de Mayo & el Grito are just Mexico. People always think 5 de Mayo = our independence day. Their confused cuz the Fourth of July is U.S. independence day, so they think the Fifth of May must be Mexico's independence day. So many Americans celebrate Cinco de Mayo, but they don't know anything about El Grito. Its really important to Mexcio's history tho. So I'm sticking with El Grito for my topic. Why its special: ringing the bell + shout, the music. Going to Zocolo in Mexico City. The food is really great. I miss it! Everybody gets involved--like decorating, making food, dancing, etc.

2 Now read your writing prompt again. Then review the ideas that you brainstormed in Section 1 on page 69. Include ideas from the Your Turns throughout the unit. Finally, brainstorm more ideas. Freewrite for five minutes. Write everything that comes to mind. You will probably not use every idea, but it is good to write as many ideas as possible.

Your Freewriting
WRITING PROMPT: Choose one object or event from a country that you know. Describe the object or event and explain why it is important to the national identity of people from that country.

STEP 2: MAKE AN OUTLINE

Complete the outline below with ideas for your paragraph from Step 1 on page 94.

PARAGRAPH OUTLINE

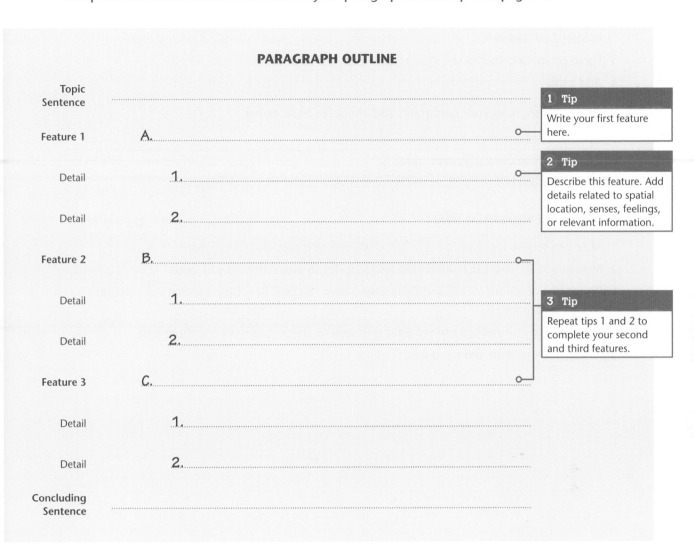

Topic Sentence	....
Feature 1	A. ....
Detail	1. ....
Detail	2. ....
Feature 2	B. ....
Detail	1. ....
Detail	2. ....
Feature 3	C. ....
Detail	1. ....
Detail	2. ....
Concluding Sentence	....

1 Tip

Write your first feature here.

2 Tip

Describe this feature. Add details related to spatial location, senses, feelings, or relevant information.

3 Tip

Repeat tips 1 and 2 to complete your second and third features.

STEP 3: WRITE YOUR FIRST DRAFT

Now it is time to write your first draft. Here are some suggestions on how to get started.

1 Use your outline, notes, and the sentences that you wrote in the Your Turns in this unit and in Step 2 on page 95.

2 Focus on making your description as clear and vivid as possible.

3 Add a title.

After you finish, read your paragraph and check for basic errors.

1 Check that all sentences have subjects and verbs.

2 Check that you used adjectives correctly.

3 Check that you did not include run-on sentences, comma splices, or fragments.

STEP 4: WRITE YOUR FINAL DRAFT

1 After you receive feedback on your first draft, review it carefully. Fix any errors.

2 Make a note of errors that were most frequent. Try to avoid them as you write.

3 Review the academic Words and Collocations from this unit. Are there any that you can add to your paragraph?

4 Turn to page 257 and use the Self-Editing Review to check your work one more time.

5 Write your final draft and hand it in.

DEFINITION PARAGRAPHS
BUSINESS: WORKPLACE BEHAVIOR

> *"Never go to a doctor whose office plants have died."*
>
> Erma Bombeck
> (1927–1996)

About the Author:

Erma Bombeck was a popular American newspaper writer. She became famous for her humorous articles about everyday life in suburban America. She wrote thousands of newspaper stories and 15 books.

Work with a partner. Read the quotation about doctors. Then answer the questions.

1   Why does Ms. Bombeck recommend avoiding doctors with dead plants?

2   What are some of the characteristics of a good doctor or a bad doctor?

3   How would you complete the sentence? Give as many examples as possible. One example is done for you.

Never go to a <u>hairstylist</u> who <u>has bad hair</u>.

Never go to a _____ who _____.

Ⓐ Connect to Academic Writing

In this unit, you will learn skills to help you write a definition paragraph. Some of the skills may seem new to you, but the skill of defining words and ideas is not new. In your everyday life, you often use defining skills. For example, when you describe an object or idea whose name you cannot remember or when you explain a new website or app, you are using defining skills.

Ⓑ Reflect on the Topic

In this section, you will be given a writing prompt and reflect on it. You will develop ideas throughout the unit and use them to practice skills that are necessary to write your final paragraph.

The writing prompt below was used for the Student Model paragraph on page 104. The student reflected on his topic and used a cluster diagram to brainstorm possible ideas for his paragraph.

WRITING PROMPT: The following words are used when talking about social skills in the workplace. Choose one and define it: *team player*, *communication skills*, or *leader*.

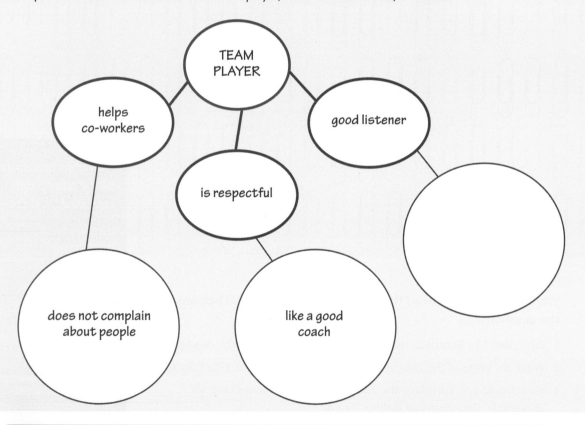

 1.1 Notice

Work with a partner. Look at the cluster diagram above. Discuss one more idea the student could write about and add it to the diagram. Share your idea with the class.

1.2 Apply It to Your Writing

Follow the directions below to reflect on your topic.

Read the prompt below. Then follow the instructions to brainstorm ideas.

WRITING PROMPT: Write your own definition of a boss or a co-worker. Explain your definition in detail.

1 Choose the word you will define and write it in the red circle in the cluster diagram below.

2 Consider what you know about this word. Write as many ideas as you can in the other circles. Add more circles if needed. Ask yourself these questions to help you get ideas:

- What are some characteristics of the kind of person this word describes?
- What does this kind of person do?
- How is this person different from others?
- Who is this person similar to?

3 Compare cluster diagrams with a partner.

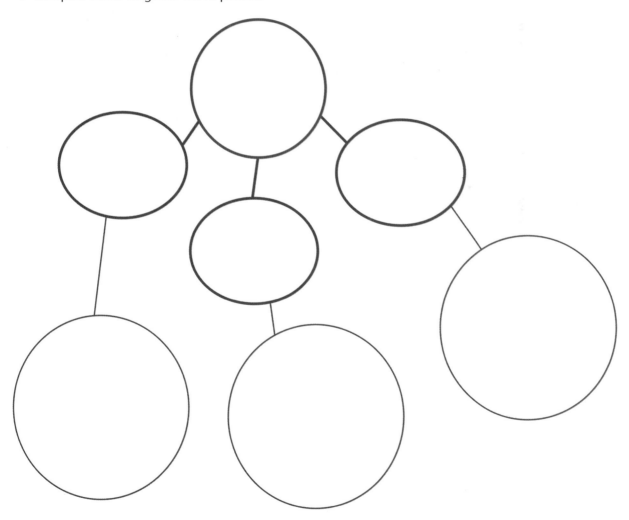

In this section, you will learn academic language that you can use in your definition paragraph. You will also notice how a professional writer uses this language.

Ⓐ Academic Vocabulary

The words below appear throughout the unit. They are from the Academic Word List or the General Service List. Using these words in your writing will make your ideas clearer and your writing more academic.

behave (v)	control (n)	encourage (v)	policy (n)
conflict (n)	distinguish (v)	habit (n)	request (v)

 2.1 Focus on Meaning

Work with a partner. Read the sentences. Decide the meaning of the bold words and circle the correct definitions.

1 Some companies **encourage** employees to bring their pets to work. This policy helps employees focus on their work and not worry about their pets at home. **Encourage** means

   a to explain an action.   b to support and approve of an action.

2 Some managers do not have **control** of their employees, so the employees do whatever they want to do. **Control** means

   a attention to someone.   b power over someone.

3 Some co-workers wear headphones and like to sing along with the music. This **habit** is rude. **Habit** means

   a regular activity.   b thoughts.

4 If employees have a **conflict** in the workplace, they will need to talk to their supervisor to help solve it. **Conflict** means

   a a disagreement.   b a meeting.

5 Some people cannot **distinguish** between polite and impolite actions at work. For example, they do not understand that checking your texts in a meeting is rude, but taking notes is polite. **Distinguish** means

   a to ignore differences.   b to recognize differences.

6 You must **request** vacation time from your supervisor. **Request** means

   a to ask for something.   b to plan for something.

7 Co-workers should always **behave** professionally with each other. They should act nicely. **Behave** means

   a to act a certain way.   b to say something a certain way.

8 Some people are sensitive to strong odors. As a result, many workplaces have a **policy** about not wearing cologne or perfume. **Policy** means

   a an opinion.   b a rule.

B Academic Phrases

Research tells us that the phrases in bold below are commonly used in academic writing.

ACTIVITY **2.2** Focus on Purpose

Read the sentences. Then match the phrases in bold to the purpose, or reason why, the writer used them.

PHRASE	PURPOSE
1 A barista is **a kind of** food worker who makes coffee at high-priced coffee shops.	a explain an idea in the previous sentence
2 Co-workers should respect each other. **In other words**, they should treat each other nicely.	b explain how two things are connected
3 Working hard **is related to** success. Employees who work hard get promotions.	c give a category

C Writing in the Real World

The author of "Workplace Tips for the 21st Century Worker" uses definitions to make sure that her reader understands certain terms. These terms are important in order to explain her ideas.

Before you read, answer these questions: What do you know about office workplaces? What issues do you think the author's tips will discuss?

Now read the article. Think about your answers to the questions above as you read.

Workplace Tips for the 21st Century Worker

by Caitlin Takeshita

1   If you've seen movies from the 1970s or 80s, you probably laughed when you saw the office spaces. The workers typed on typewriters or huge computers. They talked into large phones. Everyone did their job at their desks. Back then, companies had clear **policies** that explained appropriate[1] behavior for everyone. Workers knew exactly how to **behave**. Today's workplace looks and feels very different. It is often an open space. This type of space makes it easy for people to work together and share information. However, many companies do not have clear **policies** that explain how to work together. As a result, workers sometimes aren't sure what the rules are. Here are some tips to avoid unnecessary problems in the work space and keep friendly relationships with co-workers.

2   Today about 70 percent of workers work in open work spaces. Open work spaces are areas that have no walls. Co-workers sit next to each other. Open work spaces are a type

[1]**appropriate:** right or necessary

of design that **encourages** employees to work together. However, this design causes an increase in noise. As a result, there are more **conflicts** between co-workers because they can hear every sound, like coughing and laughing noisily. The bigger problem is people's bad **habits**. **Habits** like tapping the desk or listening to music can annoy co-workers at the next desk. There may not be a **policy** for these behaviors, but workers should be sensitive to the noise they make.

3 Another workplace problem **is related to** cell phones. These gadgets[2] cause more problems than any other because people have become addicted to them. An article in the *Chicago Tribune* stated that Americans check their phones every 5 to 10 seconds. I'm sure you have seen people answer a call in the middle of a meeting or send a text message in the middle of a face-to-face conversation. This behavior is very rude to the people around them. Don't do it. You will seem less professional if you do it.

[2]**gadget:** a small machine

4 In addition to issues with cell phones and open work spaces, social media can also cause problems. On websites like Facebook or Twitter, people often post personal photos or information about their personal lives. This is fine, but if they post complaints about their job or about other co-workers, they can get into serious trouble. For example, a waiter was fired because he posted a complaint about a customer. People need to have **control** over their actions. They are old enough to **distinguish** between good and bad behavior. If you really want to be careful, say no to a co-worker who wants to "friend" you. Keep your personal life private.

5 Work is an important part of our lives these days, so it is important to know how to make the right choices at work. HR[3] may not always tell you what to do, so you need to discover it for yourself and do what is right.

[3]**HR:** the abbreviation for *Human Resources*, which is the department at a company that hires new employees; it is an administrative office

2.3 Check Your Understanding

Answer the questions.

1 The author describes three types of problems. What are they?

2 Have you ever experienced these types of problems? Describe the situation.

3 What other twenty-first-century issues would you include in this article?

2.4 Notice the Features of Definition Writing

Answer the questions.

1 Look at the second paragraph. What term does the author define? What are some details that the author includes to help you understand the term?

2 Look at the fourth paragraph. What examples does the writer give to help define *social media*?

In Section 1, you saw how the writer of the Student Model reflected on his topic. In this section, you will analyze the final draft of his paragraph. You will learn how to organize your ideas for your own paragraph.

Ⓐ Student Model

Read the prompt and answer the questions.

WRITING PROMPT: The following words are used when talking about social skills in the workplace. Choose one and define it: *team player*, *communication skills*, or *leader*.

1 Read the title of the Student Model paragraph. What term is the writer defining?

2 Think about the term. What do you think the writer will say about it?

Read the paragraph twice. The first time, think about your answers to the questions above. The second time, answer the questions in the Analyze Writing Skills boxes. This will help you notice the key features of the paragraph.

STUDENT MODEL

Definition of a Team Player

The *Cambridge Learner's Dictionary* definition of *team player* is "member of a group who tries to do what is good for the group rather than what is good for just himself or herself." This is very true. However, it has a different meaning in the workplace. A team player is a co-worker who communicates clearly. **In other words**, he is a good speaker and listener. For example, he shares his opinions, but he **encourages** people to give their ideas, too. He avoids **conflict**. He talks to his co-workers about problems before they become serious. When he **requests** something, he is always polite. In addition, a team player supports his co-workers. For example, when his co-workers need help, he helps them. He **behaves** respectfully, and he does not try to make people feel bad. When someone does not follow a **policy** or has a bad **habit**, he explains the problem nicely. He is like a coach because he gives co-workers encouragement. Finally, a good team player does any job. He does not say, "That's not my job." For instance, waiters who are team players help clean off each other's tables when the restaurant gets busy. In brief, a team player is a valuable player on any workplace team.

1 Analyze Writing Skills

Underline the topic sentence. Circle the term that the writer is defining.

2 Analyze Writing Skills

What is the purpose of this sentence? Circle the answer.
a It gives information about the term.
b It gives another definition of the term.

3 Analyze Writing Skills

Underline a sentence that tells you what a team player does *not* do.

4 Analyze Writing Skills

What does the writer compare a team player to?
....

5 Analyze Writing Skills

Underline the sentence that gives a specific example of a team player.

Answer the questions.

1 The writer gives important characteristics of a team player. What are they? Do you agree that they are important?

2 What do you think is the most important characteristic of a team player? Why?

3 The writer describes a team player in many different ways. Which way was the most helpful, in your opinion?

ACTIVITY **3.2** Outline the Writer's Ideas

Complete the outline for "Definition of a Team Player" from page 104. Use the phrases in the box.

co-worker who communicates clearly	shares opinions
does any job	waiters who clean each other's tables
like a coach; gives encouragement	

STUDENT MODEL

PARAGRAPH OUTLINE

Topic Sentence The Cambridge Learner's Dictionary definition of team player is "member of a group who tries to do what is good for the group rather than what is good for just himself or herself."

Supporting Sentence 1 A. ....

    Detail   1. Good speaker and listener

    Detail   2. ....

    Detail   3. Avoids conflict

    Detail   4. Requests politely

Supporting Sentence 2 B. Supports co-workers

    Detail   1. Helps co-workers

    Detail   2. Behaves respectfully

    Detail   3. ....

Supporting Sentence 3 C. ....

    Detail   1. Does not say "not my job"

    Detail   2. ....

Concluding Sentence In brief, a team player is a valuable player on any workplace team.

Ⓑ Definition Paragraphs

Definition paragraphs are useful for explaining a word and/or a concept that may be unfamiliar to the reader.

There are several important reasons to define terms:

- The writer is using a term that the reader may not know. For example, a term might come from a different language or an earlier historical time.

- The term has a subjective meaning. In other words, people can have slightly different definitions of the term. For subjective terms, it is important for you to clarify the definition you will use throughout your writing.

  (Writer A): *Success means **reaching your career goals**.*

  (Writer B): *Success means **finding love and having a family**.*

- The writer has a different definition from experts or the dictionary.

- Experts disagree on a definition.

 3.3 Notice

Work with a partner. Read the Student Model paragraph on page 104 again. Why is the writer defining the term *team player*? What sentence tells you the reason?

TOPIC SENTENCES FOR DEFINITION PARAGRAPHS

The topic sentence in a **definition paragraph** defines the term and explains how it is unique.

There are two common ways to write a topic sentence for a definition paragraph:

- The first is to write your own definition. You need to state the **category** that the word belongs to and the **identifier** (trait or feature) that makes the word unique in that category.

  Notice that the identifier is often a relative clause or a prepositional phrase.

  CATEGORY   IDENTIFIER
  *A co-worker is **a person** <u>who works with you</u>.*

  CATEGORY   IDENTIFIER
  *A nonprofit is **a kind of business** <u>that does not have a main goal of making money</u>.*

  CATEGORY   IDENTIFIER
  *Personal space is **the comfortable distance** <u>between two people</u>.*

- The second way is to give a dictionary definition. Remember to write the name of the source and use quotation marks to show that the definition is from a source and is not your own words.

  SOURCE
  The Cambridge Learner's Dictionary *defines team player as a "member of a group who tries to do what is good for the group rather than what is good for just himself or herself."*

- Most definitions have a similar sentence pattern. They include the term, then the category, and finally the identifier.

TERM   CATEGORY   IDENTIFIER

*An entrepreneur is a **person** who starts and operates his or her own business.*

SOURCE   TERM   CATEGORY

*According to the Cambridge Learner's Dictionary, a bonus is **"a special amount of money***

IDENTIFIER

that you are given, especially because you have worked hard."

 3.4 Identify Parts of Topic Sentences

Read the sentences. Circle the terms. Underline the categories. Double underline the identifiers.

1 An intern is a person who is learning about a job while doing it.

2 A cubicle is a work space with low walls around it.

3 Conflict resolution is the process of solving problems between two people or two groups.

4 A rookie is a person who has just started a new job or activity.

5 Respect is a feeling that you have when you admire someone for their qualities or abilities.

 3.5 Write Topic Sentences

A Complete the sentences below. Add categories and identifiers.

1 A work space is ....

2 A cashier is ....

3 A hairdresser is ....

4 Salary is ....

B Use a dictionary and write a dictionary definition for one of the words in A.

....

Look at the cluster diagram you created for your writing prompt in Section 1 on page 99. Write two topic sentences to define the term you chose. Write one definition of your own and one dictionary definition.

1 ....

....

2 ....

....

SUPPORTING SENTENCES FOR DEFINITION PARAGRAPHS

There are many different ways to define a word. A definition paragraph should include **supporting sentences** that help define the term in one or more of the following ways:

- **Identify** the characteristics that make the term easy to recognize.

  A person who shows deference ***follows orders and doesn't complain.***

- **Compare** the idea to similar ideas.

  Deference *is **similar to politeness**.*

- Give a **negative explanation** – what the idea is *not*.

  *A person who **does not show deference acts rudely.** He or she **does not follow orders or act respectfully**.*

- Give a **specific explanation or examples**.

  For example**, employees may disagree with a new policy. **If they follow the rules and do not complain, they are showing deference to their manager.

Read the supporting sentences. Write *I* if the sentence is identifying, *C* if comparing, *NE* if giving a negative explanation, or *SE* if giving a specific example or explanation. More than one answer may be possible.

Topic sentence: Networking in business means meeting and talking to people who can help you in your work.

.... 1 Networking is similar to meeting people at any social event, but it is often more formal.

.... 2 For example, people can network at work, at school events, and at parties.

.... 3 Networking can happen anywhere at any time, but it is more common during business events.

.... 4 Networking is not for making social friends. It is about making connections for jobs.

.... 5 A person who networks can make new contacts that can help his or her career.

3.8 Write Supporting Sentences

Work with a partner. Read the following definitions. Add a supporting sentence using the way of defining a term in parentheses.

1 A co-worker is someone who works with you. (compare)

....

2 Vacation time is time when employees are not working. (negative explanation)

....

3 Cooperation is working well with co-workers to complete a task. (specific example)

....

4 Punctuality means being on time. (identify according to your culture)

....

 3.9 Apply It to Your Writing

Write three different types of supporting sentences for the definition you wrote in Activity 3.6 on page 109.

1 ....

2 ....

3 ....

In this section, you will learn writing and grammar skills that will help make your writing more academic and accurate.

Ⓐ Writing Skill 1: Distinguishing between Fact and Opinion

Because defining terms can be subjective, definition paragraphs will often include both fact and opinion. Most people will agree with facts. Not everyone will agree with opinions. Therefore, strong paragraphs use mostly facts because they are more convincing.

What is the difference between fact and opinion?

- **Facts** are true statements. Experts and scientists agree with them. They can be found in more than one source.

  Google is a large Internet company.

  United States companies can choose to give or not give employees paid vacation, according to the Fair Labor Standards Act.

- **Opinions** are judgments or beliefs. People can more easily disagree with opinions. Opinions may or may not be true.

  Google is a better place to work than other Internet companies.

  Companies should give their employees four weeks of paid vacation.

Here are some ways to identify opinions.

IDENTIFYING OPINIONS	
1 Certain verbs and modals are used to express opinions. These include: *believe, think, feel, should.*	*I **believe** that recycling will save money.* *Employees **should** bring their own lunches to work.*
2 Words that express a subjective view or judgment often show opinions. These include words such as *smart, useful, responsible, friendly, successful, success, pleasant, good, bad, better, worse, best, worst, very, quieter, smarter.*	*David was **successful** in his job. His **success** was well known.* *Co-workers who behave in a **friendly** way help make the work environment more **pleasant**.* *Email is the **best** way to communicate at work.* *Networking is the **worst** way to succeed in business.*

4.1 Notice

Read the sentences. Write *F* if the sentence is a fact or *O* if it is an opinion.

1 .... Teachers work harder than doctors.

2 .... The price of a product always shows the quality.

3 .... In the United States, less than 9 percent of top managers are women.

4 .... The president of the company pays all employees a fair salary.

5 .... The minimum wage in New York State in 2013 was $8.00 an hour.

6 .... Success is related to working hard because if you keep trying, you will succeed.

4.2 Apply It to Your Writing

Think about the term that you are going to define for your paragraph. Look at the supporting sentences you wrote in Activity 3.9 on page 110. Write two sentences to support your ideas. Work with a partner. Are your sentences opinions or facts?

1 ....

....

2 ....

....

B Writing Skill 2: Verb Tense Consistency

Verb tense consistency means using the same verb tense throughout a paragraph. In academic writing, it is important to have verb tense consistency. Writers usually use one tense in a paragraph or essay because unnecessary verb tense changes can confuse the reader. They only change the tense when there is a clear reason to change it, and they usually signal the change with a time phrase.

The following paragraph uses the present tense of the verb for most of the paragraph. The present tense is the usual tense for explaining facts and common opinions. The writer uses the past tense to compare the present and the past. Notice the time words and verbs in bold that help signal the change to past tense and then back to present tense.

According to the Cambridge Learner's Dictionary Online, *networking is "the activity of using social events to meet people who might be useful for your business." In other words, networking is making social connections that can help a person's career. It is like socializing because people meet and talk. They meet at restaurants, at parties, or at people's homes. However, it is a little different because the people want to talk about work. They discuss jobs and future opportunities.* **In the past,** *most networking* **happened** *when people* **met** *face-to-face. However,* **today** *people* **network** *on the Internet. In fact,* **within the last few years,** *several professional websites such as LinkedIn* **have started** *to connect people from far away.*

Use the following guidelines to help you choose appropriate verb tenses for your paragraphs.

1 Use **present tenses** for:
   - facts
   - definitions
   - current events

According to the Cambridge Learner's Dictionary Online, *a shuttle **is** "a bus, train, or plane that **travels** regularly between two places." It **takes** people a short distance. However, Google **uses** shuttle buses to pick up employees in San Francisco and take them to Google offices in Silicon Valley. This **is** a distance of over 40 miles. Lately, there **have been** many news stories about Google shuttle buses.*

2 Use **past tenses** for:
   - historical facts or events
   - past events at a stated time
   - specific examples from the past

*Smoking policies **changed** over time. In the late twentieth century, many cities and states **passed** laws that **made** smoking illegal in public workplaces.*

3 Use **future tenses** for:
   - predictions
   - future events

*Technology **will continue** to develop newer and better ways to communicate over the Internet. Because of this, many more employees **will choose** to work from home.*

4 If you need to change tenses, use **time phrases** or **time clauses** or signal the change.

*Telecommuting **means** to work from home over the phone or Internet. This **has become** a more popular way to work in the last 20 years. **In the past**, it **was** difficult to communicate with co-workers from an employee's home. But **today**, there **are** high-speed Internet connections and cell phones. As a result, employees **are** able to contact co-workers very quickly.*

4.3 Notice Verb Tense Consistency

Work with a partner. Underline the verbs in the paragraph. Correct the seven mistakes in verb tense consistency.

A Wallet by Any Other Name Is Still a Wallet

According to the *Cambridge Learner's Dictionary Online*, a *wallet* is a "small, folding case for paper money and credit cards." In other words, it is a way to carry money. A wallet was similar to a bank because both hold money. Also, people put money into both a bank and a wallet. In addition, people took money out of both a bank and a wallet. However, a wallet is different from a bank in some ways. A bank is a safe way to keep money, and it can hold a great deal of money. A wallet is not a safe way to keep money. Wallets were not very big, so they cannot hold a lot of money. For example, my wallet does not have very much money right now. A year ago, it has a lot of money because I have a good job at that time. I don't have enough money to fill a bank then, but I had enough money to fill my wallet. Someday, I had a good job again, and my wallet will be full of money again.

 4.4 Use the Appropriate Verb Tense

Complete the paragraph with the correct tense of the verbs in parentheses.

The Meaning of a Living Wage

A living wage ....is....... (be) a type of wage, or the amount of money, a
(1)
company .... (pay) per hour. This wage .... (allow)
(2)   (3)
a person to pay bills and to buy food. It .... (be) similar to the minimum
(4)
wage, but it .... (have) an important difference. A minimum wage
(5)
is the least amount of money that a company can pay by law. In contrast, the living wage
.... (be) the amount of money a company should pay to give employees
(6)
a good life. Usually, the living wage .... (exceed), or is larger than, the
(7)
minimum wage. For example, where I live, I .... (make) the minimum
(8)
wage of $8.00 an hour. However, the living wage where I live .... (be)
(9)
$10.00 an hour. Some people .... (say) that the living wage
(10)
.... (hurt) businesses, but I .... (believe) that in the
(11)   (12)
future it .... (help) families and society grow.
(13)

4.5 Apply It to Your Writing

Think about the ideas you brainstormed for your writing prompt in Section 1 on page 99. Write three supporting sentences. Check your sentences for verb tense consistency.

1 ....

2 ....

3 ....

C Writing Skill 3: Coordinating Conjunctions

Writers use conjunctions to put ideas together in one sentence. Use **coordinating conjunctions** like *and*, *but*, *or*, and *so* to combine words, phrases, and independent clauses. When a conjunction connects two independent clauses, it is called a compound sentence. Read the examples:

- Words: *Some employees have to work on <u>evenings</u> **and** <u>weekends</u>.*

- Phrases: *Employees can work <u>in separate offices</u> **or** <u>at separate desks</u> in one big room.*

- Independent clauses: *<u>Many employees work at night</u>, **so** <u>they sleep during the day</u>.*

Use a comma before the coordinating conjunction when it is used to combine two independent clauses.

Read the chart below to understand how to use coordinating conjunctions correctly in your writing.

USING COORDINATING CONJUNCTIONS	
1 Use *and* to add more ideas.	*Some employees ride **and** work together.* *Workers in the nineteenth century didn't have electricity, **and** they rarely used machines.*
2 Use *but* to add a contrasting idea.	*Many employees have desktop computers at work **but** laptops at home.* *You can request vacation time, **but** you may not always get it.*
3 Use *or* to show a choice.	*Many workers take the bus **or** ride a bike to work.* *Some workers have to pay for parking, **or** they can take the bus to work.*
4 Use *so* to show a result. Use it between clauses.	*Some employees receive the minimum wage, **so** they have difficulty paying for rent and food.* *One employee had the habit of listening to music at work, **so** the manager moved her far from the other workers.*

4.6 Use Coordinating Conjunctions

Complete the sentences using *and, or, but,* or *so.* Use each conjunction at least one time. Use a comma with compound sentences.

1 Full-time employees can work for a salary .... by the hour.

2 Salaried employees need to be at work on time .... they do not usually lose money for being late.

3 Hourly employees lose money for being late .... they try very hard to be on time.

4 Hourly employees earn money for working 40 hours a week .... extra money for any additional hours.

5 Salaried employees do not earn more money for working over 40 hours .... they often need to work up to 50 hours per week even though they are not paid for this overtime.

6 Many employees want salaries .... overtime pay.

 4.7 Add Ideas

Complete the sentences. Add your own ideas with *and, or, but,* and *so.*

1 Many companies are trying to protect the environment ....

2 Recycling takes a lot of time and energy ....

3 Working in an office all day long is tiring ....

4 Doing a good job is very satisfying ....

5 It is important to distinguish between ....

6 Some people like Google's pet policy ....

Ⓓ Grammar for Writing: Count and Noncount Nouns

Using **count nouns** and **noncount nouns** correctly in your writing can be challenging. Follow the basic rules below to help you use them correctly.

RULES FOR COUNT NOUNS

1 Count nouns are nouns that you can count. They can be singular or plural.	The **company** has <u>three</u> **locations** in Canada. <u>One</u> **location** has <u>two</u> **offices** in the same **city**. <u>Some</u> **employees** have <u>one</u> **boss**, but others have <u>two</u> **bosses**.
2 Singular count nouns need to have words (determiners) introduce them, such as *a, an, the, my, his, her, that,* or *this.*	<u>An</u> **employee** can put <u>his</u> **sandwich** in <u>the</u> **refrigerator** in <u>the</u> **break room**.
3 Plural count nouns do not need a determiner, but they can use determiners, such as *the, some, my, their, these,* or *those.*	<u>Some</u> **companies** have **cafeterias** for <u>their</u> **employees**.

RULES FOR NONCOUNT NOUNS

1 Noncount nouns are nouns that you cannot count. They cannot be plural. Common noncount nouns are concepts, such as *education, behavior, communication, etiquette, encouragement,* and *control.*	The **Internet** is a good source of **information** for businesses. A good boss gives her employees **encouragement** when appropriate.
2 Noncount nouns take a singular verb.	**Communication** <u>is</u> much faster through email.
3 Noncount nouns do not need a determiner, but they can use determiners, such as *the, some, my, their, these,* or *those.*	<u>Their</u> **behavior** at **work** is more formal than at **home**. Many companies let employees have <u>some</u> **control** of <u>their</u> work **schedules**.

 ACTIVITY **4.8** Identify Count and Noncount Nouns

Work with a partner. Underline the nouns in the sentences. Then label them *CS* (count singular), *CP* (count plural), or *NC* (noncount).

1 A working <u>lunch</u> is a kind of <u>meal</u> where <u>employees</u> eat and discuss <u>work</u>.
   - CS (lunch), CS (meal), CP (employees), NC (work)

2 These meals can happen at the workplace or another location.

3 The conversation may include small talk about topics such as the news, sports, or movies.

4 The behavior is more casual at these lunches.

5 Employees often dislike work lunches because they do not get a break from work.

Avoiding Common Mistakes

Research tells us that these are the most common mistakes that students make when using count and noncount nouns in academic writing.

1 **Use a determiner with singular count nouns.**

   Many employees carry <u>a</u> *bag to work.*

2. **Do not use *a/an* with a noncount noun.**

   Spoiled
   A spoiled food is often found in office refrigerators.

3. **Do not make noncount nouns plural.**

   advice
   Bosses often give employees ~~advices~~ about their careers.

4. **Use *much* – not *many* – with noncount nouns.**

   much
   It is not appropriate to wear too ~~many~~ perfume in the workplace.

 4.9 Editing Task

Find and correct six more mistakes in the following paragraph.

The Definition of Job Success

Job success is achieving goals and feeling satisfied with your work. Many people believe that ~~a~~ success is making a lot of moneys, but money does not bring many satisfaction to everybody. However, workers can feel success and a satisfaction from setting goal and reaching that goal. In addition, if employee is happy with his or her duties, he or she is more likely to do well. Enjoying work and meeting goals are very important for successes.

E Avoiding Plagiarism

Finding good information can be difficult. Knowing how to find it will help you.

My teacher says I need to find information about my topic, and she wants to see my sources. I'm not sure what she means when she says "sources." What are they, and why are they so important?

Hans

Dear Hans,

In academic writing, writers use sources to provide information for their writing assignment. Some common sources are books, newspapers, and magazines. There are also a lot of online sources like government reports and online journals, or audio and video online. Sources are important because they give you information and support for your own ideas.

Regards,

Professor Wright

FINDING GOOD SOURCES

There are many places to get information, but not all are good sources. Good sources include information you can trust.

Sources should be:	Examples of more academic sources are:	Examples of less academic sources are:
reliable up to date written by an expert	websites that end in: .gov (government sites) .org (nonprofit sites) .edu (educational sites) newspapers or magazines with good reputations for well-researched articles	personal websites, including blogs commercial websites that end in .com popular newspapers and magazines with less academic articles

ACTIVITY 4.10 Notice

A student wrote this topic sentence for a paragraph about cell phones in the workplace. Work with a partner. Check (✓) the best two sources of information for this paragraph. Explain your answer.

Most workers bring a cell phone to work, but it can affect their work and other employees.

☐ 1 A new government report on the impact of cell phones on the workplace

☐ 2 A blog with seven tips on how to create a good cell phone policy in offices

☐ 3 An article in a popular magazine that discusses cell phone etiquette at work

☐ 4 An academic article from a university on how phones affect people's work

ACTIVITY 4.11 Practice

Read the situations. Check (✓) the source you would use.

1 If you want to find information on effective teamwork on the job, go to:

☐ a a personal blog about the importance of teamwork.

☐ b an article from a newspaper about research on how companies view teamwork.

2 If you are interested in information about workplace stress, go to:

☐ a a professional association of psychologists' website.

☐ b *Workplace Wellness Massage* company's website.

3 If you are looking for information about women in the workplace today, go to:

☐ a a 2003 article on women choosing not to work.

☐ b a current government report on the number of women working now.

5 WRITE YOUR PARAGRAPH

In this section, you will follow the writing process to complete the final draft of your paragraph.

STEP 1: BRAINSTORM

Work with a partner. Follow the steps below to brainstorm more ideas for your definition paragraph.

1 Before you start, read the student's brainstorm chart. He wrote ideas from the cluster diagram he used to reflect on this topic in Section 1 on page 98. Then he brainstormed and wrote down more ideas as he thought about the topic. Finally, he crossed out the items that he thought were the least strong.

STUDENT MODEL

BRAINSTORM CHART		
Dictionary definition Cambridge Learner's Dictionary Online: "member of a group who tries to do what is good for the group rather than what is good for just himself or herself."		
Topic: Term that you are defining team player	**Category: Category it belongs to** member of a group	**Identifier: How it is different** - does what is right for the group - thinks of others and not just himself
Identifying characteristics - communicates clearly - avoids conflict - ~~honest~~ - supports co-workers - ~~behaves well~~ - ~~friendly~~ - does any job	**Comparison to similar ideas** friend helper family coach	**Negative explanation** - makes people feel bad - says "That's not my job." - ~~comes to work late~~ - ~~is competitive~~ - doesn't help
Examples and explanations Different definition in the workplace - shares opinions, listens - good speaker, talks about problems - asks for opinions - doesn't get upset - respects people - helps people	- doesn't make people feel bad - doesn't say "not my job" - waiters clean off others' tables - ~~has fun~~ - ~~doesn't insult people~~ - ~~mechanics and tools~~	

2 Now read your writing prompt again. Then review the ideas that you brainstormed in Section 1 on page 99. Write the best ones in the chart below. Include ideas from the Your Turns throughout the unit. Finally, brainstorm more ideas. You will probably not use every idea, but it is good to write as many ideas as possible.

BRAINSTORM CHART		
Dictionary definition		
Topic: Term that you are defining	**Category: Category it belongs to**	**Identifier: How it is different**
Identifying characteristics	**Comparison to similar ideas**	**Negative explanation**
Examples and explanations		

STEP 2: MAKE AN OUTLINE

Complete the outline below with ideas for your paragraph from Step 1 on page 122.

PARAGRAPH OUTLINE

Topic Sentence	....
Supporting Sentence 1	A. ....
Detail	1. ....
Detail	2. ....
Supporting Sentence 2	B. ....
Detail	1. ....
Detail	2. ....
Supporting Sentence 3	C. ....
Detail	1. ....
Detail	2. ....
Concluding Sentence	....

STEP 3: WRITE YOUR FIRST DRAFT

Now it is time to write your first draft. Here are some suggestions on how to get started.

1 Use your outline, notes, and the sentences you wrote in the Your Turns in this unit and in Step 2 on page 123.

2 Focus on making your ideas as clear as possible. Use coordinating conjunctions to join your ideas.

3 Add a title.

After you finish, read your paragraph and check for basic errors.

1 Check that all sentences have subjects and verbs. Check that your subjects and verbs agree.

2 Check that you have a topic sentence and a concluding sentence.

3 Check that you used explanations, facts, comparisons, and examples for your supporting sentences.

STEP 4: WRITE YOUR FINAL DRAFT

1 After you receive feedback on your first draft, review it carefully. Fix any errors.

2 Make a note of errors that were most frequent. Try to avoid them as you write.

3 Review the Academic Words and Academic Phrases from this unit. Are there any that you can add to your paragraph?

4 Turn to page 258 and use the Self-Editing Review to check your work one more time.

5 Write your final draft and hand it in.

5 INTRODUCTION TO THE ESSAY: OPINION ESSAYS

PSYCHOLOGY: CREATIVITY

"You can't use up creativity. The more you use, the more you have."

Maya Angelou
(1928–2014)

About the Author:

Maya Angelou was an influential American author and civil rights activist. She was most famous for her memoirs, poetry, essays, and plays.

Work with a partner. Read the quotation about creativity. Then answer the questions.

1 What is creativity? Give an example of a time when you did something creative.

2 According to Maya Angelou, being creative makes people more creative. Do you agree or disagree?

3 Maya Angelou was a famous writer. Besides writers, what other jobs require a lot of creativity?

Ⓐ Connect to Academic Writing

Up to now, you have been learning how to write a paragraph in academic English. In this unit, you will learn skills to organize your ideas in an essay. You will also learn how to give and support your opinion in an essay. Some of the skills may seem new to you, but the skill of giving opinions is not new. In your everyday life, you give opinions when you talk about why you like or don't like a movie, or when you recommend a restaurant to a friend.

Ⓑ Reflect on the Topic

In this section, you will choose a writing prompt and reflect on it. You will develop ideas throughout the unit and use them to practice skills that you need to write your essay.

The first step in writing opinion essays is deciding on an opinion. One way to decide is to brainstorm reasons why a person would agree or disagree with the idea in the writing prompt.

The writing prompt below was used for the Student Model essay on pages 132–133. The student reflected on her topic and used a chart to brainstorm possible ideas for her essay.

WRITING PROMPT: Some people believe that all high school students should be required to take a class in the arts (music, drama, art history, etc.). Do you agree? Why or why not?

Reasons to AGREE	Reasons to DISAGREE
- improves students' creativity	- takes time away from other subjects
- helps students with other subjects	- too expensive – should spend money on science
- makes students more interesting	- not everyone is creative
-	- ....
-	- ....

ACTIVITY 1.1 Notice

Work with a partner. Add two more reasons to each side of the chart. Share your ideas with the class.

1.2 Apply It to Your Writing

A Choose one of the prompts below for your essay.

- Some people believe that the best kinds of jobs are creative ones, such as jobs in art, design, or music. Do you agree? Why or why not?
- Should universities accept students who have poor grades but are very creative? Why or why not?
- Many successful people, such as Steve Jobs of Apple, have been very creative. Do you think that creative people are more successful than other people? Why or why not?
- A topic approved by your instructor

B Complete the chart below.

C Compare charts with a partner.

Reasons to AGREE	Reasons to DISAGREE
-	- ....
-	- ....
-	- ....
-	- ....
-	- ....
-	- ....
-	- ....
-	- ....

In this section, you will learn academic language that you can use in your opinion essay. You will also notice how a professional writer uses this language and writes an opinion.

Ⓐ Academic Vocabulary

The words below appear throughout the unit. They are from the Academic Word List or the General Service List. Using these words in your writing will make your ideas clearer and your writing more academic.

capable (adj)	create (v)	explore (v)	range (n)
concept (n)	design (v)	motivate (v)	relevant (adj)

 2.1 Focus on Meaning

Work with a partner. Read the sentences. Decide the meaning of the bold words and circle the correct definitions.

1 Many professional artists are **capable** of making perfect drawings of things they see. **Capable** means

   a able to do something.   b able to get money to do something.

2 Most art classes begin by teaching **concepts** such as color, light, and composition. **Concept** means

   a a test.   b an idea.

3 The artist Vincent van Gogh **created** more than 2,000 paintings and drawings, but he only sold one. **Create** means

   a to buy something new.   b to make something new.

4 One of the most creative people today is Jony Ive, the man who **designed** the iPod, iPhone, and iPad for Apple. He made drawings of what these products would look like. **Design** means

   a to make plans for building something.   b to build something in a factory.

5   Before they start a painting, many artists make smaller drawings to **explore** the subject they want to paint. This helps them understand their subject better. **Explore** means

   a   to make many copies of something.   b   to search and discover more about something.

6   Money probably doesn't **motivate** people who choose to become painters because most artists are not paid well. **Motivate** means

   a   to make someone want to do something.   b   to know clearly about something.

7   Over his lifetime, Pablo Picasso made a **range** of art, including paintings, sculptures, and drawings. **Range** means

   a   a selection of very different things.   b   a selection of similar things.

8   People who study the sciences do not usually take many art classes because they are not **relevant** to their majors. **Relevant** means

   a   based on math.   b   related to.

B Academic Collocations ⊙

Collocations are words that are frequently used together. Research tells us that the academic vocabulary in Part A is commonly used in the collocations in bold below.

ACTIVITY 2.2 Focus on Meaning

Work with a partner. Match the collocations in bold to their meanings. Write the letters.

.... 1   The musician Miles Davis worked with **a wide range of** musical styles, including jazz, rock, and experimental music.

.... 2   With his trumpet, Davis was **capable of expressing** many different emotions, such as excitement, sadness, anger, and joy.

.... 3   One of the **basic concepts** of photography is to put the subject of your picture in the center.

.... 4   Because he grew up poor, Charles Dickens' **main motivation** for writing novels was to show the difficult lives of poor children.

.... 5   People who want to **explore the possibility** of becoming an artist can begin by taking a short art course at a local school.

a   to see if something can be done

b   the first thing you need to learn

c   able to show

d   many different kinds

e   the most important reason

C Writing in the Real World

The author of "This Math Teacher Wants More Classes in the Arts" expresses her opinion about the arts in schools.

Before you read, answer this question: Why do you think a math teacher wants more classes in the arts?

Now read the article. Think about your answer to the question above as you read.

THIS MATH TEACHER WANTS MORE CLASSES IN THE ARTS

BY PATRICIA BLANC

1   In my 23 years as a high school math teacher, there have been only a few students I couldn't reach. Mark was one of them. A small, shy boy, he slumped[1] quietly in the back of my algebra class, looking bored. Mark didn't have any motivation, struggled to pay attention in class, and had trouble with **basic concepts** like long division. I helped him after class, I found tutors for him, but nothing worked. Mark even began to miss classes, and I worried that he might drop out.[2]

2   Then, suddenly, I noticed big differences in Mark's behavior. Mark began to sit up straight in class. He took notes, asked questions, and smiled. His homework improved, and his test scores got better, too.

3   Why did Mark change? It wasn't because of anything I did. Mark's performance improved because he started taking an art class. For the first time, he found a subject he liked and was good at. Even though he was shy and quiet in person, he was **capable of expressing** his ideas and feelings with a paintbrush. Art class **motivated** Mark to stay in school and gave him confidence to try harder in other subjects.

4   Mark is not alone. Many experts believe that classes in the arts – music, painting, theater, film, and more – do more than develop a student's creativity. They can also help students in math and other subjects. Also, students who take arts classes drop out of school less often. This is why 40 states in the United States require high school students to take classes in the arts. Sadly, our state is not one of them, but it should be.

5   There is strong evidence[3] that classes in the arts can help students in other subjects. A 2007 study found that students who took music classes scored more than 20 percent

[1]**slump:** sit with the head and shoulders bent forward
[2]**drop out:** stop going to school before graduation

[3]**evidence:** anything that helps to prove something is or is not true

higher on math and English tests. According to a different study, children who began to take singing and piano lessons improved their scores on IQ tests. A third study found that children who learned about paintings were better at remembering information. A report from the President's Committee on the Arts and the Humanities mentions **a wide range** of studies that say that arts classes help students solve problems and think creatively and critically.

6   That is not all. Researchers also believe that classes in the arts improve student motivation. When schools teach the arts, students **pay attention** more in class, and more students hope to go to college. One study, by the anthropologist Shirley Brice Heath, found that students who received arts education were "three times more likely to have high attendance."[4] Some of these students are like Mark – art class is their **main motivation** for staying in school. Other students simply feel more confident and interested in school after taking these classes.

7   For all of these reasons, our schools must give the arts the importance – and the money – they deserve. I strongly believe that our state must join the other 40 that have made high school classes in the arts a requirement. If we do not, what will happen to other students like Mark, who could be helped so much by the arts? Thanks to art class, Mark not only finished high school, he also finished college and graduate school, and is now a teacher himself. What subject does he teach? He has just joined my own department as a new algebra teacher.

[4]**attendance:** being at an event or going to a place

 2.3 Check Your Understanding

Answer the questions.

1   What are the main reasons why the author thinks high schools should require classes in the arts?

2   What evidence (facts, stories, examples, details) does the author give for her opinion? Which evidence do you think is the strongest? Why?

3   Have you ever had an experience like Mark's? If so, what happened?

 2.4 Notice the Features of Opinion Writing

Answer the questions.

1   Look at the first four paragraphs. In which paragraph does the author try to make the reader interested in the topic? In which paragraphs does the author give her opinion on the topic?

2   How many reasons does the author give to support her opinion? In which paragraphs can you find those reasons?

3   Look at the last paragraph. In which sentence does the author restate her opinion?

In Section 1 on page 126, you saw how the writer of the Student Model reflected on her topic. In this section, you will analyze the final draft of her essay. You will learn how to organize your ideas for your own essay.

Ⓐ Student Model

Read the prompt and answer the questions.

WRITING PROMPT: Some people believe that all high school students should be required to take a class in the arts (music, drama, art history, etc.). Do you agree? Why or why not?

1 What are some reasons to agree?

2 What are some reasons to disagree?

3 Read the title. What opinion do you think the writer has? What reasons do you think she will give?

Read the essay twice. The first time, think about your answers to the questions above. The second time, answer the questions in the Analyze Writing Skills boxes. This will help you notice the key features of an opinion essay.

High School Students Do Not Need the Arts

1   In today's world, education is very important because you need a college degree for many good jobs. High schools need to do many things to prepare students for college. For example, students have to learn math, English, science, and history, and they must also study for college entrance exams. Recently, some people have said that high schools should also make students take classes in the arts, for example, painting, theater, fashion, film, or music. The arts are nice, but this is not a good idea. High schools should not make students take classes in the arts for three main reasons: these classes do not prepare students for college, they are too expensive, and students do not have time for them.

2   The first reason why classes in the arts should not be required is that these classes do not prepare students for college. This is true in two ways. First, students do not need to take arts classes to get into college. Most college applications ask for three things: the student's grades, scores on achievement tests, such as the SAT, and a personal essay. Students do not have to do a dance, **design** a dress, or **create** a painting when they apply to college. Second, unless they are going to an art school, most students do not plan to major in[1] the arts. Since they are not going to **explore the possibility** of being a painter or dancer in college, the arts are not **relevant** to them in high school.

[1]**major in:** to study something as your main subject in college

> **1 Analyze Writing Skills**
>
> Underline the sentence in paragraph 1 that gives the writer's opinion and her reasons for it.

> **2 Analyze Writing Skills**
>
> Underline the topic sentences in paragraphs 2–4. Circle: The topics are **the same as / different from** the topics in the last sentence in paragraph 1.

3   Another reason for my opinion is that classes in the arts cost too much money. These classes need a **wide range of** expensive equipment such as paint, musical instruments, or video cameras. Most schools do not have the money to give these things to every student. If the school buys them, it will not have enough money for more important subjects, such as chemistry and biology, which also need expensive supplies. The school could make students buy their own art supplies, but many students cannot afford them. Also, this is not fair because people should not have to spend money on a class they are required to take.

4   The final reason that high school students should not have to take classes in the arts is that they do not have enough time to **explore** these subjects. High school students are already busy with many important things. First, they have to take classes they need for college. Second, they have homework in all of these subjects. Third, students have to spend time preparing for important college entrance tests, such as the SAT. Many students already spend all of their evenings and weekends doing these things, so they do not have enough time to act in a play or practice the piano as well.

3 Analyze Writing Skills

Circle the words that show that this will be the last paragraph of the essay.

5   In conclusion, the goal of high school is to prepare students for college. Classes in the arts do not prepare students for college, and there is not enough money or time for those classes, so they should not be required. If high schools force students to study these subjects, it is possible that fewer students will go to college, and they will be less successful as adults. Instead of spending money on the arts, high schools should offer more tutoring and test preparation.

4 Analyze Writing Skills

Circle: The last sentence is **a prediction / a recommendation / an example.**

ACTIVITY 3.1 Check Your Understanding

Answer the questions.

1 Does the writer think high schools should require classes in the arts?

2 What three reasons does the writer give?

3 Do you agree with the writer? Why or why not?

ACTIVITY 3.2 Outline the Writer's Ideas

Complete the outline for "High School Students Do Not Need the Arts." Use the phrases in the box.

arts not required on applications	musical instruments	test scores
homework	other subjects more important	

STUDENT MODEL

ESSAY OUTLINE

I. Introductory paragraph

Thesis Statement High schools should not make students take classes in the arts for three main reasons:

These classes do not prepare students for college, they are too expensive, and students

do not have time for them.

Body Paragraph 1: Reason 1 II. Doesn't prepare students for college

Supporting Sentence A. What college applications require

Detail 1. Grades

Detail 2.

Detail 3. Essay

Supporting Sentence B.

Supporting Sentence C. Most students not art majors

Body Paragraph 2: Reason 2 III. Classes too expensive

Supporting Sentence A. Equipment is expensive

Detail	1. Paint
Detail	2.
Detail	3. Video cameras
Supporting Sentence	B.
Detail	1. Chemistry
Detail	2. Biology
Supporting Sentence	C. Students can't afford equipment
Body Paragraph 3: Reason 3	IV. No time for arts classes
Supporting Sentence	A. Students already busy
Detail	1. Classes
Detail	2.
	3. Preparing for college entrance tests
Supporting Sentence	B. No time for the arts
	V. Concluding paragraph
Concluding Sentence	Instead of spending money on the arts, high schools should offer more tutoring and test preparation.

B From Paragraph to Essay

The paragraph and the essay are similar in many ways. A paragraph is a group of sentences about one topic. An essay is a group of paragraphs about one topic. Each paragraph presents a key point about the topic.

You have already learned that a paragraph has three important parts:

- a **topic sentence** that introduces the main idea to the reader
- **supporting sentences and details** that are in the **body** of the paragraph. They give specific information about the topic sentence.
- a **concluding sentence** that ends the paragraph and usually restates the topic sentence.

As you can see below, an essay is similar to a paragraph because it has three parts, too. However, each part is much longer and gives more information about the supporting sentences and details. This additional information gives more support to the writer's ideas and makes them stronger and more convincing.

PARAGRAPH	ESSAY
Topic sentence	Introductory paragraph – Background information – Thesis statement
Supporting sentence 1 details	Body paragraph 1 – Topic sentence – Supporting statements and details
Supporting sentence 2 details	Body paragraph 2 – Topic sentence – Supporting statements and details
Supporting sentence 3 details	Body paragraph 3 – Topic sentence – Supporting sentences and details
Transition word + restatement of topic sentence	Concluding paragraph – Transition word – Restatement of thesis sentence – Comment or recommendation

3.3 Notice

Look at the chart on page 136. Circle the correct words to complete the sentences.

1 The topic sentence in a paragraph is **similar to** / **different from** the thesis statement in an essay.

2 A supporting sentence in a paragraph is similar to a **topic sentence** / **thesis statement** in an essay.

3 The last sentence of a paragraph usually restates the topic sentence of the paragraph. The concluding paragraph of an essay **usually restates** / **does not restate** the topic sentence of the essay.

 3.4 Identify Parts of the Essay

Work with a partner. Read the Student Model essay on pages 132–133 again. Then circle the answers.

1 In the introductory paragraph, which is the thesis statement?

  a "In today's world, education is very important because you need a college degree for many good jobs."

  b "High schools should not make students take classes in the arts for three main reasons: these classes do not prepare students for college, they are too expensive, and students do not have time for them."

2 How are the other paragraphs related to the thesis statement?

  a They explain and support the thesis statement in the first paragraph.

  b They give new opinions and topics that are not in the thesis statement.

3 In each body paragraph, what does the topic sentence do?

  a It gives another reason for the writer's opinion.

  b It makes a comment or recommendation.

4 In the concluding paragraph, which sentence restates the thesis statement?

  a "Classes in the arts do not prepare students for college, and there is not enough money or time for those classes, so they should not be required."

  b "In conclusion, the goal of high school is to prepare students for college."

5 In the concluding paragraph, which recommendation does the writer make?

  a Schools should make fewer students go to college.

  b Schools should spend more money on tutoring.

C Opinion Essays

At the end of this unit, you will write your first academic essay. This will be a special kind of essay called an **opinion essay**. In this type of essay, you give your opinion on a topic. You also give the reasons for your opinion.

THE INTRODUCTORY PARAGRAPH OF OPINION ESSAYS

The **introductory paragraph** is always the first paragraph of an essay. It does two important things:

- It invites the reader into the essay with interesting **background information** about the topic.
- It tells the reader what the essay is about in the **thesis statement**. The thesis statement is usually the last sentence or last two sentences in the paragraph.

In an opinion essay, the **background information** helps readers understand the topic and why it is important. Background information can include:

- general information about the topic

- important facts about the topic

- a story that helps readers understand why the topic is important

- historical information about a topic

- issues that people relate with the topic

In an opinion essay, the thesis statement gives the writer's opinion about the topic. The purpose of the essay is to persuade readers of this opinion.

- Make sure the thesis statement gives only one opinion on the topic.

- Introduce the opinion with expressions such as *in my opinion, in my view, I believe*, or with modal verbs such as *should, ought to, need to*, or *must*.

- The thesis statement often mentions the main reasons for the opinion. Each body paragraph in the essay will be about one of these reasons.

For every writing prompt, there are many possible good thesis statements that answer the question in the prompt. Here are two examples:

WRITING PROMPT: In many countries, the government gives money to support artists and creative people. Do you think this is a good idea? Why or why not?

Good thesis statement: *In my opinion, government support for artists is a good idea because art can improve a country's image, increase tourism, and attract new businesses.*

Good thesis statement: *In my view, government support of artists is a bad idea. It takes money away from more important things, and it could increase taxes.*

A good thesis statement always gives only one opinion that clearly answers the question in the writing prompt. The following are *not* good thesis statements:

Poor thesis statement: *There are many reasons why governments should not support creative people, but there are also reasons why supporting creative people is a good idea.* (The statement has two opinions. There should only be one.)

Poor thesis statement: *In my opinion, creative people struggle to earn money because they do not make art that average people can understand or enjoy.* (The statement does not answer the question. The question in the prompt is about government support of the arts, but the thesis statement is about why many artists are not well paid.)

 3.5 Notice

A **Read the introductory paragraph below. Underline the background information and circle the thesis statement.**

Government Support for Artists

Throughout history, there have always been artists and other creative people, and they have often struggled to earn a living. One example of this is the famous painter Vincent van Gogh. He only sold one painting during his life, and he was often poor and hungry. Today, we all enjoy van Gogh's work, and he might have made even more wonderful paintings if he had received more support. Luckily, today there are many programs that give money to help artists, including some government programs. In my view, the city government ought to do more to support artists because this will create more art for everyone to enjoy, it will attract tourists, and it will encourage more young people to be artists.

B **Answer the questions.**

1 What will the essay be about?
2 Why does the writer mention Vincent van Gogh?
3 What is the writer's opinion about the topic?
4 How many reasons does the writer give for his opinion? What are they?

3.6 Notice Background Information

Work with a partner. Read the writing prompt and the background information about the topic in each sentence. Circle the kind of information each sentence gives.

WRITING PROMPT: In many countries, the government gives money to support artists and creative people. Do you think this is a good idea? Why or why not?

1   Vincent van Gogh only sold one painting in his life. He might have painted more if he had received more support.

    a   issues related to the topic   b   a story about the topic

2   Government support of the arts raises questions about taxes, poverty, the economy, and more.

    a   issues related to the topic   b   historical information

3   Since the first cave paintings were made more than 40,000 years ago, art has been part of human culture.

    a   historical information   b   a story

4   In 2014, a United States government program called the National Endowment for the Arts (NEA) gave over $75 million to artists and arts organizations.

    a   issues related to the topic   b   an important fact

 3.7 Notice Thesis Statements

Read the writing prompt. Check (✓) the good thesis statements. Then compare answers with a partner. Discuss why the others are not good thesis statements for the prompt.

WRITING PROMPT: Most artists do not earn much money. Should parents discourage their children from being artists?

☐ 1   Most artists do not earn enough money because most people are not interested in art and would prefer to spend their time on other forms of entertainment.

☐ 2   Even though most artists are not rich, parents should allow their children to be artists because this will make the children happier and more interesting people.

☐ 3   I believe that parents should not encourage their children to be artists because art is an expensive hobby, most artists are very poor, and children need to earn and save money for their future.

☐ 4   In my view, children who are very talented in the arts should be encouraged, but sometimes it is better for children to make money to support their families because it is so hard to succeed in the arts.

☐ 5   If a child wants to be an artist, it is the parents' job to encourage the child, because he or she will be a better artist with the family's support, and he or she could become very successful and wealthy.

3.8 Apply It to Your Writing

Look at the brainstorm chart you created for your writing prompt in Section I on page 127. Write a thesis statement for your essay. Include one clear opinion.

....

....

....

BODY PARAGRAPHS OF OPINION ESSAYS

Body paragraphs give more information about the ideas in the thesis statement. Each body paragraph should be about one of the reasons in the thesis statement. For example, if your thesis statement gives three reasons for your opinion, your essay should have three body paragraphs – one paragraph for each reason.

Each body paragraph:

- starts with a **topic sentence** that gives one reason for your opinion. This reason should be one of the reasons mentioned in the thesis statement.
- includes **supporting examples**, **details**, or **expert opinions** that support your reasons.
- uses phrases like *one reason, another reason, finally* to help connect one paragraph to the next paragraph:

    The first reason/One reason *why classes in the arts should not be required is that these classes do not prepare students for college.*

    Another reason for my opinion is *that classes in the arts cost too much money.*

    The most important reason *why these classes should not be required is that most students are not interested in them.*

    The final reason *that high school students should not have to take classes in the arts is that they do not have enough time to explore these subjects.*

    Finally*, high school students should not have to take classes in the arts because they do not have enough time to explore these subjects.*

 **3.9** Notice

Work with a partner. Read the thesis statement and the two body paragraphs. Then answer the questions.

Thesis statement: Art today often costs millions of dollars, but in my view it is not worth that much because anyone could make it, and it is often made from worthless things.

Body paragraph 1: The first reason why modern and contemporary art should not be worth very high prices is that anyone can make it. Today's art can be made with very little skill or talent. For example, paintings by the artist Jackson Pollock have sold for over $100 million, but Pollock did not even use paintbrushes. He just dripped, poured, and squirted paint on the canvas. Anyone can do that. Also, some artists do not even make the things that they display as art. One example of this is the French artist Marcel Duchamp. In 1917, Duchamp bought a toilet at a hardware store and put it in an art gallery. The critics said he was a genius, but anyone could have done that. More recently, the British artist Tracy Emin "made" a work of art by moving her bed into an art gallery. Someone paid £150,000 for it (about $250,000). This price is not reasonable because nearly all of us already have a bed and do not need to buy one – especially not for $250,000.

Body paragraph 2: Another reason for my opinion is that today's art is often made from materials that have no value. Some artists work with very cheap materials. The American artist Tom Friedman is an example of this. He has made expensive art from toothpicks, pieces of tape, plastic cups, and drinking straws. Recently, Friedman put a single green pea on a gallery wall and sold it for $35,000. This is not a reasonable price. No one will want to eat a pea that has been on a wall, so it really has no value. There are even artists, such as the American artist Joseph Cornell, who make art from things they find in the garbage. Today, people pay more than $100,000 for Cornell's work even though it is actually made of trash.

1 Circle the topic sentence in each paragraph.

2 Each topic sentence gives a different reason for the writer's opinion. What is the reason in each topic sentence?

3 Underline the supporting sentences in each paragraph.

4 Put a dotted line under the details in each paragraph. Is each detail a fact, an explanation, or an example?

5 Read the thesis statement again. Circle the two reasons in the thesis statement. Are they the same as the reasons in the topic sentences of the body paragraphs?

 3.10 Write Topic Sentences for Body Paragraphs

Read the thesis statement at the top of page 143. Complete the topic sentences for each body paragraph. Make sure each body paragraph makes a different point.

Thesis statement: There should be more television programs about the arts because these programs are educational, they make viewers more creative, and they help support artists.

Body paragraph 1: One reason why we need more programs about the arts is ....

....

Body paragraph 2: Another reason for my opinion is that ....

....

Body paragraph 3: Finally, television channels ought to have more programs about the arts because ....

....

ACTIVITY **3.11** Organize Ideas

Work with a partner. Read the opinion below. Think of three reasons for the opinion and write a few words or important phrases to suggest these reasons.

Opinion: It's a good idea for everyone to have a creative hobby like painting or making music.

Reason 1: ....

Reason 2: ....

Reason 3: ....

ACTIVITY **3.12** Write Topic Sentences

Look at the reasons in Activity 3.11. Use your ideas to write a topic sentence for each body paragraph. Use some of the expressions below to begin your topic sentences.

the first reason for my opinion is	the most important reason is
one reason why I believe this is	the final reason is
another reason for my opinion is	finally

Body paragraph 1

Topic sentence: ....

....

Body paragraph 2

Topic sentence: ....

....

Body paragraph 3

Topic sentence: ....

....

3.13 Write Supporting Sentences

Work with a partner. Look at your sentences in Activity 3.12. Write one supporting sentence for each of the topic sentences. Add a detail (a fact, an explanation, or an example) for each supporting sentence.

Body paragraph 1

Supporting sentence: ....

Detail: ....

Body paragraph 2

Supporting sentence: ....

Detail: ....

Body paragraph 3

Supporting sentence: ....

Detail: ....

 3.14 Write a Body Paragraph

Look at Activities 3.11–3.13. Choose a topic sentence, supporting sentence, and detail. Write one body paragraph on a separate sheet of paper. Add one more supporting sentence and detail to the paragraph.

 3.15 Apply It to Your Writing

YOUR TURN

Look at your brainstorm chart in Section 1 on page 127 and the Your Turns in this unit. Write a body paragraph explaining one reason for your opinion. Use the steps in this section as a guide.

CONCLUDING PARAGRAPH

The **concluding paragraph** is the last paragraph of the essay. It does not add any new topics or main points. Instead, the concluding paragraph summarizes what you have written and ends the essay in an interesting way. The concluding paragraph usually:

- begins with a **transition phrase** to show that you are concluding. These phrases include: *in conclusion, in short, in sum, to summarize,* and *to conclude.*

  In conclusion*, the goal of high school is to prepare students for college.*

- **restates** the thesis statement from the introductory paragraph. You can do this in the first or second sentence of the concluding paragraph.

- ends with a **final comment**. This could be one or both of the following:

  - a recommendation (something that people should do):

    Instead of spending money on the arts, high schools should offer more tutoring and test preparation.

  - a prediction:

    If high schools force students to study these subjects, fewer students will go to college, and they will be less successful as adults.

  The final comment will show readers that your essay is finished. You do not need to end the concluding paragraph by writing, "This is the end of my essay," or something similar.

HOW TO RESTATE THE THESIS STATEMENT

You have already learned how to restate the topic sentence of a paragraph in a concluding sentence. You can use the same skills to restate the thesis statement.

Thesis statement in introductory paragraph: *High schools should not make students take classes in the arts because these classes do not prepare students for college, they are too expensive, and students do not have time for them.*

Restated thesis in concluding paragraph: *Classes in the arts do not prepare students for college and there is not enough money or time for them, so they should not be required.*

The writer used a few strategies to restate the thesis:

- **Change the order:** In the introductory paragraph, the writer gave her opinion first, then her reasons; in the concluding paragraph, she gave the reasons first, then her opinion.

- **Repeat phrases:** In both sentences, the writer used the phrases *classes in the arts* and *prepare students for college.*

- **Use different words for the same idea:** In the introductory paragraph, the writer wrote that arts classes *are too expensive, and students do not have time for them*. In the concluding paragraph, she wrote that *there is not enough money or time for them*.

When you restate the thesis, make sure you include all of the important points in the thesis statement. Do not leave any ideas out, and do not add ideas that were not in the thesis statement.

 **3.16** Notice

Read the introductory and concluding paragraphs of the opinion essay below. Then do the following:

1 Underline the thesis statement in the introductory paragraph.

2 Underline the sentence in the concluding paragraph that restates the thesis.

3 Circle the reasons given in the thesis and the restatement of it in the concluding paragraph.

4 Put a dotted line under the transition phrase used in the concluding paragraph.

5 Put a box around the final comment. Does the writing end with a recommendation, a question, or a prediction?

WRITING PROMPT: Many people are creative as children but become less creative as adults. Is this a good thing or a bad thing? Why do you think so?

Introductory Paragraph

People change in many ways as they become adults. Many of us were very creative as children but became less creative and artistic as adults. In my view this is a bad thing because the world needs creative adults to invent new products, to entertain us with books and movies, and to solve important problems in the world.

Concluding Paragraph

To summarize, most adults are less creative than they were as children. Because we need creativity for inventions, entertainment, and solutions to major problems, in my opinion it is a shame that so many adults are not creative. For this reason, all adults should spend at least an hour each day doing something creative, such as writing or painting.

 3.17 Restate the Thesis

Work with a partner. For each thesis statement, choose the sentence that best restates it. Why do you think it is the best restatement?

1 **Thesis statement:** In my view, everyone should have a creative hobby such as painting because it keeps your mind sharp, it is relaxing, and it can be a good way to make friends.

Restatements:

a Because painting and other creative hobbies relax you and keep your mind sharp, I believe that everyone should have one.

b In my opinion, it is a good idea for all people to have creative hobbies so they can relax, keep their minds sharp, make friends, and possibly even become famous artists.

c Creative hobbies like painting help people relax, improve their minds, and meet new people, so in my view everyone should have one.

2 **Thesis statement:** Television channels do not need to make more programs about the arts because there are already enough videos about art online, few people will watch these programs on television, and the channels will lose money.

Restatements:

a In my view, there should not be more programs about the arts on television because very few people will watch them, the TV channels will lose money, and the art might offend some viewers.

b There is no need for more arts programming on television because the Internet is full of these programs, and not enough people will watch them on TV, so a network will not make money.

c Because there are already so many websites for the arts, I believe there is no reason for television channels to show more programs about these subjects.

3 **Thesis statement:** I believe that imagination is more important than knowledge because we need imagination to solve important problems, to make valuable inventions, and to entertain ourselves.

Restatements:

a Because imagination is necessary to invent, entertain, and solve critical problems in the world, in my view, it is more important than knowledge.

b In my opinion, the main reason why imagination is more important than knowledge is that we need imagination to solve major problems in the world, such as global warming.

c Imagination is more important than knowledge in my view because imagination lets us invent things, entertain ourselves, find solutions to important problems, and most importantly it lets us dream.

 3.18 Make a Final Comment

Choose the best final comment for the concluding paragraph below. Write it at the end of the paragraph. Discuss your answer with a partner.

In summary, television is an important issue because almost everyone watches it, including young children. Television can be entertaining, but it should also be educational. I believe there should be more television programs about the arts because they will help teach our children, they will make viewers more creative, and they will also help support artists. ....

a Thank you for taking the time to read my essay, which is now finished.

b If television channels make more of these programs, in a few years we will probably see our children's test scores get better.

c Another thing people should do is give money to museums because many museums also have educational activities for children.

In this section, you will learn writing and grammar skills that will help make your writing more academic and accurate.

Ⓐ Writing Skill 1: Background Information

In the introductory paragraph of an essay, writers give background information. This helps readers understand the topic and gets them interested in it. You have already seen that background information can include facts, a story, general information, historical information, or issues. There are also many different ways to order background information. One way is to begin with a very general statement and then write sentences that become more and more specific, until you get to the specific topic of the essay. Notice how the writer of the Student Model essay wrote her background information.

In today's world, education is very important because you need a college degree for many good jobs. High schools need to do many things to prepare students for college. For example, students have to learn math, English, science, and history, and they must also study for college entrance exams. Recently, some people have said that high schools should also make students take classes in the arts, for example, painting, theater, fashion, film, or music.

The writer begins with a sentence about the general topic of education.

The next sentence is about something more specific: high school education.

Next, the writer gives more specific information about what high school students need to do.

Finally, the writer adds a sentence that is about the specific topic of the essay.

For the general sentences, you can use phrases such as *in today's world*, *throughout history*, *is an important issue today*, and *most people are familiar with*.

In today's world, education is extremely valuable.

Schools and education have been important to people **throughout history**.

Education **is an important issue today**.

Most people are familiar with the issue of education.

4.1 Order Information

Read the prompt and the background information for an introductory paragraph.
Number the sentences from 1 (most general) to 4 (most specific).

WRITING PROMPT: Most artists do not earn much money. Should parents discourage their children from being artists?

.... a   Therefore, parents worry about the subjects their children study and the careers they choose.

.... b   They do not approve of careers in the arts because these jobs often pay very little money.

.1........ c   Throughout history, parents have always wanted their children to grow up to be happy and successful adults.

.... d   Many parents want their children to be doctors, lawyers, or engineers because these jobs pay well.

 4.2 Write a General Sentence

Read the prompt, background information, and thesis statement. Then choose the most general sentence to begin the introductory paragraph. Write it on the line.

WRITING PROMPT: Some people think that having a creative hobby like painting or photography is good for you. Should everyone have a creative hobby? Why or why not?

....

Background information: People need hobbies that help them relax, challenge their minds, and socialize with friends. There are very few hobbies that help people do all three of these things. Sports are social but not always relaxing, and hobbies like collecting or doing puzzles are relaxing and stimulate the brain, but are not very social. However, a creative hobby like painting or photography can do all three of these things.

Thesis statement: In my view, everyone should have a creative hobby because it is a great way to relax, keep your mind sharp, and meet new friends.

a   In today's world, people have hobbies for a few different reasons.

b   Photography is a creative hobby that helps people in many ways.

c   Painting and photography are all examples of creative hobbies.

4.3 Write Specific Information

Read the prompt, background information, and thesis statement for an introductory paragraph. The last sentence of background information is missing. Write a specific sentence that completes the background information and connects it to the thesis statement. Then compare sentences with a partner.

WRITING PROMPT: Many people are creative as children but become less creative as adults. Is this a good thing or a bad thing? Why?

Background information: There are many differences between adults and children in our society. In addition to physical differences, children and adults also have different minds. One of the biggest differences between the minds of children and adults is in the area of creativity.

....

Thesis statement: In my view, it is actually a good thing that adults are less creative because many adults need to do very important but uncreative work like building things, fixing things, and keeping people safe.

4.4 Apply It to Your Writing

Think about your opinion for the writing prompt you chose and the ideas you brainstormed in Section 1 on page 127. On a separate sheet of paper, write four sentences of background information for your topic. Make sure each sentence is more specific and is connected to the topic of the previous sentence.

Ⓑ Writing Skill 2: The Thesis Statement

In most academic essays, the last sentence of the introductory paragraph is the thesis statement. The thesis statement answers the question in the writing prompt and gives the controlling idea that the rest of the essay will be about. A good opinion thesis statement includes the following:

- the topic of the essay

- the writer's idea, opinion, or point of view about the topic

- the main reasons for the writer's opinion

Notice how the thesis statements below include each of these things:

|———————— IDEA/OPINION ————————||——— TOPIC ———| |———— REASON ————|
High schools should not make students take classes in the arts because these classes do not prepare
|———————— REASON ————————| |———— REASON ————|
students for college, they are too expensive, and students do not have time for them.
|———— TOPIC ————||——— IDEA/OPINION ———| |———— REASON ————|
Government support for artists is a good idea, in my opinion, because art can improve a country's
|——— REASON ———| |——— REASON ———|
image, increase tourism, and attract new businesses.

4.5 Complete Thesis Statements

A Work with a partner. Read the incomplete thesis statements. Write the letter of the missing parts. Write *T* for topic, *O* for opinion, and *R* for reason.

WRITING PROMPT: These days, some works of art costs millions of dollars. Do you think people should pay so much money for art? Why or why not?

O ...... 1 Some art is extremely expensive today, but in my view people should buy it if they want to because it helps the economy and also because it is their money and they can buy whatever they want.

.... 2 It is now common for some art to cost millions of dollars, but I believe people should not spend so much money on art because ....

.... 3 These days, ..., and in my view this is a good thing because these are beautiful works of art, and buying them will support artists.

.... 4 People .... because, in my opinion, today's art could be made by anyone, and it would be better to spend that money to help the poor.

B Now complete the thesis statements in A with the missing parts. Read the example above. Then compare your answers with a partner.

 4.6 Write Thesis Statements

Read the topic sentences for three body paragraphs for three essays. Write a thesis statement for each essay. Make sure your thesis statement matches the opinion and reasons in the topic sentences of the body paragraphs.

1 **Thesis statement:** ....
....

Body paragraph 1: One reason why there should be more art on TV is to educate people.

Body paragraph 2: Another reason to have more art on TV is that it is relaxing.

Body paragraph 3: Finally, it is a good idea to have more art on TV because it will support artists.

2 **Thesis statement:** ....

....

Body paragraph 1: The first reason why knowledge is more important than imagination is that we need knowledge to make useful things, such as bridges.

Body paragraph 2: Another reason is that children need knowledge to do well in school.

Body paragraph 3: The most important reason for my opinion is that people need knowledge to get a good job.

3 **Thesis statement:** ....

....

Body paragraph 1: One reason why people should not buy expensive art is that artists today are making art out of garbage and ordinary materials, so people should not have to pay a lot of money for it.

Body paragraph 2: Another reason for my opinion is that art should be affordable for everyone.

Body paragraph 3: Finally, people should not buy expensive art because it should be in public museums and not in private collections.

 4.7 Apply It to Your Writing

Think about the writing prompt you chose in Section I on page 127 and the Your Turns in this unit. Write a thesis statement for your essay.

....

ⓒ Grammar for Writing: Word Forms

Knowing the different forms of words is an essential skill in good writing because writers connect an idea across sentences by changing the forms of a word. Look at this example:

> *Children who **create** art benefit from this hobby later in life. Research shows that they are often more **creative** as adults, and **creativity** is linked to effective problem solving.*

You usually change the form of a word using a suffix. Common suffixes are *-er/-or* and *-tion*. Suffixes are syllables you can add to a word to change its form, that is, its meaning or part of speech. For example, five new words are formed by adding suffixes to the verb *create*:

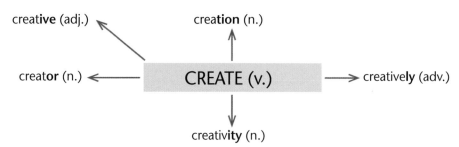

Different suffixes form different parts of speech. Here are some common suffixes.

COMMON SUFFIXES	
1 Add a suffix to a verb to make a noun. Common suffixes: *-sion/-tion, -er/-or,* *-ment*	apply → applic**ation** conclude → conclu**sion** educate → educa**tion** explore → explora**tion** motivate → motiva**tion** prepare → prepara**tion** design → design**er** explore → explor**er** invent → invent**or** paint → paint**er** achieve → achieve**ment** require → require**ment**
2 Add a suffix to a verb or adjective to make a noun. Common suffixes: *-ance/-ence, -ness, -ity*	attend → attend**ance** enter → entr**ance** important → import**ance** perform → perform**ance** relevant → relev**ance** confident → confid**ence** independent → independ**ence** friendly → friendl**iness** great → great**ness** happy → happ**iness** open → open**ness** equal → equal**ity**
3 Add a suffix to a noun or verb to make an adjective. Common suffixes: *-able, -ful*	comfort → comfort**able** love → lov**able** value → valu**able** help → help**ful** success → success**ful** use → use**ful**
4 Add a suffix to a verb to make an adjective. Common suffix: *-ive*	act → act**ive** create → creat**ive**

(CONTINUED)

5 Add a suffix to an adjective to make an adverb. Common suffix: *-ly*	*creative → creatively* *different → differently* *extreme → extremely* *final → finally* *quiet → quietly* *real → really* *recent → recently* *sad → sadly* *sudden → suddenly*

 4.8 Write the Correct Word Form

Complete the concluding paragraph. Add the correct forms of the words in parentheses. Sometimes you do not need to add a suffix.

In .... (conclude), there are a few reasons why the government
 (1)
should give money to support artists. First, many .... (create)
 (2)
people have to work other jobs to survive. Government help would give them freedom
and .... (independent) so they can spend more time on their
 (3)
art. Second, these programs give artists more .... (confident)
 (4)
that they can make a living as artists. This is important because people who feel
.... (confident) are generally more likely to be
 (5)
.... (success). .... (final), government programs
 (6)   (7)
to support the arts will .... (motivate) young children to explore the
 (8)
possibility of becoming artists when they are older. This is a good thing because too many
people lose their .... (create) when they become adults. For
 (9)
these reasons, the city and state government should include more money for the arts in this
year's budget.

Avoiding Common Mistakes

Research tells us that these are the most common mistakes that students make when using suffixes in academic writing.

1 Write *-ful* for words like *useful, helpful, wonderful, successful, powerful.* Do not write *-full.*

 Some people say that classes in the arts are not ~~usefull~~ useful or ~~helpfull~~ helpful, but in fact these classes increase student test scores in math and reading.

2 Use the *-ence* ending for nouns like *difference, patience,* and *self-confidence.* Do not use *-ance.*

 Artists and engineers both need creativity, but the ~~differance~~ difference is that engineers earn more money.

3 Write *-lly* for adverbs like *really, finally, especially, totally,* and *personally.* Do not write *-ly.*

 ~~Finaly~~ Finally, arts classes are necessary because they help students stay in school.

 4.9 Editing Task

Find and correct six more mistakes in the paragraph below.

One ~~differance~~ difference between children and adults is that adults are often less creative. In my view, that is a good thing because we need adults to do jobs that are usefull and helpful but are not always creative. For example, we need people to build important things like bridges, and people need to know that these are safe so they can use them with confidance. This work is not realy creative, but it has a lot of importance. If adults were as creative as children, they might not want to do this sort of work. We also need doctors and nurses to keep us healthy. These are wonderfull and important jobs that require a lot of patience, skill, and knowledge. However, they do not require as much creativity as a career in the arts. Finaly, our country needs police officers and soldiers to protect us. People in these jobs have to follow orders and do not have many chances to be creative. In sum, because there are many important jobs that do not require creativity, it is a good thing that many adults are less creative than children.

D Avoiding Plagiarism

Finding information is the first step to writing a good academic paper.

Q

My instructor told us that good writers support their thesis statements. I sometimes see quotation marks around text from sources, but I don't see them all the time. How do writers use information they find to support their thesis statement without plagiarizing?

Ken

A

Dear Ken,

There are a few ways to use information that you find. Using the author's words in quotation marks is one way. You can also write the information in your own words. In both cases, the important thing is that you always mention the author. That is called citing your sources. That is how writers use information without plagiarizing.

Sincerely,

Professor Wright

USING INFORMATION WITHOUT PLAGIARIZING

For each source that you use, you must cite your source. It doesn't matter if it is a quote or if it is your own words. The original author's name is an important part of any information you use. If you use the MLA style, you will also include the page number if it is available.

Here are three ways to use information without plagiarizing.

How to use information to support your writing	Examples
1 Put the author's exact words in quotation marks. Choose interesting phrases or unusual ideas to quote. Also, choose things that are not easy to paraphrase. Be careful! Don't quote too much.	*Csikszentmihalyi says, "When we're creative, we feel we are living more fully than during the rest of life" (56).*
2 Write the author's ideas in your own words and use the author's name in the sentence with a phrase like *according to.* We call this a signal phrase, or an in-text citation.	*According to Root-Bernstein, schools can model creativity, but they can't teach it (4).*
3 Write the author's ideas in your own words and cite the author at the end of the sentence.	*Both taking a shower and working in a blue room can increase creativity (Zielinski 21).*

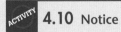 **4.10** Notice

Work with a partner. Read a paragraph from a student's essay. How many ways did the writer use information to support his writing? Use the chart on page 156 to help you.

There are many ways for older people to stay creative. According to Stacia Pierce, people should write and keep journals (3). It is also important to think about things in new ways (Secord 15). Csikszentmihalyi suggests that we should "make time for reflection and relaxation" (5).

 4.11 Practice

Read a paragraph from a student's essay. Underline the sentence that uses quotation marks. Double underline the sentence that uses a signal phrase. Circle the sentence that puts the name of the author at the end.

Some argue that older people are not as creative as younger people. According to Moody, it is true that older people take longer to learn new things, and their reactions are slower (359). However, he believes older people can still be creative. Moody says, "Creativity can mean doing old things in a new way, or in a different way" (qtd. in Collins 3). If people learn new things, they can be creative all of their life (Bahrampour 6).

In this section, you will follow the writing process to complete the final draft of your opinion essay.

STEP 1: BRAINSTORM

Work with a partner. Follow the steps below to brainstorm more ideas for your topic.

1   Before you start, read the student's brainstorm chart. She wrote ideas from the chart she used to reflect on her topic in Section 1 on page 126. Then she brainstormed and wrote down more ideas. After reading the reasons to agree and disagree, she formed an opinion and checked the box with ideas she could use in her essay.

STUDENT MODEL

BRAINSTORM CHART
WRITING PROMPT: Some people believe that all high school students should be required to take a class in the arts (music, drama, art history, etc.). Do you agree? Why or why not?

☐ Reasons to AGREE	✓ Reasons to DISAGREE
- improves students' creativity	- takes time away from other subjects
- helps students with other subjects	- too expensive – should spend money on science
- makes students more interesting	- not everyone is creative
- opportunity to explore new subjects	- does not prepare students for college
- helps support local artists, museums, etc.	- many arts classes are not interesting

2 Now read your writing prompt again and write it in the chart. Then review the ideas you brainstormed in Section 1 on page 127. Write the best ones in the chart below. Include ideas from the Your Turns throughout the unit. Finally, brainstorm more ideas. You will probably not use every idea, but it is good to write as many ideas as possible. Form an opinion and check (✓) the box with ideas that will help you write about your opinion.

BRAINSTORM CHART

WRITING PROMPT: ....
....

☐ Reasons to AGREE	☐ Reasons to DISAGREE
-	- ....
-	- ....
-	- ....
-	- ....
-	- ....
-	- ....
-	- ....
-	- ....

STEP 2: MAKE AN OUTLINE

Complete the outline below with ideas from Step 1 on page 159.

ESSAY OUTLINE

I. Introductory paragraph

Thesis Statement

Body Paragraph 1: Reason 1

II.

Supporting Sentence

A.

Detail

1.

Detail

2.

Supporting Sentence

B.

Detail

1.

Detail

2.

Body Paragraph 2: Reason 2

III.

Supporting Sentence

A.

Detail

1.

Detail

2.

Supporting Sentence

B.

Detail

1.

Detail

2.

Body Paragraph 3: Reason 3	IV. ....
Supporting Sentence	A. ....
Detail	1. ....
Detail	2. ....
Supporting Sentence	B. ....
Detail	1. ....
Detail	2. ....
	V. Concluding paragraph ....
Concluding Sentence	....
	....

STEP 3: WRITE YOUR FIRST DRAFT

Now it is time to write your first draft. Here are some suggestions on how to get started.

1 Use your outline, notes, and the sentences you wrote in the Your Turns in this unit and in Step 2 on pages 160–161.

2 Focus on making your ideas as clear as possible.

3 Add a title.

After you finish, read your essay and check for basic errors.

1 Check that all sentences have subjects and verbs.

2 Check that you have used the correct word forms and suffixes.

3 Check that your background information explains the topic and makes the reader interested in it.

4 Check that your thesis statement includes the topic, your opinion, and your reasons for your opinion.

STEP 4: WRITE YOUR FINAL DRAFT

1 After you receive feedback on your first draft, review it carefully. Fix any errors.

2 Make a note of errors that were most frequent. Try to avoid them as you write.

3 Review the Academic Words and Collocations from this unit. Are there any that you can add to your essay?

4 Turn to page 259 and use the Self-Editing Review to check your work one more time.

5 Write your final draft and hand it in.

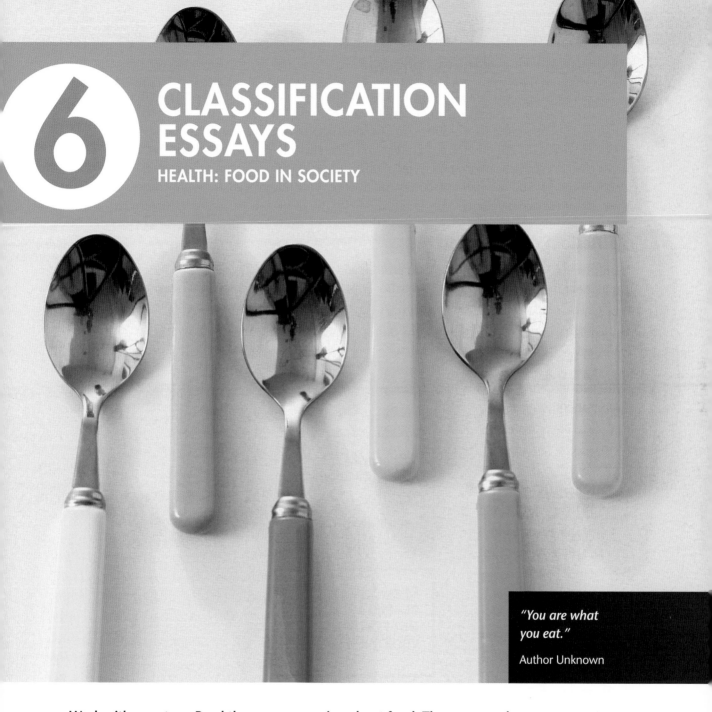

6 CLASSIFICATION ESSAYS

HEALTH: FOOD IN SOCIETY

> *"You are what you eat."*
>
> Author Unknown

Work with a partner. Read the common saying about food. Then answer the questions.

1 Think of someone you know who has a special diet, for example, a vegetarian or someone who eats a certain food on special days. What does this eating habit tell you about the person's culture, values, or interests?

2 What is something you love to eat and something you never eat? What can people learn about you from these preferences?

3 Do you agree with the saying that "you are what you eat"? Why or why not? Give examples.

A Connect to Academic Writing

In this unit, you will learn skills to write a classification essay. Some of the skills may seem new to you, but the skill of classifying is not new. In your everyday life, you use the skill of classifying when you talk about the style of shoe that is appropriate for certain jobs or the kind of car that is best for people in cities. When you classify, you put items into groups based on what the items have in common. For example, you might group cars with two doors and cars with four doors. This helps you compare categories and discover their advantages or disadvantages, and their similarities and differences.

B Reflect on the Topic

In this section, you will choose a writing prompt and reflect on it. You will develop ideas throughout the unit and use them to practice skills that you need to write your essay.

The writing prompt below was used for the Student Model essay on pages 170–171. The student reflected on his topic and used a cluster diagram to brainstorm possible ideas for his essay.

WRITING PROMPT: What are three places where people can get fruit and vegetables? What is special about each place?

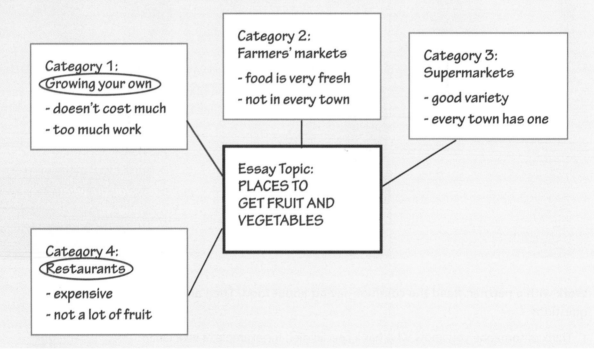

ACTIVITY 1.1 Notice

Work with a partner. Look at the cluster diagram above. *Doesn't cost much* and *expensive* are both information about price. What other kinds of information are similar to each other? Share your ideas with the class.

1.2 Apply It to Your Writing

A **Choose a writing prompt for your essay and follow the directions below.**

- What are three types of healthy diets?
- What are three things that influence a person's eating habits?
- What are three ways to improve your health and quality of life?
- A topic approved by your instructor

B **Complete the cluster diagram below. Write an essay topic, three categories related to the topic, and everything you know about the categories. You can add more boxes if you want to write about more categories.**

C **Compare cluster diagrams with a partner.**

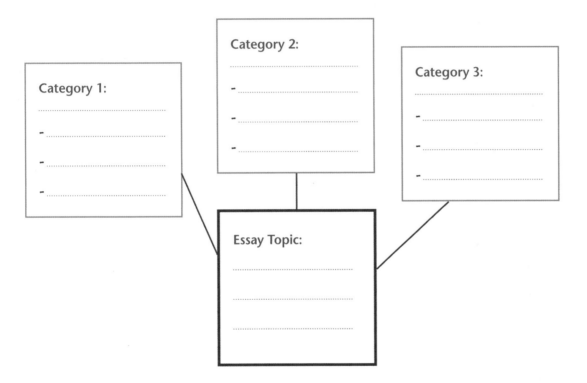

In this section, you will learn academic language that you can use in your classification essay. You will also notice how a professional writer uses this language and classifies items.

A Academic Vocabulary

The words below appear throughout the unit. They are from the Academic Word List or the General Service List. Using these words in your writing will make your ideas clearer and your writing more academic.

approach (n)	contemporary (adj)	medicine (n)	traditional (adj)
condition (n)	eliminate (v)	suffer (v)	treat (v)

 2.1 Focus on Meaning

Work with a partner. Read the sentences. Decide the meaning of the bold words and circle the correct definitions.

1 One **approach** to preventing heart disease is to eat green vegetables and avoid eating red meat. **Approach** means

   a a problem.   b a method.

2 Doctors advise people who have a heart **condition** to avoid red meat and foods high in fat, and to be careful when they run or exercise. If you have a **condition**, you are

   a sick.   b healthy.

3 Many restaurants in the United States serve a kind of food called "**contemporary** American." They cook well-known dishes in new ways and with new ingredients. **Contemporary** means

   a old.   b modern.

4 More and more people are **eliminating** red meat from their diets and eating only fruit and vegetables. **Eliminate** means

   a remove something.   b reduce something.

5 According to some scientists, chicken soup fights a cold better than **medicine** sold at pharmacies. You take **medicine** because you feel

   a hungry.   b sick.

6 People who **suffer** from lactose intolerance cannot drink milk. If they drink milk, they become sick. If you **suffer** from something, you

   a have an illness.   b have a bad habit.

7 In the United States, the **traditional** Thanksgiving meal always includes a turkey. **Traditional** means

   a unusual or unique.   b following a custom.

8 Many people believe that the best way to **treat** a cold is to rest and drink plenty of water or tea. If you **treat** an illness, you

   a try to stop it.   b make it worse.

B Academic Phrases

Research tells us that the phrases in bold below are commonly used in academic writing.

^{ACTIVITY} **2.2** Focus on Purpose

Read the paragraph. Then match the phrases in bold to the purpose, or reason why, the writer used them.

Farming in the United States

The United States is a large country with a lot of open land, and as a result, the country has always had many farms. From TV shows and movies, these farms may **appear to be** small, simple places that one family owns. **It is possible** to farm that way today, of course, but more and more farms are actually corporate farms owned by large companies. Overall, there are **a variety of** kinds of farms in the United States, including family farms, corporate farms, and cooperative farms owned by several farmers.

PHRASE	PURPOSE
.... 1 appear to be	a show there is more than one kind
.... 2 It is possible	b show that something seems a certain way
.... 3 a variety of	c show that something can be done

C Writing in the Real World

The author of "Eat Healthy the Chinese Way" uses classification to talk about food.

Before you read, answer these questions: What kinds of food do you think the article will say are healthy? What foods will it probably say are not healthy?

Now read the article. Think about your answers to the questions above as you read.

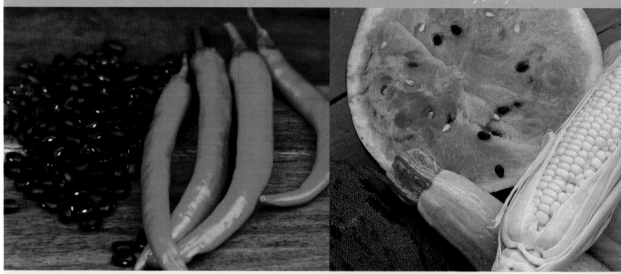

EAT HEALTHY THE CHINESE WAY
by Jenny Cho

1   We all know that food affects[1] our health. Everyone can think of **a variety of** food that fights illness, such as chicken soup or broccoli. There are also unhealthy junk foods, like burgers and candy. But what about the foods that aren't on either extreme,[2] such as watermelon, cherries, or cinnamon? These foods don't **appear to be** bad for us, but they also don't prevent disease. Most Americans don't know how to classify these foods in the middle. However, in **traditional** Chinese culture, nearly every food can be classified as healthy or unhealthy, depending on how it is eaten.

2   **Traditional** Chinese **medicine** is complex, but the basic concepts are easy. All food is divided into two categories: hot and cool. These categories aren't based on the temperature of the food on your plate. Instead, these categories are based on how the food affects the body: hot foods make you warmer, and cool foods make you cooler. Hot foods are usually high in calories, have spicy or bitter flavors, and sometimes have hot colors like red or orange. Examples of hot foods are lamb, peppers, cinnamon, and ginger. Cool foods have fewer calories and have cool colors like white and green. Watermelon, corn, and tofu are all cool foods.

[1]**affect:** have an influence on something
[2]**extreme:** a point that is very far from another point

3 So which kind of food is better for your health, hot or cool? The answer is not that simple. In **traditional** Chinese **medicine**, the goal is balance. You don't want to be too hot or too cold. So, it is not always a good idea to eat hot foods in the summer because the weather is already raising your body's temperature. If you eat too much hot food, you may feel nervous and have digestive[3] trouble. Similarly, you don't want to eat a lot of cool foods in winter. Eating too much cool food can make you feel weak or depressed. Instead, the **traditional** Chinese **approach** is to eat cool foods when your body is too hot, and eat hot foods when your body is too cool.

4 Hot and cool foods also help when you feel sick. In **traditional** Chinese **medicine**, most illnesses can also be classified as hot or cool. When you **suffer** from a hot illness such as a rash[4] or a sore throat, try **treating** it by eating something cool like cucumbers or strawberries. If you have a cool **condition** such as a stomachache or the chills, have some beef, black beans, or other hot foods. By learning a little bit about these Chinese traditions and treatments, people from any country can make better choices to improve their health.

[3]**digestive:** related to what happens in your body after you eat

[4]**rash:** a skin problem

 2.3 Check Your Understanding

Answer the questions.

1 What are the two kinds of food in traditional Chinese medicine? Give some examples of each kind.

2 In traditional Chinese culture, when should you eat each kind of food?

3 What foods are considered healthy or unhealthy in your culture?

 2.4 Notice the Features of Classification Writing

Answer the questions.

1 Read the second paragraph. Which sentence introduces the two categories of food? What phrase does the author use to introduce the categories?

2 Read the last paragraph. Which sentence introduces the two categories of illness. What phrase does she use to introduce the categories?

In Section 1, you saw how the writer of the Student Model reflected on his topic. In this section, you will analyze the final draft of his essay. You will learn how to organize your ideas for your own essay.

Ⓐ Student Model

Read the prompt and answer the questions.

WRITING PROMPT: What are three places where people can get fruit and vegetables? What is special about each place?

1 What places do you think the writer will mention?

2 What are some good points and bad points about each place?

Read the essay twice. The first time, think about your answers to the questions above. The second time, answer the questions in the Analyze Writing Skills boxes. This will help you notice key features of a classification essay.

STUDENT MODEL

Three Places to Find Healthy Food

1   To stay healthy, more and more people are **eliminating** junk food and are eating more fruit and vegetables. **A variety of** places now sell these foods, so it is easier for people to eat well today. However, not all fruit and vegetable sellers are the same. In the United States, the main places to get fruit and vegetables are at supermarkets, at farmers' markets, and in your own garden, and each place has advantages and disadvantages.

2   One place to get fruit and vegetables is at a supermarket. The cost of grocery store produce[1] can be low or very high. An apple costs fifty cents at some places. At other places, it costs two dollars. One reason for the difference is the quality of the produce. Some supermarkets import[2] produce cheaply from other countries. It does not cost much to import, but the produce is not always the freshest. Also, **it is possible** that farmers used chemicals to grow it. Other supermarkets sell organic[3] fruit and vegetables from local farms that do not use chemicals. The quality is often higher, but so is the price. In most towns, there is usually at least one supermarket, so for most people, it is a convenient place to buy produce.

> **1 Analyze Writing Skills**
>
> Underline the categories mentioned in the thesis statement. How many categories are mentioned?

> **2 Analyze Writing Skills**
>
> Underline the phrase the writer uses to introduce the first category.

> **3 Analyze Writing Skills**
>
> Check (✓) the kinds of information that the writer gives in the first body paragraph.
>
> ☐ cost
> ☐ convenience
> ☐ healthiness
> ☐ popularity
> ☐ quality

[1] **produce:** fruit and vegetables
[2] **import:** bring in products from another country
[3] **organic:** made without artificial chemicals

3   Another place to get fruit and vegetables is at farmers' markets. These are places where local farmers come to sell the fruit and vegetables they grow. Produce usually costs less than at supermarkets. The quality is often better because the fruit and vegetables are fresh and often do not contain chemicals. In the United States, some neighborhoods in big cities have a farmers' market, but most places do not have one, so this place is not convenient for everyone.

4 Analyze Writing Skills

Does the writer give the same kinds of information in the remaining body paragraphs as in the first body paragraph? Circle *yes* or *no*.

4   The final place to get fruit and vegetables is to grow them at home. This can be inexpensive. All you need are some cheap seeds, dirt to plant them in, water, sun, and time. If you are good at gardening, the quality of the produce can be very good. Perhaps your vegetables do not look as pretty as the ones in the store, but they are fresher and will probably taste better. However, growing food at home is not convenient for everyone. It requires space, special tools, and a lot of time and hard work.

5   In conclusion, farmers' markets, supermarkets, and your own garden are three places to get fruit and vegetables, and all of them have good points and bad points. Supermarkets prices are often cheap, but the quality varies,[4] and growing your own vegetables is healthy but takes time and hard work. The best place to buy produce is probably at farmers' markets, if one is nearby, because the prices are often low and the quality is usually high.

5 Analyze Writing Skills

Underline the sentence that restates the thesis statement of the essay.

[4]**vary:** be different in different places or times

3.1 Check Your Understanding

Answer the questions about the student essay on pages 170–171.

1 What places does the writer mention?

2 What does the writer say about the cost, quality, and convenience of each place?

3 Which place does the writer think is best? Why does he think so?

3.2 Outline the Writer's Ideas

An outline helps you see the structure of the essay and the connection between ideas. Complete the outline for the student essay on pages 170–171. Use the phrases in the box.

expensive in others	better than supermarkets	not pretty but fresh
farmers' markets	lower than supermarkets	sometimes organic

STUDENT MODEL

ESSAY OUTLINE

I. Introductory paragraph

Thesis Statement
In the United States, the main places to get fruit and vegetables are at supermarkets, at ...., and in your own garden, and each place has advantages and disadvantages.

Body Paragraph 1: Category 1
II. Supermarkets

Detail/ Characteristic
A. Cost

Explanation
1. Cheap in some places

Explanation
2. ....

Detail/ Characteristic
B. Quality

Explanation
1. Sometimes imported, not fresh, chemicals

Explanation
2. ...., fresher, more expensive

Detail/ Characteristic	C. Convenience
Explanation	1. Usually one in every town
Explanation	2. Convenient for most people
Body Paragraph 2: Category 2	III. Farmers' markets
Detail/ Characteristic	A. Cost:
Explanation	1. Local farmers
Explanation	2. Local produce
Detail/ Characteristic	B. Quality:
Explanation	1. Fresh
Explanation	2. No chemicals
Detail/ Characteristic	C. Convenience: not for everyone
Explanation	1. Sometimes in big cities
Explanation	2. Not in most places
Body Paragraph 3: Category 3	IV. Growing your own
Detail/ Characteristic	A. Cost: low
Explanation	1. Cheap seeds
Explanation	2. Needs dirt, water, time
Detail/ Characteristic	B. Quality: very good
Explanation	1.
Explanation	2. Taste better

(CONTINUED)

Detail/ Characteristic	C. Convenience: not for everyone
Explanation	1. Requires special tools
Explanation	2. Takes time and space
	V. Concluding paragraph
Concluding Sentence	The best place to buy produce is probably at farmers' markets, if one is nearby, because the prices are often low and the quality is usually high.

B Classification Essays

PURPOSE AND STRUCTURE

The purpose of a classification essay is to reveal interesting points about a topic by dividing it into its main categories. The structure of a classification essay is similar to other academic essays. A classification essay includes:

- an **introductory paragraph** that gives background information to introduce the topic and make the reader interested in it. The introductory paragraph also gives a thesis statement that mentions the topic and the main categories.

- **body paragraphs** that give more information about the categories. Each body paragraph is about a different category. However, each body paragraph gives the same kinds of information about each category, for example, information about price, convenience, and quality.

- a **concluding paragraph** that restates the thesis statement and ends with a final comment or recommendation.

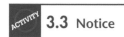 **3.3** Notice

Read the Student Model essay on pages 170–171 again. Answer the questions.

1 Circle the main categories in the essay.

    a convenience stores   c farmers' markets   e home gardens

    b large farms   d restaurants   f supermarkets

2 How many categories does each body paragraph describe?

    a one   b two   c three

3 Find a sentence in the introductory paragraph that mentions the topic and the main categories. Write it on the line. ....

....

4 Find a sentence in the concluding paragraph that restates the topic and the main categories. Write it on the line. ....

....

CHOOSING CATEGORIES

In classification essays, writers explain a topic by dividing it into categories. For example:

- the main types of meals: *breakfast, lunch, dinner, dessert, snacks*
- the main types of items on a menu: *appetizers, entrées, drinks, desserts*

When writers choose the main categories for their topic, they keep the following rules in mind:

Rules

1 The categories should cover the topic completely.

2 Each category should be different from the others so that everything belongs in only one category and nothing can be put into two or more categories.

3 All of the categories should be related to the topic.

4 There is something interesting to write about each category.

Here are some examples of categories that do *not* follow the rules above:

The main places to eat a meal are at home, in a car, or on a plane. (These categories do not cover the topic well because they do not include eating at restaurants or eating outside in a park.)

The main ways to eat a meal are with friends, at a party, or in a restaurant. (These categories are not different enough. A meal at a party is usually the same as a meal with friends.)

The main ways to eat a meal are because you are hungry, to lose weight, or for enjoyment. (These are not related to the topic of *ways* to eat a meal. They are reasons why a person might eat a certain kind of food.)

The main ways to eat a meal are with your right hand, your left hand, or both hands. (Although these categories are related to the topic, there are probably not enough interesting things to write equally about each one.)

3.4 Evaluate Categories

Work with a partner. Check (✓) the student who chose good categories for the writing prompt. Write X next to the students who did not follow the rules mentioned on page 175. Which rules didn't the students follow?

WRITING PROMPT: We need food to survive, but food is also a business. What are the main types of businesses that are based on food?

☐ **Student 1:** supermarkets, farmers' markets, and shopping malls

☐ **Student 2:** farms, supermarkets, restaurants, and packaged food companies

☐ **Student 3:** local supermarkets, online supermarkets, and supermarket chains

☐ **Student 4:** vegetarians, people trying to lose weight, and people with food allergies

3.5 Write Categories

Work with a partner. Read the writing prompts. Write three categories for each prompt.

1 **WRITING PROMPT:** What are the main types of restaurants or places that serve food?

....

....

....

2 **WRITING PROMPT:** What are the main types of reasons why a person would not want to eat a certain food?

....

....

....

3 **WRITING PROMPT:** In many countries, different regions (parts) of the country serve different kinds of food. What are the main types of regional food in your country?

....

....

....

3.6 Apply It to Your Writing

YOUR
TURN

Look at the cluster diagram you created for your writing prompt in Section 1 on page 165. Write the essay topic and three categories below. Discuss your categories with a partner. Are all the categories good for the topic?

Essay Topic ....

Category 1: ....

Category 2: ....

Category 3: ....

POINTS OF CLASSIFICATION

In classification essays, writers explain each category with the same criteria or characteristics. For example, in the Student Model essay, the writer described the *cost*, *quality*, and *convenience* of each place to get fruit and vegetables. By using the same criteria or characteristic for each category, it is easy for readers to see the advantages, problems, or interesting points about each category.

Look at the notes below about places to eat a meal. Notice that the writer gives the same kind of information about each category: *cost*, *atmosphere*, and *taste*. This kind of information is called a **point of classification.** Most essays have three points of classification.

It is important to choose points of classification that are relevant to the categories you are writing about. In the example above, the points are relevant because you can describe the cost, atmosphere, and taste for each category.

An example of a point of classification that is *not* relevant in the discussion of places to eat is *weather*. This is *not* a good point of classification for the prompt and categories. You can only talk about the weather for the last category, eating a meal outdoors. The other categories, at home and in a restaurant, are indoors, so you cannot talk about the weather for these categories.

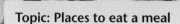

Topic: Places to eat a meal

Category 1: At home
Cost: very low
Atmosphere: Familiar and comfortable, but not special
Taste: It depends on how well you can cook.

Category 2: In a restaurant
Cost: high, higher than at home
Atmosphere: Interesting and new
Taste: Usually very good, and you can try new/foreign flavors.

Category 3: Outdoors (a picnic)
Cost: Depends. Food you bring from home: low; prepared food from supermarket or special food stores: high
Atmosphere: Excellent. You can enjoy nature or watch people while you eat.
Taste: Depends on how you get the food.

3.7 Choosing Points of Classification

Read the writing prompts and the categories. For each prompt, write three points of classification. Write a word or two for each point of classification, for example, cost, taste, atmosphere. Compare with a partner. Is each point of classification interesting and relevant?

1 **WRITING PROMPT:** What are the main types of restaurants or places that serve food?

Categories: street vendors, fast-food places, sit-down restaurants

Points of classification:

1 ....
2 ....
3 ....

2 **WRITING PROMPT:** What are three popular types of international food where you live?

Categories: Chinese food, Italian food, Mexican food

Points of classification:

1 ....
2 ....
3 ....

3 **WRITING PROMPT:** What are three types of businesses that are based on food?

Categories: farms, supermarkets, restaurants

Points of classification:

1 ....
2 ....
3 ....

3.8 Give Details about Points of Classification

Read the writing prompt, categories, and points of classification below. For each category, write a sentence about each point of classification.

WRITING PROMPT: What are the main types of restaurants or places that serve food?

Category 1: Street vendors

Cost: Food from street vendors is usually not very expensive.

Convenience: Street vendors are very convenient for people who live or work in a big city.

Health: Street food is often high in fat and can sometimes make people sick.

Category 2: Fast-food places

Cost: ....

Convenience: ....

Health: ....

Category 3: Sit-down restaurants

Cost: ....

Convenience: ....

Health: ....

3.9 Apply It to Your Writing

Think about the categories you wrote for your writing prompt in Activity 3.6 on page 176. Write three points of classification for your categories. Make sure your points of classification can describe all of your categories. (You may need to change some of your categories to make this easier.)

Categories:

1 ....

2 ....

3 ....

Points of classification:

1 ....

2 ....

3 ....

BODY PARAGRAPHS

In a classification essay, each body paragraph is about a different category. For example, if you write about three categories, your essay will have three body paragraphs.

Each body paragraph begins with a topic sentence that introduces one of the categories. You can introduce the category with expressions such as:

One (name the category) *is …*

> One **place to eat** is at home.

… is/are another (name the category)

> Restaurants are another **place to eat** a meal.

The first/second/last (name the category) *is …*

> The last **place to eat** a meal is outdoors, for example, at a picnic.

After the topic sentence introduces the category, the points of classification give interesting and relevant explanations about the category. The categories in each body paragraph are different, but the points of classification in each body paragraph should be the same.

Notice the topic sentence and the points of classification in the body paragraph below:

Topic sentence introducing the category	Point of classification: cost

One place to eat a meal is at home. The cost of a meal at home is very low because you can use food from the supermarket and you do not have to pay for a cook, waiter, tax, or tips. A meal at home can have a familiar, comfortable, and relaxing atmosphere, but it might not feel exciting or special. The best thing about a meal at home is the taste, if you or your family can cook well. You can enjoy flavors that remind you of your family, your friends, and happy memories.

Point of classification: atmosphere

Point of classification: taste

3.10 Write Topic Sentences

Write topic sentences for the two body paragraphs below.

WRITING PROMPT: What are the main types of restaurants or places that serve food?

Body paragraph 1:

....

Food from street vendors is usually not very expensive. You can often eat a meal for only a few dollars. Street vendors are also very convenient for people who live or work in a big city. In many cities, there are parks or other places where a lot of different food trucks sell meals. One negative thing about street vendors is that the food is not always very healthy. Street food like hot dogs and hamburgers are high in fat, and sometimes street vendors are not very clean and their food can make people sick.

Body paragraph 2:

....

The price of fast food is usually fairly low. For example, many fast-food places sell hamburgers for only a dollar, or a complete meal with a hamburger, fries, and a drink for about five dollars. These restaurants are also extremely convenient. You can find fast-food places in almost every town, so they are nearby. They are also convenient because they can prepare a meal for you in just a minute or two. One bad thing about fast food is that it is unhealthy. These meals are very high in calories and fat, and it is not good to eat this type of food every day.

 3.11 Write a Body Paragraph

A Write three categories for the writing prompt. Then compare your categories with a partner.

WRITING PROMPT: What are three types of businesses that are based on food?

Category 1: ....

Category 2: ....

Category 3: ....

B Write three points of classification to describe each category. For each point of classification, add some interesting details about each category. Then compare your ideas with a partner.

Point of classification A: ....

Point of classification B: ....

Point of classification C: ....

C Write a body paragraph about one of the categories on a separate sheet of paper. Use your ideas in A and B.

INTRODUCTORY AND CONCLUDING PARAGRAPHS

The **introductory paragraph** of a classification essay is similar to other kinds of academic essays. It begins with **background information** that introduces the topic and makes your readers interested in it. The introductory paragraph then gives a **thesis statement** that states the three main categories you will write about in your essay. When you write your thesis statement, you may want to use expressions such as:

- The main types / ways / kinds of … are …

  *In most cultures, **the main types of meals** are breakfast, lunch, dinner, dessert, and snacks.*

- … can be classified as …

  ***Almost all meals** can be classified as breakfast, lunch, dinner, dessert, or snacks.*

The **concluding paragraph** of a classification essay is the same as in other academic essays. The concluding paragraph:

- begins with a **transition phrase**, such as *in conclusion* or *in sum*
- restates the **thesis statement**
- ends with a **final comment**, such as a recommendation or prediction.

3.12 Write Thesis Statements

Read the writing prompts. For each prompt, write a thesis statement. Include three categories in each thesis statement. Use the expressions you learned on page 182.

1 **WRITING PROMPT:** What are the main ways to eat a meal?

The main ways to eat a meal are with your hands, with a fork and knife, or with chopsticks.

2 **WRITING PROMPT:** What are the main types of food on a restaurant menu?

....

3 **WRITING PROMPT:** What types of international food are popular where you live?

....

4 **WRITING PROMPT:** What are the main types of restaurants in your city or town?

....

 3.13 Apply It to Your Writing

Look at the thesis statement you wrote in Section 1. Does it mention all three categories? Does it use the expressions you learned on page 182? Rewrite your statement to include them if needed.

....

....

....

In this section, you will learn writing and grammar skills that will help make your writing more academic and accurate.

Ⓐ Writing Skill: Sentence Variety

In academic writing, it is important to use sentences with different lengths and different structures. This is called **sentence variety**. Using different sentence types makes writing more natural and more academic.

Here are a few ways to add sentence variety to your writing.

- **Vary the order of time clauses:** Do not always use time clauses at the beginning of the sentence. Use them in the beginning sometimes and at the end other times.

  TIME CLAUSE AT BEGINNING
  When you buy produce at farmers' markets, it usually costs less than at supermarkets.

  TIME CLAUSE AT END
  Produce usually costs less than at supermarkets when you buy it at farmers' markets.

- **Use a mix of simple, compound, and complex sentences:** Combine two or more sentences to make one sentence.

  Simple sentence: *This can be an inexpensive approach.*

  Compound sentence: *It does not cost very much to import, but it is not always the freshest.*

  Complex sentence: *If you are good at gardening, your vegetables may not look as pretty as the ones in the store.*

- **Start or end with a prepositional phrase:** Adding this phrase to the beginning or end of the sentence gives it a different structure and style.

  PREPOSITIONAL PHRASE
  An apple costs fifty cents at some places.

  PREPOSITIONAL PHRASE
  At other places, it costs two dollars.

- Use synonyms to avoid repeating words: Instead of using the same word or phrase again and again, replace it with a new word that has a similar meaning.

  One place to get <u>fruit and vegetables</u> is at a <u>supermarket</u>.

  SYNONYM
  *The cost of **grocery store produce** can be very low or very high.*

4.1 Add Sentence Variety

Rewrite the sentences so there is more sentence variety. Use the ways in parentheses.

1 When it is winter, people in China eat hot foods. When it is summer, they eat cool foods. (vary order of time clauses) ....

....

2 In many cultures, garlic is considered medicine. It is used as a medicine for colds and other illnesses. (use synonyms) ....

....

3 China is a place. Many people there do not like to drink ice water. (use a prepositional phrase)

....

....

4 Fast food tastes good. It can be very bad for your health. (use a compound sentence)

....

....

 4.2 Apply It to Your Writing

Think about the writing prompt you chose and the ideas you brainstormed in Section I. On a separate sheet of paper, write four varied kinds of sentences about your topic.

ⓑ Grammar for Writing: Simple Present and Present Progressive

In academic essays, it is important to use the most appropriate verb form to make your ideas clear. If you use the simple present and the present progressive, remember the following points.

SIMPLE PRESENT AND PRESENT PROGRESSIVE	
1 Use the simple present for routines, habits, and things that are generally true.	*An apple* **costs** *fifty cents at some places.* *It* **does not cost** *much to import fruit and vegetables, but it* **is not** *always the freshest.*
2 Use the present progressive for things that are in progress now, or for temporary or changing actions.	*To stay healthy, more people* **are eliminating** *junk food and* **are eating** *more fruit and vegetables.*
3 Use the simple present with stative verbs such as *be, believe, have, know, like, look, need, seem,* and *want.* Do not use the present progressive with stative verbs.	*Perhaps your vegetables* ~~are not looking~~ do not look *as pretty as the ones in the store.*
4 Some verbs have both an active meaning and a stative meaning. Use present progressive if the verb's meaning is active.	STATIVE MEANING: *Many supermarkets* **have** *organic produce now.* ACTIVE MEANING: *More people* **are having** *fish for lunch and dinner to help improve their memory.*

4.3 Complete the Paragraph

Complete the paragraph with the correct form of the verbs in parentheses. Use the simple present or present progressive.

Coffee and Mental Health

A type of diet that can improve mental health is one that includes coffee. Coffee is more popular than ever, and at this moment millions of people .... (enjoy)
_(1)_
a cup of coffee around the world. However, it is important to understand coffee's effects on your health. Coffee .... (have) caffeine. According to research, caffeine
_(2)_
usually .... (improve) people's memory and their ability to concentrate.
_(3)_
However, these effects are temporary. Imagine you .... (have) a cup of
_(4)_
coffee at the moment. You .... (be) probably alert right now, but in a
_(5)_
few hours you will not feel as good. Caffeine also .... (make) people feel
_(6)_
more anxious, according to research, and coffee drinkers .... (not sleep)
_(7)_
as well.

Avoiding Common Mistakes

Research tells us that these are the most common mistakes that students make when using the simple present and present progressive in academic writing.

1 Use the simple present with stative verbs such as *be, believe, have, know, like, need, seem,* or *want.* Do not use the present progressive.

   Many people today are becoming vegetarians because they ~~are wanting~~ **want** *to have a healthier diet.*

2 Use the simple present for routines and habits that are not likely to change. Do not use the present progressive.

   Fast-food restaurants ~~are serving~~ **serve** *meals that can be prepared quickly at a low cost.*

3 Use the present progressive to talk about something temporary. Do not use the simple present.

   Now, many people ~~start~~ **are starting** *to learn about the importance of good nutrition.*

4 Use the *-ing* form of the verb in the present progressive. Do not use the base form.

   Organic food brands are ~~grow~~ **growing** *at a fast rate throughout the United States.*

 4.4 Editing Task

Find and correct six more mistakes in the paragraph below.

Another type of diet that is good for your mental health is a diet with a lot of fish. Scientists are ~~do~~ **doing** a lot of research on the effects of fish these days. We already are knowing that fish improves memory and concentration, especially for older people. This is because fish are having a fatty acid called Omega-3 that is helping our brains. Right now, scientists research the effect of fish on people's mood. Many of them believe that fish can help people who are suffer from depression. According to research, fish also is improving sleep. If you are having trouble sleeping these days, you might want to try eating more fish for a few days.

C Avoiding Plagiarism

Citing sources can seem confusing.

I'm not doing research for my essays yet, but I'd like to know a little bit about citing sources in my essay and in Works Cited. I want to understand when and why I see citations. Also, there are so many kinds of print and electronic sources. Do I write the names of all sources the same way?

Sofia

Dear Sofia,

The reason you see citations is because the writer is using another writer's words or ideas. You might see them in the body of the essay, and you will see them at the end of the essay in Works Cited. Citations for print and electronic sources are slightly different. In all cases, though, you will need to know the author, title, and date of publication.

Best regards,

Professor Wright

CITING PRINT SOURCES

Different schools and departments may use different styles for citing sources. This book uses the MLA style. Ask your instructor which style he or she prefers. In this lesson, you will look at print sources only, such as printed books, magazines, and newspapers.

There are two places where you will cite your print sources: in the text (as in-text citations) and in the Works Cited page at the end of an essay.

In-text citations	Method 1
There are two methods of citing your print sources. Both methods include the author's name and the page number.	Write the author's first and last name in the sentence and the page number in parentheses at the end.
	Maria Rodale says that education is important to help children make good food choices (26).
	Method 2
	Write the author's last name and page number in parentheses at the end of the sentence.
	Eating at a restaurant is as unhealthy as eating fast food (Smith 2).

Works Cited

At the end of the essay, include a Works Cited page. Write a citation for each in-text citation. Include the author's first and last name, title, place, and date of publication. Notice the order of the information and the punctuation of the citation and the indentation of the lines.

List citations alphabetically, not in the order the citation appears in the essay.

Books

Write the author's last name, a comma, and the first name. Italicize names of books and magazines. Include the medium (such as print) at the end.

Robbins, John. *Diet for a New America*. Tiburon: Kramer, 1998. Print.

Newspapers or Magazines

Put names of newspaper or magazine articles in quotation marks. Write the day, month, and year of the article's publication.

Bittman, Mark. "Yes, Healthful Fast Food Is Possible." *New York Times Magazine*, 7 Apr. 2013: MM26. Print.

 4.5 Practice

A Read the in-text citations. Circle the information that is missing in each one.

1 Frances Moore Lappe argued that meat production was not good for the planet.

   a the name of the author   b the page number   c the publisher

2 Many Americans choose foods based on cost and convenience (25).

   a the date   b the name of the author   c the page number

B Correct the order of the citations from the Works Cited page. Write the information in the correct order. Use correct punctuation.

1 Book: *Fast Food Nation*. Eric Schlosser. 1992. Print. Harper. New York.

2 Magazine: Pollan, Michael. *The Nation*. "How Change Is Going to Come in the Food System." Print. Oct. 3, 2011: 7.

In this section, you will follow the writing process to complete the final draft of your classification essay.

STEP 1: BRAINSTORM

Work with a partner. Follow the steps below to brainstorm more ideas for your topic.

1 Before you start, read the student's cluster diagram. He brainstormed more ideas for the cluster diagram he started in Section 1 on page 164. Finally, he crossed out the ideas that he thought were the least strong, the least interesting, or not relevant to the topic.

Category 1:
Growing your own

- doesn't cost much
- too much work
- not pretty but fresh
- not very popular

Category 2:
Farmers' markets

- food is very fresh
- not in every town
- often not expensive
- nice atmosphere

Category 3:
Supermarkets

- ~~good variety~~
- every town has one
- some cheap, others expensive
- quality varies; not always fresh
- ~~sometimes too crowded~~

Essay Topic:
PLACES TO GET FRUIT AND VEGETABLES

Category 4:
Restaurants

- expensive
- not a lot of fruit

2 Now read your writing prompt again. Then review the ideas you brainstormed in Section 1 on page 165. Write the essay topic, categories, and details in the diagram. Include ideas from the Your Turns throughout the unit. Finally, brainstorm more ideas. You will probably not use every idea, but it is good to write as many ideas as possible.

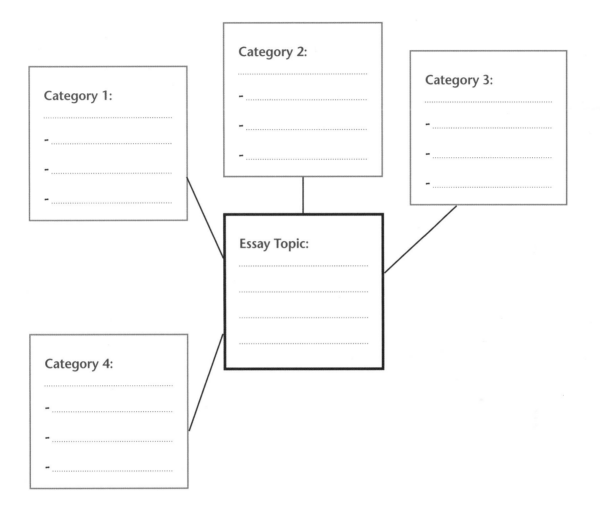

STEP 2: MAKE AN OUTLINE

Complete the outline below with ideas from Step 1 on page 191.

ESSAY OUTLINE

I. Introductory paragraph

Thesis Statement

Body Paragraph 1: Category 1

II.

Point of Classification   A.

Detail   1.

Detail   2.

Point of Classification   B.

Detail   1.

Detail   2.

Point of Classification   C.

Detail   1.

Detail   2.

Body Paragraph 2: Category 2

III.

Point of Classification   A.

Detail   1.

Detail   2.

Point of Classification | B. ....

Detail | 1. ....

Detail | 2. ....

Point of Classification | C. ....

Detail | 1. ....

Detail | 2. ....

Body Paragraph 3: Category 3 | IV. ....

Point of Classification | A. ....

Detail | 1. ....

Detail | 2. ....

Point of Classification | B. ....

Detail | 1. ....

Detail | 2. ....

Point of Classification | C. ....

Detail | 1. ....

Detail | 2. ....

V. Concluding paragraph ....

STEP 3: **WRITE YOUR FIRST DRAFT**

Now it is time to write your first draft. Here are some suggestions on how to get started.

1 Use your outline, notes, and the sentences you wrote in the Your Turns in this unit and in Step 2 on pages 192–193.

2 Focus on making your ideas as clear as possible.

3 Add a title.

After you finish, read your essay and check for basic errors.

1 Check that all sentences have subjects and verbs.

2 Check that you have used commas and periods correctly.

3 Check that you have used the present progressive and simple present correctly.

4 Make sure that your sentences have variety so that your ideas flow well and are clear.

STEP 4: **WRITE YOUR FINAL DRAFT**

1 After you receive feedback on your first draft, review it carefully. Fix any errors.

2 Make a note of errors that were most frequent. Try to avoid them as you write.

3 Review the Academic Words and Academic Phrases from this unit. Are there any that you can add to your essay?

4 Turn to page 260 and use the Self-Editing Review to check your work one more time.

5 Write your final draft and hand it in.

7 PROCESS ESSAYS

SOCIAL WORK: SOCIAL ACTIVISIM

"Be the change that you wish to see in the world."

Mahatma Gandhi
(1869–1948)

About the Author:

Mahatma Gandhi used peaceful and nonviolent protest to fight for freedom, civil rights, and justice in India. Throughout history, he inspired many leaders, such as Dr. Martin Luther King, Jr.

Work with a partner. Read the quotation about change. Then answer the questions.

1 Gandhi believed that anyone could help change the world. Do you agree or disagree? Why?

2 What are some social problems in today's world?

3 What steps can you take to start changing the world and helping to solve social problems?

Ⓐ Connect to Academic Writing

A process shows how to do something. In this unit, you will learn skills to write a process essay. Some of the skills may seem new to you, but the skill of organizing the steps of a process is not new. In your everyday life, you use the skill of organizing the steps of a process when you tell someone how to set up a new laptop or teach your roommate how to cook your favorite food.

Ⓑ Reflect on the Topic

In this section, you will choose a writing prompt and reflect on it. You will develop ideas throughout the unit and use them to practice skills that you need to write your essay.

The writing prompt below was used for the Student Model essay on pages 202–203. The student reflected on her topic and used a process diagram to brainstorm possible ideas for her paragraph.

WRITING PROMPT: Some companies and groups of people make products – such as jewelry, candy, or clothing – and use the money to help themselves or others who need help. Choose a product. Tell how people make the product and who it helps.

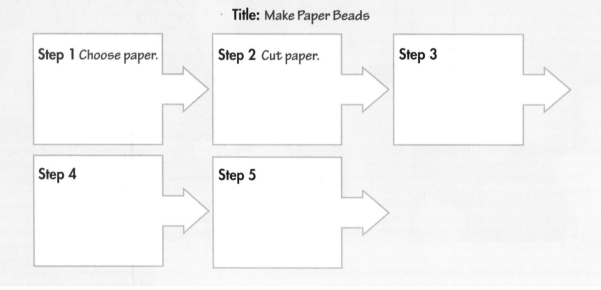

Title: Make Paper Beads

Step 1 *Choose paper.*

Step 2 *Cut paper.*

Step 3

Step 4

Step 5

ACTIVITY 1.1 Notice

Work with a partner. Look at the process diagram above. Where do the steps below fit? Add them to the diagram. Share your ideas with the class.

String the completed beads.

Glue the ends of the beads.

Roll paper strips to make beads.

1.2 Apply It to Your Writing

A Choose a prompt for your essay.

- Sick people, elderly people, and children often need help. Many communities create programs, called service projects, to provide support for these people. Think about a service project that people could start in your community, for example, visiting sick or elderly members, organizing after-school activities for children and teens, collecting food or clothes for the needy. Describe the steps you would take to organize a service project in your community.

- Choose something people can do for others, such as cooking, cleaning, running errands, or making clothes or furniture. Describe the steps someone would take to personally do something for others.

- One way people can assist organizations, such as schools and community groups, is to raise money for them. Choose a fundraiser, such as a sports event, a car wash, or a garage sale. Explain the steps that someone could take to plan this fundraising event.

- A topic approved by your instructor.

B Complete the process diagram below. Write an essay title and five steps. You can add more boxes if you need to write about more steps.

C Compare process diagrams with a partner.

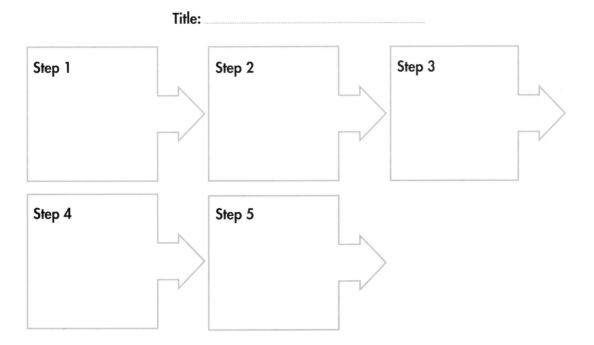

Title: ....

| Step 1 | Step 2 | Step 3 |

| Step 4 | Step 5 |

In this section, you will learn academic language that you can use in your process essay. You will also notice how a professional writer uses this language and describes the steps in a process.

Ⓐ Academic Vocabulary

The words below appear throughout the unit. They are from the Academic Word List or the General Service List. Using these words in your writing will make your ideas clearer and your writing more academic.

assist (v)	organization (n)	provide (v)	requirement (n)
commitment (n)	primary (adj)	recover (v)	volunteer (n)

 2.1 Focus on Meaning

Work with a partner. Read the sentences. Decide the meaning of the bold words and circle the correct definitions.

1 Often people want to **assist** children. They try to make their lives better by tutoring them or working at an after-school program. **Assist** means

   a help.   b be with.

2 Meals on Wheels is an **organization** that delivers meals to seniors and people who are ill. It is one example of how a group of people can serve the community. **Organization** means

   a a group of people who live together but are not related.

   b a group of people who work together for the same purpose.

3 There are many different types of community service people can choose. For example, the **primary** focus of some community groups is to rescue animals. For others, the most important focus is to protect the environment. **Primary** means

   a most important.   b easiest.

4 People can work with groups like the Red Cross. The Red Cross helps communities **recover** after natural disasters, such as floods or earthquakes, by providing medical care or building safe housing. **Recover** means

   a create something new   b return to normal.

5 Most community service groups do not pay their workers. Their **volunteers** do the work because they want to help people or make a positive change even though they are not paid. **Volunteer** means

   a a part-time worker.   b an unpaid worker.

6 People who want to serve with groups like Meals on Wheels or the Red Cross must make a **commitment**. They must decide to show up on time and work hard. **Commitment** means

   a a donation of money.   b a firm decision.

7 Many groups like the Red Cross have a training **requirement**. These groups insist that people who work with them learn the necessary skills to do their jobs. A **requirement** is

   a a necessity.   b a choice.

8 Service groups usually **provide** training to their volunteers for free. The groups give volunteers all of the information that they need and supply any necessary materials or resources. **Provide** means

   a give.   b make.

B Academic Collocations 👁

Collocations are words that are frequently used together. Research tells us that the academic vocabulary in Part A is commonly used in the collocations in bold below.

ACTIVITY 2.2 Focus on Meaning

Work with a partner. Match the collocations in bold to their meanings. Write the letters.

.... 1 Hospital volunteers **provide support** to patients and their families. They talk to the families, run errands for families, or visit patients.

.... 2 Volunteers also **provide information** to hospital guests. These volunteers work at the front desk to answer questions or give directions.

.... 3 The **primary goal** of a hospital volunteer is to care for patients and their families so that they feel more comfortable.

.... 4 Volunteers must **make a commitment** to serve all people with respect.

.... 5 Volunteers must **meet the requirements** of the hospital. For example, a volunteer needs to be 16 or older.

a the most important thing that you want to accomplish

b give facts about a situation, person, or event

c have the necessary experiences, qualifications, and characteristics

d help or encourage

e firmly decide something

C Writing in the Real World

The author of "Doctors without Borders" describes the steps an organization takes to help people.

Before you read, answer these questions: Have you heard of Doctors without Borders? What does this organization do? Why is there a need for an organization like this?

Now read the article. Think about your answers to the questions above as you read.

Doctors without Borders

by Bruce Parker

1 Doctors without Borders, or *Médecins Sans Frontières* (MSF), is an international **organization** that **provides** medical assistance to millions of people around the world. The **organization** was created in 1971 by journalists and doctors in France. Now it works in over 60 countries. Through its effective and responsible medical and humanitarian aid, Doctors without Borders has helped millions of people. Its **primary goal** is to help people in crisis situations, such as wars, natural disasters, or extreme poverty.

2 MSF raises money from private donors.[1] This allows the **organization** to work independently from other governments, religions, or militaries. MSF can fulfill[2] its **commitment** to **assist** people regardless of race, religion, or political affiliation.[3] With this money, MSF creates medical teams of doctors, nurses, and other health-care professionals. MSF requires these teams to have experience in the medical field and to **make a commitment** to their work.

3 MSF sends medical teams to countries where there are major needs. For example, a team might go to a refugee[4] camp. Another team might go to a poor country with a lack of doctors and medicines. The teams study the situation and decide what care is needed so that they can create a program to **provide information** and support. MSF can offer many different types of services. During a war, they may **provide** mental health services. After a natural disaster like an earthquake, they may rebuild hospitals and shelters to help the country **recover**.

4 While MSF's medical teams are working in a country, their **primary** concern is quality medical assistance. However, if a team learns about a new problem,

---

[1]**donor:** a person who gives money to an organization
[2]**fulfill:** do something as promised
[3]**affiliation:** a relationship or connection with a group or organization

[4]**refugee:** a person who leaves his or her home or country to find safety

they will speak out so that the international community becomes aware of the situation. MSF will use media, such as newspaper articles or Twitter feeds, to inform the world. For instance, MSF created a campaign called "Starved for Attention." The campaign informed Americans, Europeans, and Africans about the problem of childhood malnutrition. In this way, MSF encouraged people and governments to give food assistance and nutrition programs to starving children.

5   After MSF has helped a country, they may leave and give its programs to the local citizens of that country. This allows MSF to use its resources to help the next country. However, MSF will not leave a country until the emergency situation has improved. MSF must feel that the people are able to support themselves. MSF wants to be sure that the country will continue to get medical care after they leave. Through this process, MSF continues to have a positive impact on a community even after the organization has left a country.

 2.3 Check Your Understanding

Answer the questions.

1   Use the information from "Doctors without Borders" to put the steps below in order. Number the steps from 1 (first step) to 5 (last step).

.... Evaluate the country's needs.

.... Give the MSF program to local citizens.

.... Provide information and assistance to the country and educate the international community.

.... Raise money and recruit medical professionals.

.... Send a medical team to a country in crisis.

2   Based on your knowledge of current events, where do you think Doctors without Borders is working today?

3   Would you be interested in working for an organization like Doctors without Borders? Why or why not?

 2.4 Notice the Features of Process Writing

Answer the questions.

1   Look at the first paragraph. The author describes the work of Doctors without Borders. Does the author think this organization and its work are important? Why or why not?

2   Look at the second, third, and fourth paragraphs. Does the author use chronological order, spatial order, or rank order to describe the steps in the organization's work?

3   Look at the fourth paragraph again. Which step in Doctors without Borders' work is the main point of this paragraph? What specific example does the author provide to support this step?

In Section 1, you saw how the writer of the Student Model reflected on her topic. In this section, you will analyze the final draft of her essay. You will learn how to organize your ideas for your own essay.

Ⓐ Student Model

Read the prompt and answer the questions.

WRITING PROMPT: Some companies and groups of people make products – such as jewelry, candy, or clothing – and use the money to help themselves or others who need help. Choose a product. Tell how people make the product and who it helps.

1 In your own words, what will this essay be about?

2 Have you ever purchased a product from a company or organization that donates money to help others? If so, what was it?

Read the essay twice. The first time, think about your answers to the questions above. The second time, answer the questions in the Analyze Writing Skills boxes. This will help you notice key features of a process essay.

Paper Bead Jewelry

1   BeadforLife is an **organization** that helps poor women in Uganda. It teaches them to make beautiful beads from recycled paper and simple materials. They make jewelry with the beads. The **organization** sells the jewelry all over the world. BeadforLife takes the money and gives it to the women in Uganda. The money from the sale of the jewelry **provides** an income for the women. It takes a lot of time to create this beautiful paper bead jewelry. The women of Uganda follow a careful step-by-step process to make the beads and jewelry. Here are the steps. If you follow these steps carefully, perhaps you can make this jewelry, too.

> **1 Analyze Writing Skills**
> Underline the sentence that tells you the process the writer will describe.

2   First, choose the paper. You can use any kind of paper that you have in your home. BeadforLife customers often like bright, colorful beads, so paper from magazines or posters works well. Next, cut the paper into long triangular[1] shapes. Make wide and thin triangles so that the beads are different sizes and shapes. Third, roll the paper strips into beads. This step requires a small stick, such as a toothpick or needle. Roll the paper around the stick very tightly. The stick creates a hole. It is a little difficult to roll the paper correctly, so be patient. It may take a minute or two to make one bead. After that, put some glue on the end of the paper. Hold

> **2 Analyze Writing Skills**
> Circle the words that show the order of the steps in the process.

> **3 Analyze Writing Skills**
> Underline the details that help the reader understand how to roll the paper strips into beads.

[1]**triangular:** shaped like a triangle

the paper tightly for a few moments. Wait for the glue to dry. When you have made many beads, you can make a bracelet. Take a string and put the string through the beads. Then put varnish[2] on the beads with a brush. It is like painting. The varnish is clear. It makes the beads hard and shiny. Finally, let the beads dry. This step can take two to three days. After the beads are completely dry, you can wear your paper bead jewelry.

3   In short, making bead jewelry is a simple but long process, and it is a process that the women of Uganda have mastered. Thanks to BeadforLife and the creativity of the women, you can buy paper bead bracelets and necklaces and save yourself time. At the same time, you will have something wonderful and will help the women of Uganda support themselves.

[2]**varnish:** a clear liquid that you paint onto wood or paper to protect it and make it shine

4 **Analyze Writing Skills**

Circle the words that introduce the concluding paragraph. Underline the opinion, suggestion, or prediction the writer makes.

3.1 Check Your Understanding

Answer the questions.

1 How many steps are there in making paper bead jewelry?

2 If you wanted to make a blue and white paper bead necklace, which material would you use?

  a an article from an old newspaper

  b a large poster with a picture of the earth

  c a magazine page with photos of people

3 Who does BeadforLife help? How does buying paper bead jewelry help?

 3.2 Outline the Writer's Ideas

Complete the outline for "Paper Bead Jewelry" from pages 202–203. Use the phrases in the box.

apply varnish	create a hole	make a bracelet	wide and thin triangles
choose the paper	glue the paper	two to three days	

STUDENT MODEL

ESSAY OUTLINE

I. Introductory paragraph ....

Thesis Statement If you follow these steps carefully, perhaps you can make this jewelry, too. ....

Body Paragraph II. The process of making beads ....

Step 1 A. ....

Detail 1. Bright and colorful ....

Detail 2. Magazines or posters ....

Step 2 B. Cut the paper ....

Detail 1. ....

Detail 2. Different sizes and shapes ....

Step 3	C. Roll the strips into beads
Detail	1. Roll paper around a stick or needle
Detail	2.
Step 4	D.
Detail	1. Hold tightly
Detail	2. Wait until dry
Step 5	E.
Detail	1. Have enough beads
Detail	2. Put string through beads
Step 6	F.
Step 7	G. Let the beads dry
Detail	1.

III. Concluding paragraph

Concluding Sentence In short, making bead jewelry is a simple but long process, and it is a process that the women of Uganda have mastered.

B Process Essays

A process essay tells the steps in a process. One way writers use process essays is to teach readers how to do something. For example, in the Student Model essay the writer described how to make paper bead jewelry. As in other essays, each paragraph in a process essay has a purpose:

- The **introductory paragraph** tells the reader what process the writer will describe. It explains why this process is important and often gives background information to interest the reader.

- The **body paragraph** describes each step of the process in chronological order. The supporting sentences give details about each step.

- The **concluding paragraph** ends the essay by restating the main idea. In addition, writers often offer a suggestion, give an opinion, or make a prediction.

 3.3 Notice

Read the Student Model essay on pages 202–203 again. Match each sentence to its purpose in the essay.

INTRODUCTORY PARAGRAPH

Sentence	Purpose
.... 1 The money from the sale of the jewelry provides an income for the women.	a gives background information
.... 2 The women of Uganda follow a careful step-by-step process to make the beads and jewelry.	b explains why this process is important
.... 3 BeadforLife is an organization that helps poor women in Uganda.	c tells the reader what process the writer will describe

BODY PARAGRAPH

Sentence	Purpose
.... 1 Third, roll the paper strips into beads.	a describes a step in the process
.... 2 This step requires a small stick, such as a toothpick or needle.	b provides more information about a step

CONCLUDING PARAGRAPH

Sentence	Purpose
.... 1 In short, making bead jewelry is a simple but long process, and it is a process that the women of Uganda have mastered.	a gives an opinion
.... 2 Thanks to BeadforLife and the creativity of the women, you can buy paper bead bracelets and necklaces and save yourself time.	b restates the main idea
.... 3 At the same time, you will have something wonderful and will help the women of Uganda support themselves.	c makes a suggestion

THE INTRODUCTORY PARAGRAPH

In a process essay, the writer includes background information and a thesis statement that answers these questions:

- What process will the writer explain?

- Why is this process important?

- What are the steps in the process? OR How many steps are there?

In the thesis statement, a writer needs to state that the essay will describe a process. The thesis statement may list the steps or tell the number of steps in the process.

NUMBER OF STEPS   PROCESS

*If you follow this simple **seven-step process**, you **can create this beautiful paper bead jewelry**.*

Writers often use phrases like the ones below to write a thesis statement for a process essay:

Follow these steps to start *a home recycling program.*

If you follow these steps, *you can make this comforting soup for a sick person.*

The three steps *in holding a clothing drive **are** advertising the event, collecting the clothing, and distributing the donations.*

 3.4 Notice Introductory Paragraphs

Work with a partner. Read this introductory paragraph from a process essay. Then answer the questions.

   Many high school students participate in service learning with their class. Some students visit the elderly in nursing homes and talk to them. Some students read to children in libraries. Some students make sandwiches for poor people. These are wonderful opportunities for students. They learn important skills. They learn how to be kind and to be responsible. Starting a service-learning project takes time and good planning. Things can go wrong and people can be disappointed. If you want to start a service learning project for your class that works well, follow these four steps.

1 What process will the writer explain?
2 Why is this process important?
3 How many steps are there?

ACTIVITY 3.5 Apply It to Your Writing

Look at the process diagram you created for your writing prompt in Section 1 on page 197 and think about your topic. Answer the following questions. You may decide to use this information later in your introductory paragraph.

1 What process will you explain? ....

2 Why is this process important? ....

3 How many steps are there? ....

BODY PARAGRAPHS

In the **body paragraphs** of a process essay, writers clearly break down the process into steps. They use words and phrases such as *first, second, next*, and *after that* to present the steps in chronolocial order.

> **First**, *contact your garbage service to add recycling if you do not already have this service.*
>
> **Second**, *ask for information about what you can recycle and what you have to throw away.*
>
> **Next**, *learn how to separate items for recycling.*
>
> **After that**, *create recycling bins in your home for the separate items. Label them and put them next to your trash can.*
>
> **Finally**, *take your recycling bins out with your trash cans before each pickup time.*

Writers ask themselves questions like the following to help them clearly state each step, explain it, and add details that make it easier to understand. Be sure to answer these questions when you write your own process essay.

1 How do I state the step?

2 What do I need to explain to make sure that the reader does the step correctly? What tips can I give?

3 How much time does the step take?

4 What materials or tools does the reader need for the step?

ACTIVITY 3.6 Notice Supporting Details

Work with a partner. Read the step from the Student Model essay. Then follow the directions.

Third, roll the paper strips into beads. This step requires a small stick, such as a toothpick or needle. Roll the paper around the stick very tightly. The stick creates a hole. It is a little difficult to roll the paper correctly, so be patient. It may take a minute or two to make one bead.

1 Underline the sentence that states the step.

2 Double underline the sentence that explains what to do or tells how to do the step correctly.

3 Put a box around how much time the step takes.

4 Find the sentence that describes a tool. Circle the tool.

3.7 Write Supporting Details

Read the essay prompt. Then complete the activity.

WRITING PROMPT: One of the most common ways to help others is to prepare and serve food for a sick person. For this reason, most cultures have a food or drink that they commonly use to comfort sick people. In the United States, people often make chicken noodle soup, for example. Describe the steps someone would take to prepare a common food or drink for a sick person in your culture.

A Outline the steps and provide details for each step. Add as many steps as necessary.

Step 1: ....

    Detail(s): ....

....

Step 2: ....

    Detail(s): ....

....

Step 3: ....

    Detail(s): ....

....

Step 4: ....

    Detail(s): ....

....

B Work with a partner. Read your partner's outline. Does your partner present the steps in chronological order? Are the steps clear? Are there enough details to help you understand the process?

3.8 Apply It to Your Writing

Think about the writing prompt you chose on page 197. Write one step for your process essay. Be sure to add details and make the step easy for your reader to understand.

....

....

....

....

CONCLUDING PARAGRAPH

To successfully conclude a process essay, writers do the following:

- Use a transition word or phrase, such as *to conclude, in sum, in short, in conclusion.*
- Restate the main idea of the essay.
- Give a suggestion, an opinion, or a prediction.

 3.9 Notice Concluding Paragraphs

Work with a partner. Read the concluding paragraph. Then complete the activities.

In sum, you can follow these five steps to plan a successful bake-sale fundraiser and have fun, too. A bake sale is a quick and easy way to make money to assist people in your community. These kinds of activities will make the people in your community become better neighbors and friends.

1 Circle the transition phrase.

2 Underline the sentence that restates the main point of the essay.

3 Double underline the sentence that gives a suggestion, an opinion, or a prediction.

 3.10 Complete the Concluding Paragraph

Read the essay prompt. Use the words and phrases in the box to complete the concluding paragraph for this essay.

WRITING PROMPT: One of the most common ways to serve others is to prepare and serve food for a sick person. For this reason, most cultures have a food or drink that they commonly use to comfort sick people. Describe the steps someone would take to prepare a common food or drink for a sick person in your culture.

> help a sick family member recover quickly
>
> in conclusion
>
> want to serve it to everyone in the family

_____, if you follow these five easy steps, you can make a delicious soup that will _____. In fact, the soup is so delicious that you will _____, whether they are sick or not.

 3.11 Apply It to Your Writing

Think about the topic you chose for your essay. Write a concluding sentence. Give a suggestion, an opinion, or a predication.

....

....

....

In this section, you will learn writing and grammar skills that will help make your writing more academic and accurate.

Ⓐ Writing Skill 1: Clarity

Writers need to use **precise adjectives** so that ideas are really clear. They also need to use correct **pronoun references** when referring to nouns to make sure the reader can follow the ideas more easily.

Precise Adjectives: First, cut the paper into ˄shapes.
long, triangular

Pronoun Reference: The varnish is clear. ~~The varnish~~ makes the beads hard and shiny.
It

PRECISE ADJECTIVES

Below are some guidelines for using precise adjectives.

USING PRECISE ADJECTIVES	
Use specific adjectives. Try to avoid general words, such as the following: *a lot of, big/small, good/bad, nice, old/young,* and *some.*	Doctors without Borders provides assistance for **millions** ~~a lot~~ *of people around the world.* *Put a* **drop** ~~small amount~~ *of glue on the end of the piece of paper.* *It helps people in* **disastrous** ~~bad~~ *situations, such as wars, natural calamities, or extreme poverty.* *Customers often like* **bright, multi-colored** ~~nice~~ *beads.* *Even* **six-year-old** ~~young~~ *children can become volunteers in service-learning projects.* *The primary goal of the project was to raise* **one thousand dollars** ~~some money~~ *for Honduran students to buy books.*

4.1 Choose Clear Adjectives

Work with a partner. Look at the general adjectives below. Write three more specific adjectives for each one. Use the ideas in this unit, a dictionary, or a thesaurus.

1	a lot of	*dozens*	*countless*	*hundreds*
2	bad			
3	big			
4	good			
5	nice			
6	small			
7	old			
8	young			

4.2 Write Specific Adjectives

Rewrite the sentences below. Replace the underlined words with specific adjectives.

1 <u>Young</u> students have participated in service-learning projects.

....

2 The students created a <u>good</u> recycling system for the school.

....

3 San Francisco General Hospital has a <u>big</u> volunteer program to assist patients and their families.

....

4 The women use <u>nice</u> paper beads to make their necklaces.

....

PRONOUN REFERENCES

Another way to add clarity to your writing is by using correct pronoun references.

Below are some rules for using the correct pronouns when referring to nouns.

USING CORRECT PRONOUNS	
1 Use a pronoun when referring to nouns in previous sentences.	You can volunteer to help older <u>people</u>. You can help ~~him~~ **them** in many ways.
2 Make sure that nouns and their pronouns and possessive adjectives agree in person and number.	When you volunteer, <u>you</u> must remember to keep track of ~~their~~ **your** hours.

4.3 Correct Pronoun References

The introductory paragraph below has pronoun reference problems. The nouns are underlined. Correct the incorrect pronouns in bold.

The TOMS shoe company has the <u>slogan</u> "One for One" on all of its boxes. You might wonder what **he** means. In fact, this slogan means that you have given a new pair of shoes to a child who does not have any <u>shoes</u>. TOMS makes a commitment to give a pair of shoes away every time a customer buys a new pair of TOMS shoes. TOMS gives **him** to <u>organizations</u> that have experience working in poor countries or communities. TOMS counts on **it** to hand out the shoes in an effective way. TOMS has given 10 million pairs of shoes to poor children. <u>The company</u> follows a six-step process. With this process, **they** provides shoes to children in more than 60 countries. <u>TOMS</u> encourages support from people like you. You can follow these steps to support **his** "One for One" program.

4.4 Apply It to Your Writing

Read the sentences you wrote for the Your Turns in this unit. Check each sentence for clarity. Did you use specific adjectives? Are your pronoun references correct? Rewrite the sentences if necessary to add clarity.

ⓑ Writing Skill 2: Transition Words and Phrases for Sequential Order

In a process essay, transition words and phrases for sequential order will help your reader follow the order of the steps in the process. These transition words and phrases include:

- *first, second, third*: Use these transitions to number the steps in order.

  First, do online research to learn about the organization's primary goal.

  Second, find out if you meet the organization's requirements.

- *next, then, after that*: Use these transitions to introduce another step.

  Next, make an appointment to meet the person who coordinates the volunteers.

  After that, write a résumé to provide information about your experience.

- *last, finally*: Use these transitions to present the final step in the process.

  Last, find out how much time the job requires.

  Finally, ask yourself: "Am I able to make a commitment?"

4.5 Use Transition Words and Phrases

Number the steps in order from 1 to 5. On a separate sheet of paper, write them in order using transitions to form a paragraph.

Charity organizations often use walks or runs to raise money. Anyone can use this popular fundraising idea by following these steps.

.... On the day of the event, have volunteers register the walkers and hand out water during the walk.

.... After you have a definite location for the walk, find volunteers to help you at the event.

.... Once you have a location and some volunteers, advertise the walking event. Make sure to describe the primary goal of the walk and the time and place of the walk.

.... Choose a place for the walk. A good place for a fundraising walk is a city park.

.... Go to the city government office to get permission for your event.

C Grammar for Writing: Phrasal Verbs

Writers often use phrasal verbs like the ones below to describe a process. They usually have a verb + a preposition. Together, the verb + preposition have a special meaning:

count on (to trust someone/something for something)

fill out (to complete something by writing or typing)

find out (to learn something new)

hand out (to give something to someone by hand)

log in/on (to connect to a computer with a username and/or password)

sign up (to agree to do an organized activity)

work out (to calculate or make a plan)

Follow these rules when using phrasal verbs.

PHRASAL VERBS

1	Intransitive phrasal verbs do not have an object. Intransitive verbs include: *log in/on* *sign up*	**PHRASAL VERB** *When volunteers arrive for their shift, they **log in** so that they can enter their start time.* **PHRASAL VERB** *People can **sign up** any time.*
2	Transitive phrasal verbs have an object. Transitive verbs include: *count on* *fill out*	**PHRASAL VERB + OBJECT** *Many hospitals **count on** <u>volunteers</u> to provide support and information to patients and their families.*
3	Most transitive verbs are separable. This means that noun objects can come before or after the preposition. The following phrasal verbs are separable: *fill (something) out* *find (something) out* *hand (something) out* *work (something) out* Some transitive verbs are inseparable. This means that noun objects cannot come before the preposition, for example: *count on* *go over* *care for*	**VERB + OBJECT + PREPOSITION** *Students can **hand** <u>flyers</u> **out** to advertise their bake sale.* **VERB + PREPOSITION + OBJECT** *Students can **hand out** <u>flyers</u> to advertise their bake sale.* **VERB + PREPOSITION + OBJECT** *Doctors without Borders **counts on** <u>donors</u> to provide funding for their important work.* *NOT: Doctors without Borders **counts ~~donors on~~** to provide funding for their important work.*
4	With separable transitive verbs, long objects usually go after the preposition.	*Before they start, race planners often must* **VERB + PREPOSITION + OBJECT** ***fill out** <u>the necessary city paperwork</u>.*
5	When the phrasal verb is separable, object pronouns come before the preposition. Do not put an object prounoun after the preposition with a separable phrasal verb.	*TOMS provides new shoes to children in need. They* **VERB + PRONOUN + PREPOSITION** *ask organizations to **hand** <u>them</u> **out**.* *NOT: TOMS provides new shoes to children in need. They ask organizations to **hand out ~~them~~**.*

4.6 Use Phrasal Verbs

Work with a partner. Read the steps to volunteering at a soup kitchen. Complete the sentences with the correct phrasal verbs from the box.

count on	fill out	find out	hand out	sign up

1 Use the Internet to .... the location of the nearest soup kitchen in your area.

2 Call the soup kitchen and .... for a date and time to volunteer.

3 When you call, ask if you need to .... any forms or get any training. Complete any requirements before you volunteer.

4 Arrive at your shift on time. The soup kitchen staff will .... you and the other volunteers to serve food that day.

5 Follow the soup kitchen staff's instructions. They may ask you to prepare or .... food, or they might need you to clean up.

Avoiding Common Mistakes

Research tells us that these are the most common mistakes that students make when using phrasal verbs in academic writing.

> 1 Use *fill out*, not *write* or *answer*, when talking about forms.
>
> $\quad$ **fill out**
> You must ~~write~~ an application form.
>
> 2 Use *find out*, not *know*, *learn*, or *check*, when the meaning is "to discover."
>
> **found out**
> I ~~knew~~ that the company helps immigrants.
>
> $\quad\quad$ **find out**
> Go to the organization's website to ~~learn~~ if they need volunteers.
>
> 3 Use *sign up (for)*, not *sign in* or *subscribe to*, when you talk about joining something officially, such as a class at school, a program, or an organization.
>
> $\quad\quad$ **sign up**
> It is easy to get people to ~~sign in~~ for the organization.
>
> $\quad\quad$ **sign up for**
> I am going to ~~subscribe to~~ a volunteer program at the library.

 4.7 Editing Task

Find and correct six more mistakes in the paragraph below.

First, decide the date and location for your blood drive. You need to work with the Red
$\quad\quad\quad\quad\quad\quad\quad\quad\quad\quad\quad\quad\quad\quad\quad\quad\quad\quad\quad\quad$ **find out**
Cross to choose a date when they are available. Also, ~~know~~ how much space the Red Cross requires for their equipment. Learn if your location will work well. After that, you can begin advertising the event. The Red Cross recommends that you begin advertising four weeks before the event. At the same time, you can subcribe donors. Sign people in to give blood and schedule appointments. On the day of the event, call donors to remind them of their appointment times. Next, greet the Red Cross workers and show them where to set up. When donors arrive, the Red Cross staff will do everything. They help donors write the necessary paperwork. After all the paperwork is answered, the staff safely takes the blood donations. Finally, check how many people gave blood so that you can announce the results and thank all of the donors.

Ⓓ Avoiding Plagiarism

The Internet is a wonderful resource, but sometimes it is not clear how to cite sources from the Internet.

I found some interesting Internet articles about starting up a volunteer program in a community. I'm not sure if I can use these articles because I'm having trouble finding information, like the name of the authors or the date. I think these sources are helpful, but I don't want to plagiarize. Can you give me some tips on citing Internet sources?

Zainab

Dear Zainab,

Citing sources from the Internet can be a little different from citing sources from books and magazines. Often information you usually include in a citation is missing from an Internet source. You can still use those articles, though. Be sure to provide as much information as you can from the site.

Good luck!

Professor Wright

CITING INTERNET SOURCES

Citing print and online sources is very similar. However, online sources often do not include the same amount of source information. It is common to have page numbers, dates, or even author's names and article titles missing from online sources. All sources, in spite of any missing information, should be cited in-text and in the Works Cited at the end of the essay.

In-text citations	
1 If the page number is missing: Treat the citation as you treat print citations, but do not include a page number at the end of the sentence.	*Kathy Tully reports that volunteers picked crops from already picked fields and donated the crops to food banks.* *Over 88,000 pounds of produce were gathered last year (Tully).*
2 If the author's name is missing: Treat the citation as you treat print citations, but include the name of the website or article instead of the author's name.	*According to Habitat.org, volunteers helped bring safer and cleaner water to the village of Chazanga in Zambia.* *According to a Habitat for Humanity newsletter, volunteers helped build a safe water system for 400 residents in Fiji. ("Safe Water in Fiji and Zambia").*

Works Cited

3 At the end of the essay, include a Works Cited page. Write a citation for each in-text citation. Include as much information as is available, in the same order as you do in print citations:

Author, title, publication, publisher of the website, date, medium. End with the date you visited the website (date of access).

Hannon, Kerry. "Gaining in Years and Helping Others Make Gains." *New York Times.* New York Times, 25 Oct. 2014. Web. 10 Nov. 2014.

4 If the author's name is missing: Start with the name of the article or website.

"Safe Water in Fiji and Zambia." *Habitat World.* Habitat for Humanity, Sept. 2014. Web. 10 Nov. 2014.

5 If the date is missing: Write *n.d.* in place of a missing date.

"Neglected People." *Doctors without Borders.* MSF USA, n.d. Web. 15 Oct. 2014.

 4.8 Practice

Read the citations from a Works Cited page. Circle the letter of the information that was unavailable in each of the online sources cited. There may be more than one answer.

1 "50 Young Progressive Activists Who Are Changing America." *Huffington Post.* Huffington Post, 12 Dec. 2012. Web. 20 Aug. 2014.

   a the name of the author

   b the date of publication

   c the medium

2 Gladwell, Malcolm. "Small Change." *New Yorker.* Condé Nast, n.d. Web. 4 Oct. 2014.

   a the name of the author

   b the date of publication

   c the name of the publication

3 *Createthegood.org.* Create the Good, n.d. Web. 11 Nov. 2014.

   a the name of the author

   b the name of the website

   c the date of publication

In this section, you will follow the writing process to complete the final draft of your process essay.

STEP 1: BRAINSTORM

Work with a partner. Follow the steps below to brainstorm ideas for your essay.

1 Before you start, read the student's process diagram. She wrote ideas from the process diagram she used to reflect on this topic in Section 1 on page 196. Then she brainstormed more ideas and added a step. Finally, she crossed out the ideas that she thought were the least important.

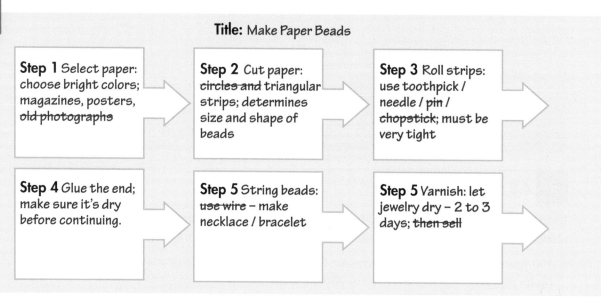

Title: Make Paper Beads

Step 1 Select paper: choose bright colors; magazines, posters, ~~old photographs~~

Step 2 Cut paper: ~~circles and~~ triangular strips; determines size and shape of beads

Step 3 Roll strips: use toothpick / needle / ~~pin~~ / ~~chopstick~~; must be very tight

Step 4 Glue the end; make sure it's dry before continuing.

Step 5 String beads: ~~use wire~~ – make necklace / bracelet

Step 5 Varnish: let jewelry dry – 2 to 3 days; ~~then sell~~

2 Now read your writing prompt again. Then review the ideas that you brainstormed in Section 1 on page 197. Include ideas from the Your Turns throughout this unit. Finally, brainstorm more ideas and add or take away steps if necessary. You will probably not use every idea, but it is good to write as many ideas as possible.

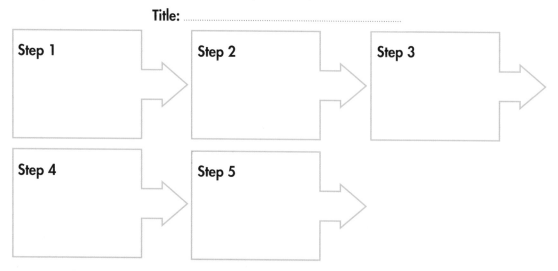

Title: ....

Step 1

Step 2

Step 3

Step 4

Step 5

STEP 2: MAKE AN OUTLINE

Complete the outline below with the ideas from Step 1.

ESSAY OUTLINE

I. Introductory paragraph ....

Thesis Statement ....

....

....

Body Paragraph II. ....

Step 1 A. ....

Detail 1. ....

Detail 2. ....

Step 2 B. ....

Detail 1. ....

Detail 2. ....

Step 3 C. ....

Detail 1. ....

Detail 2. ....

Step 4 D. ....

Detail 1. ....

Detail 2. ....

(CONTINUED)

Step 5	E. ....
Detail	1. ....
Detail	2. ....

III. Concluding paragraph ....

Concluding Sentence
....

....

....

STEP 3: WRITE YOUR FIRST DRAFT

Now it is time to write your first draft. Here are some suggestions to help you get started.

1 Use your outline, notes, and the sentences you wrote in the Your Turns in this unit and in Step 2 on pages 221–222.

2 Focus on making your ideas as clear as possible.

3 Add a title.

After you finish, read your essay and check for basic errors.

1 Check that all sentences have subjects and verbs.

2 Check that your thesis statement, paragraph topic sentences, and supporting sentences are clear.

3 Check that you have enough supporting details for each step.

4 Check that you have used specific adjectives, pronoun references, and phrasal verbs correctly.

STEP 4: WRITE YOUR FINAL DRAFT

1 After you receive feedback on your first draft, review it carefully. Fix any errors.

2 Make a note of errors that were most frequent. Try to avoid them as you write.

3 Review the Academic Words and Collocations from this unit. Are there any that you can add to your essay?

4 Turn to page 261 and use the Self-Editing Review to check your work one more time.

5 Write your final draft and hand it in.

8 COMPARISON AND CONTRAST ESSAYS

FINANCE: PERSONAL FINANCE

"A man who both spends and saves money is the happiest man because he has both enjoyments."

Samuel Johnson
(1709–1784)

About the Author:

Samuel Johnson was an English writer and philosopher. He wrote about many subjects, including literature and economics.

Work with a partner. Read the quotation about money. Then answer the questions.

1 Samuel Johnson wrote these words in the eighteenth century. Do you think his words are still true today?

2 What enjoyments do people get from spending money? What about from saving money?

3 Do you think it is more enjoyable to spend or save? Why?

Ⓐ Connect to Academic Writing

In this unit, you will learn how to write a comparison and contrast essay. Some of the skills may seem new to you, but the skill of making comparisons is not new. In your everyday life, you compare subjects when you decide whether to take the bus or walk to school, or when you decide whether you prefer the book or movie version of your favorite story.

Ⓑ Reflect on the Topic

In this section, you will choose a writing prompt and reflect on it. You will develop ideas throughout the unit and use them to practice skills that you need to write your essay.

The writing prompt below was used for the Student Model essay on pages 230–231. The student reflected on his topic and used a Venn diagram to brainstorm possible ideas for his essay.

STUDENT MODEL

WRITING PROMPT: Some students are full-time students. Some students only study part-time and work the rest of the time. Compare studying full-time to studying part-time while working.

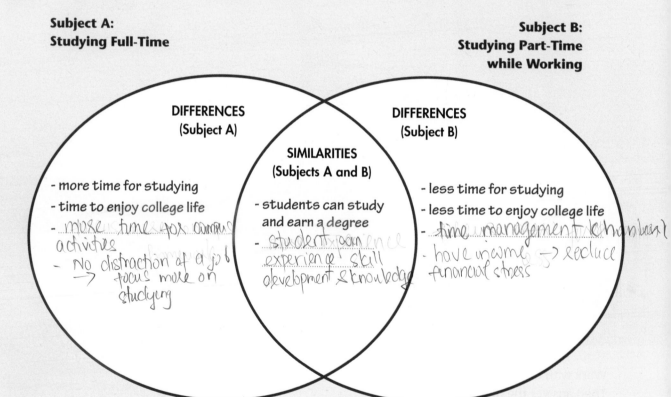

Subject A:
Studying Full-Time

Subject B:
Studying Part-Time
while Working

DIFFERENCES
(Subject A)

SIMILARITIES
(Subjects A and B)

DIFFERENCES
(Subject B)

- more time for studying
- time to enjoy college life
- more time for campus activities
- No distraction of a job → focus more on studying

- students can study and earn a degree
- students can experience skill development & knowledge

- less time for studying
- less time to enjoy college life
- time management techniques
- have income → reduce financial stress

1.1 Notice

Work with a partner. Look at the Venn diagram again. Discuss one more similarity and one more difference and add it to the diagram. Share your ideas with the class.

1.2 Apply It to Your Writing

A Choose a prompt for your essay.

- Compare two products that you are familiar with. For example, compare the costs, the customers who buy them, or their value.

- Compare the spending habits of two people that you know. For example, compare how much they spend, what they spend their money on, and where they spend it.

- Compare two ways to buy a product For example, compare buying something in a store and buying something online.

- A topic approved by your instructor

B Brainstorm ideas and complete the Venn diagram below. Think of everything you know about the subjects you chose.

C Compare Venn diagrams with a partner.

Subject A: _buying online_

Subject B: _buying in store_

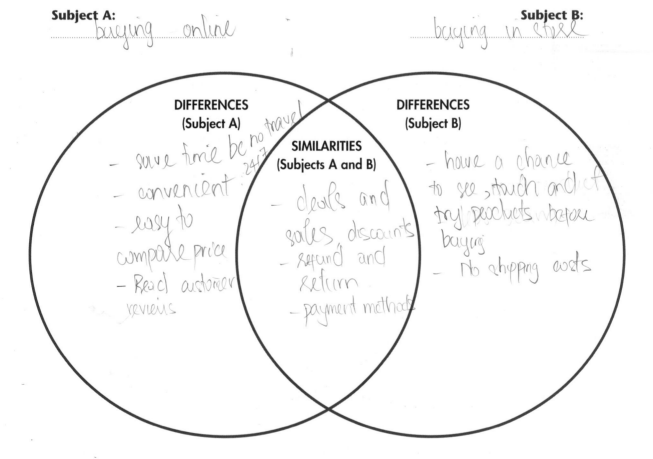

DIFFERENCES
(Subject A)

- save time bc no travel 24/7
- convenient
- easy to compare price
- Read customer reviews

SIMILARITIES
(Subjects A and B)

- deals and sales, discounts
- refund and return
- payment methods

DIFFERENCES
(Subject B)

- have a chance to see, touch and try products before buying
- No shipping costs

In this section, you will learn academic language that you can use in your comparison and contrast essay. You will also notice how a professional writer uses this language and writes about comparisons.

Ⓐ Academic Vocabulary

The words below appear throughout the unit. They are from the Academic Word List or the General Service List. Using these words in your writing will make your ideas clearer and your writing more academic.

| account (n) | credit (n) | expert (n) | income (n) |
| challenge (n) | debt (n) | finances (n) | payment (n) |

 2.1 Focus on Meaning

Work with a partner. Read the sentences. Match the words to their meanings. Write the letters.

A

.... 1 An online bank **account** is more convenient than a traditional one because people can see how much money they have at any time.

.... 2 Saving for college is a **challenge**. Many families find it difficult to save enough money for tuition costs.

.... 3 Many people use **credit** at stores. Credit lets them buy something immediately even though they do not have the money to pay for it at the time.

.... 4 Some people only use cash to buy things in order to avoid **debt**. They do not want to owe people money.

a money that you owe someone

b personal information, or money, that you allow a business to have so that it can provide services to you

c a way of buying something but paying for it later

d a difficult task

B

.... 1 Budgeting **experts** usually tell people to spend only the money that they actually have. These knowledgeable people know that this is the first step in having a balanced budget.

.... 2 Many people use apps on their phones to manage their **finances**. They can check the apps anytime to see how much money they have.

.... 3 Many students choose to work while going to school because they want an **income**. They use the money that they earn to pay for their tuition and books.

.... 4 Students who use loans to go to school will have to make **payments** for many years after they graduate.

a earned money

b the amount of money people have

c the amount of money you pay for something

d people with a lot of skill or knowledge in a subject

B Academic Phrases

Research tells us that the phrases in bold below are commonly used in academic writing.

 2.2 Focus on Purpose

Read the paragraph. Then match the phrases in bold with the purpose or reason why the writer used them.

Today's consumers **compared to** consumers of the past have more shopping choices than ever before. For generations, people had to go to a physical store to buy what they needed or wanted. Now shoppers have additional choices, **such as** shopping by mail, by phone, or online. Many businesses offer all of these options to their customers. However, **it is clear that** businesses are very interested in how customers feel about online shopping. They are constantly doing research to get information on the online shopping experience. This market research shows clear differences between shopping online and shopping in a store.

PHRASE	PURPOSE
.... 1 **compared to** consumers of the past	a to add specific examples
.... 2 **such as** shopping by mail, by phone, or online	b to introduce a conclusion
.... 3 **it is clear that** businesses are very interested in	c to compare two subjects

ⓒ Writing in the Real World

The author of "Marketing to Different Generations: X vs. Y" uses comparisons to talk about different generations.

Before you read, answer these questions: How can businesses make advertisements to interest people of different ages? What do you think *X* and *Y* mean in the title?

Now read the article. Think about your answers to the questions above as you read.

MARKETING TO DIFFERENT GENERATIONS: X VS. Y

BY MATTHEW BRYAN

1   To advertise the new name of a product, Kraft, an American food company, used social media. They created a two-minute YouTube video. In the video, *A.1. Steak Sauce* uses its Facebook **account** to break up with[1] steak. The video shows the sauce accepting "friend" requests from chicken, potato, and salmon,[2] as well as from other foods. Then *A.1. Steak Sauce* changes its relationship status to "It's complicated."[3] At the end of the video, the product changes its name to *A.1. Sauce* on its Facebook profile.

2   Kraft created the video in order to attract Millennial consumers. Millennials (Generation Y or Gen Y) are people born between 1980 and 2000. Kraft knows that this generation behaves differently from the previous[4] generation, Generation X (or Gen X). They eat and communicate differently. They also spend money differently.

3   Each generation has different ways of making financial decisions, according to **experts**. Changes in technology and economic **challenges**, for example, cause generations to behave differently. Because of the poor economy in recent years, many Millennials have more **debt** than Gen X. As a result, they use their **finances** differently.

[1]**break up with:** end a romantic relationship
[2]**salmon:** a type of fish
[3]**relationship status … "It's complicated.":** relationship status on Facebook lets people say whether they are married, single, or in another type of relationship; *It's complicated* often means a person is not sure about a relationship.

[4]**previous:** existing before someone/something else

4   Perhaps the most obvious difference between these generations is the way they use technology. Millennials use technology for almost everything. They use their phones to pay for coffee, and they use social media to communicate with friends and family. Millennials also use social media for information. Gen X, however, can remember life before the Internet or cell phones existed. They use technology in different ways. For example, they use search engines primarily to get information and email to connect with friends.

5   These differences affect the buying habits of the two generations. Typically, Gen X needs to have a lot of information to make a decision. As a result, they use the Internet to search for product information and do careful research before they make a purchase. Millennials, on the other hand, use social media to see what other people are buying. This is because they depend a lot on their peers'[5] and their families' opinions. They want products that help them fit in[6] with their friends or that their families recommend.

6   These differences explain why Kraft's *A.1. Sauce* YouTube video is effective for Millennial shoppers. Social media allows Millennials to learn about new products and to connect with other people at the same time. It gives them a way to communicate about and relate to products in a familiar environment. This marketing strategy may not work for Gen X. They are more likely to go to company websites to get detailed information about products.

7   Smart companies like Kraft advertise differently to different generations. As each new generation starts to buy products, consumers will most likely continue to see creative ads like the *A.1. Sauce* YouTube video.

[5]**peer:** someone of the same age or position
[6]**fit in:** feel that you belong to a group and are accepted by them

2.3 Check Your Understanding

Answer the questions.

1   The author describes a major difference between Gen X and Gen Y. What is the most obvious difference between these generations? How does the difference affect their spending habits?

2   Are you a part of the Millennial generation (Gen Y) or Gen X? Does your technology use affect your spending habits in the way the reading describes?

3   Imagine your clothing business is designing a marketing plan for a new pair of blue jeans. What advice would you give your company for targeting Gen X? What about Gen Y?

2.4 Notice the Features of Comparison and Contrast Writing

Answer the questions.

1   Look at the first paragraph. What is the purpose of this information? Why does the author include this information here?

2   Look at the fourth paragraph. What two subjects is the author comparing? What characteristic of the subjects is the author comparing?

3   Look at the fifth paragraph. Does the author discuss one or both subjects' buying habits in this paragraph?

In Section 1, you saw how the writer of the Student Model reflected on his topic. In this section, you will analyze the final draft of his essay. You will learn how to structure your ideas for your own essay.

Ⓐ Student Model

Read the writing prompt and answer the questions.

WRITING PROMPT: Some students are full-time students. Some students only study part-time and work the rest of the time. Compare studying full-time to studying part-time while working.

1 What two things is the prompt asking the writer to compare?

2 What similarities and differences could the writer describe?

Read the essay twice. The first time, think about your answers to the questions above. The second time, answer the questions in the Analyze Writing Skills boxes. This will help you notice key features of a comparison and contrast essay.

Paying for College

1   How long will it take to get a degree? How much will it cost? These questions are important for college students. College is expensive now. As a result, students today have to think about different ways to pay for college. For many students, there are only two solutions. They can study full-time and take out student loans, or they can study part-time and work. With both choices, students can study and earn a degree, but the choices are not the same for their lives now and in the future. Studying full-time and part-time are different because students will have different experiences, will graduate at different times, and will have different amounts of **debt** after graduation.

2   Full-time students and part-time students have different experiences. Full-time students can enjoy college life. They can take classes at any time, meet with other students, and participate in campus organizations. On the other hand, part-time students do not spend a lot of time at school. Their jobs take a lot of time and energy. They are very busy. Therefore, they have less time to socialize and participate in campus activities.

3   Another difference is the time that it takes to graduate. Full-time students usually graduate on time. This is because full-time students can take many classes each term[1] and finish more quickly. In contrast, part-time students take fewer classes each term because of their job commitments. As a result, they often have to go to school longer.

[1]**term:** a period of time in a school year (e.g., a quarter or a semester)

1 Analyze Writing Skills
Underline the questions at the beginning of the essay.

2 Analyze Writing Skills
Circle the two subjects that the writer is comparing.

3 Analyze Writing Skills
The last sentence of the introductory paragraph tells what the writer will talk about. Underline the three differences that the writer will discuss.

4 Analyze Writing Skills
Circle the difference that the writer will discuss in each body paragraph. Does the writer discuss this difference for one or both of the subjects in each paragraph?

4   The biggest difference is the amount of **debt** after graduation. Full-time students who do not work usually do not have an **income**. They use loans, or **credit**, to pay for their college tuition. For this reason, they will have loan **payments** for many years after they graduate. They may have **financial** problems later. On the other hand, part-time students can pay for the classes as they take them. They often have less **debt** after they graduate. Therefore, these graduates often are able to buy houses or cars or start a family before the people who studied full-time.

5   In conclusion, studying full-time and studying part-time are different in many important ways. Students enjoy school differently, complete school at different times, and have different amounts of **debt**. In my case, I chose to study part-time and work. It is good for me because, in the future, I want a nice house for my family.

5 Analyze Writing Skills

Underline the transition phrase that the writer uses to conclude the essay.

3.1 **Check Your Understanding**

Answer the questions.

1 According to the writer, what are the differences between full-time studying with loans and part-time studying while working?

2 What did the writer discover by comparing these two options for paying for college? Who would benefit from the information in this essay?

3 Do you agree or disagree with the writer's ideas? Why?

 3.2 **Outline the Writer's Ideas**

An outline helps you see the structure of the paragraph and the connection between ideas. Complete the outline for "Paying for College." Use the phrases in the box.

debt after graduation	graduate on time	participate in organizations
don't socialize as much	less debt	
enjoy college life	often have financial problems	

ESSAY OUTLINE

I. Introductory paragraph

Thesis Statement
Studying full-time and part-time are different because students will have different

experiences, will graduate at different times, and will have different amounts of debt after

graduation.

Body Paragraph 1
II. Student experience

Subject A
A. Full-time students

Detail
1. enjoy college life

Sub-detail
a. Take classes anytime

Sub-detail
b. Meet people

Sub-detail
c. participate in organizations

Subject B	B. Part-time students
Detail	1. Don't enjoy college life as much
Sub-detail	a. Very busy working
Sub-detail	b. don't socialize as much
Sub-detail	c. No time for school organizations
Body Paragraph 2	III. Time to graduate
Subject A	A. Full-time students
Detail	1. graduate on time
Sub-detail	a. Take many classes
Sub-detail	b. Finish quickly
Subject B	B. Part-time students
Detail	1. Go to school longer
Sub-detail	a. Take fewer classes
Sub-detail	b. Need time to work
Body Paragraph 3	IV. debt after graduation
Subject A	A. Full-time students
Detail	1. Have debt
Sub-detail	a. Need to repay loans
Sub-detail	b. often have financial problem

(CONTINUED)

Subject B	B. Part-time students
Detail	1. *less debt*
Sub-detail	a. No loans to repay
Sub-detail	b. Often can start a family earlier
Sub-detail	c. Can make big purchases sooner
	V. Concluding paragraph
Concluding Sentence	In conclusion, studying full-time and studying part-time are different in many important ways.

ⓑ Comparison and Contrast Essays

In a comparison and contrast essay, a writer shows how two subjects are the same and/or different. The comparison helps the reader see those subjects in a fresh way or discover something new about them. The writer chooses specific characteristics to compare. These characteristics help the reader understand the purpose for the comparison. One way to organize these characteristics is with **point-by-point organization**. In this way, the writer discusses each characteristic one at a time. Like with other essays, each paragraph in a point-by-point comparison and contrast essay has a specific purpose:

- The **introductory paragraph** provides background information and makes a thesis statement that names the subjects being compared. The thesis statement may list the points of comparison that will be discussed in the body paragraphs.

- Each **body paragraph** compares one **specific characteristic**, called a **point of comparison**, in both subjects.

- The **concluding paragraph** restates the thesis statement and summarizes the similarities or differences between the subjects. The writer often ends with a comment that gives an insight or a discovery that came from comparing the two subjects.

Work with a partner. Read the questions about the Student Model essay on pages 230–231. Circle the correct answers.

1 What background information does the writer include in the introductory paragraph?
   a the time and the cost of going to college
   b the importance of participating in campus activities

2 What is the point of comparison in body paragraph 1?
   a the time it takes to graduate
   b the experience of being a student

3 What is the point of comparison in body paragraph 2?
   a the number of classes needed to graduate
   b the time it takes to graduate

4 What is the point of comparison in body paragraph 3?
   a getting loans
   b having debt

5 What discovery does the writer make?
   a that being a part-time student is better
   b that enjoying campus life is the most important thing

POINTS OF COMPARISON

Writers must choose clear points of comparison in order to show the most important similarities and/or differences between two subjects. A point of comparison is a feature or characteristic that the subjects share. Writers use points of comparison to:

- support the thesis statement, such as in the Student Model essay. The writer focused on three features that both full-time and part-time students share (*experiences, time to graduate,* and *debt*). The writer's purpose was to show the challenges for each type of student, and the pros and cons.

- organize their essay logically. Writers focus on one point of comparison in each body paragraph and compare both subjects using that one point of comparison.

 **3.4** Write Points of Comparison

Work with a partner. Read the essay prompt. Then complete the activity.

WRITING PROMPT: Shoppers can choose to buy most products in a store or online. Compare these two shopping options.

Read the chart. Write two more points of comparison and complete the chart.

Points of Comparison	Subject A: Shopping in a Store	Subject B: Shopping Online
Body Paragraph 1: taxes	local sales taxes; almost always have to pay taxes	sales taxes vary by location of business and buyer; may not have to pay taxes
Body Paragraph 2:		
Body Paragraph 3:		

 3.5 Apply It to Your Writing

Look at the Venn diagram you created for your writing prompt in Section 1 on page 225. Think about your topic and the the two subjects you are comparing. Write one point of comparison and complete the chart for your two subjects.

Point of Comparison	Subject A:	Subject B:

INTRODUCTORY PARAGRAPH

The introductory paragraph in a comparison and contrast essay contains:

- background information that introduces the two subjects and helps the reader understand the purpose for comparing them.

- the thesis statement that tells the reader which two subjects the essay will compare and the points of comparison. Note that sometimes writers do not state the points of comparison.

The thesis statement should clearly show whether the essay will focus on similarities or differences. Following is common language that writers use to:

- Focus on **differences**:

  *It is clear that online shopping and traditional shopping **have some differences** that consumers should consider.* (no stated points of comparison)

Although both types of students can attend and graduate from college, they may have **different** experiences, graduate at different times, and have different amounts of debt. (stated points of comparison)

In contrast to Generation X, Generation Y makes decisions dependently, uses technology constantly, and eats differently. (stated points of comparison)

- Focus on **similarities**:

A tablet and a smartphone **may appear very different, but** they actually share some interesting similarities. (no stated points of comparison)

Although my siblings and I have very different personalities, it is clear that our spending habits **are quite similar**. (stated points of comparison)

Advertisements for fast-food restaurants **are similar to** cereal advertisements **because** they use the same techniques to target children with toys, bright colors, and cartoon characters. (stated points of comparison)

 3.6 Notice Introductory Paragraphs

A Read the introductory paragraph. Underline the sentences that provide background information.

What makes a person a saver instead of a spender? Psychologists continue to debate the factors that determine personality. Some experts argue that genetics decides our behaviors and attitudes. Others say that it is mainly environment that affects who we become. My brother and I have the same parents, but we grew up very differently. He grew up in the 1980s when our parents were poor, but I grew up in the 1990s when our family had a higher income. It is clear that this difference in our environments as children caused my brother and me to view money differently.

B Answer the questions about the paragraph in A.

1 What type of background information do the third and fourth sentences in the paragraph provide?

 a an explanation of an issue that will help the reader understand why the comparison is important

 b a story that will help the reader understand why the comparison is important

2 What type of background information do the fifth and sixth sentences in the paragraph provide?

 a background information on the subjects

 b an explanation of an issue that people associate with the subjects

3 Underline the thesis statement. What subjects will the essay compare?

 a life in the 1980s and life in the 1990s

 b the writer's view of money and his brother's view of money

ACTIVITY **3.7** Choose Thesis Statements

Work with a partner. Read the prompts and the thesis statements. (Notice that these thesis statements do not state the points of comparison.) Check (✓) the thesis statement that best answers the prompt and explain your answer.

1 **WRITING PROMPT:** There are many ways to make payments nowadays. For example, people can use cash, debit cards, credit cards, or online accounts such as PayPal. These options have different security concerns. Choose two payment options and compare them. Which one is safer for people to use?

☐ Focusing on the similarities and differences between cash and credit cards can help people decide which payment option is safer.

☐ When people pay for something, they can choose different payment options, for example cash or credit cards.

2 **WRITING PROMPT:** Some people argue that shoppers should support their community by only buying products from local companies. Compare shopping locally with shopping at large national or global chain stores. What do consumers need to know about these options?

☐ Shopping at local stores and shopping at large national chain stores have some clear differences that consumers should consider when deciding where to buy products.

☐ Consumers should realize that shopping nationally or globally does not support the local economy or help the environment.

 **3.8** Write Thesis Statements

Work with a partner. Complete the thesis statements for these prompts with another point of comparison.

1 **WRITING PROMPT:** Compare advertising styles for two different types of companies or products.

   Thesis statement: Commercials for cell phones are similar to commercials for food because they both show family situations, have memorable music, and _use attractive actors_ .

2 **WRITING PROMPT:** Compare online college classes with traditional college classes.

   Thesis statement: Although there are some differences between online classes and traditional classes, both help students learn new material, let students interact with each other, and _develop necessary skills_

3 **WRITING PROMPT:** Compare the financial attitudes of two generations.

   Thesis statement: Although both my generation and my parents' generation take finances seriously, we are different in the amount of debt we have, how we save money, and _How we pay money for_

 3.9 Apply It to Your Writing

Write a thesis statement for your comparison and contrast essay. Be sure to show whether you will discuss similarities or differences. Include your points of comparison.

Even though tothll

BODY PARAGRAPHS WITH POINT-BY-POINT ORGANIZATION

A point-by-point comparison and contrast essay will have one body paragraph for each point of comparison. Each paragraph will:

• begin with a **topic sentence** that states the point of comparison.

• discuss the **point of comparison** for Subject A with supporting details, examples, or explanations.

• discuss the **point of comparison** for Subject B with supporting details, examples, or explanations.

Writers can use these words or phrases to introduce the point of comparison in the topic sentence:

One similarity/difference between my brother and me is how comfortable we are spending money.

Another similarity/difference between fast-food advertisements and cereal advertisements is that they target children by offering a free toy with their products.

The most important similarity/difference between studying full-time with loans and studying part-time while working is the amount of debt students will have after graduating.

Finally, customers who pay by mail are the same as those who pay by phone because they do not want to shop in stores.

 3.10 Notice Point-by-Point Organization

Read the body paragraph from an essay comparing the similarities between two businesses' marketing strategies. Then outline the paragraph.

One similarity between the fast-food restaurants Wendy's and Kentucky Fried Chicken (KFC) is how they are changing their menus to target Millennial consumers. Wendy's is trying new menu items, such as a Pretzel Bacon Cheeseburger. Wendy's wants food that seems higher in quality because their research shows that Millennials prefer "fast-casual" restaurants instead of fast-food restaurants. Similarly, KFC is also testing a new menu in order to target Millennials. They are going to change some restaurants from KFC to KFC Eleven. A KFC Eleven will have a special menu of boneless wings. KFC thinks this will attract Millennials who have grown up eating chicken nuggets.

Body Paragraph 1: (point of comparison) ....
    A. (subject A) ....
        1. (example) ....
        2. (explanation) ....
    B. (subject B) ....
        1. (example) ....
        2. (explanation) ....

3.11 Write Topic Sentences

Read the thesis statements. Identify the points of comparison. Use each point of comparison to write a topic sentence.

1 **Thesis statement:** Traditional banking is similar to online banking in several ways: It offers the same choice of banks, account types, and interest rates.

Topic sentence for body paragraph 1: *One similarity between traditional banking and online banking is the choice of banks that customers have.*

Topic sentence for body paragraph 2: ....

....

Topic sentence for body paragraph 3: ....

....

2 **Thesis statement:** Online shopping and traditional shopping have some clear differences, such as the type of interaction with the products, the type of information consumers can get about the product, and the amount and type of interaction with the sales staff.

Topic sentence for body paragraph 1: ....

....

Topic sentence for body paragraph 2: ....

....

Topic sentence for body paragraph 3: ....

....

3.12 Write Body Paragraphs

Work with a partner. Read the essay prompt. Then complete the activities.

WRITING PROMPT: People purchase many expensive products that they need to use on a daily basis, such as cars, cell phones, or computers. Compare two different models of the same product, such as two cell phones. Do they have similar or different features?

1 Decide on a product and one specific feature for your first point of comparison.

2 Complete the outline for your first point of comparison.

BODY PARAGRAPH OUTLINE

Body Paragraph 1: (point of comparison) ....

    A. (subject A) ....

        1. (example) ....

        2. (explanation) ....

    B. (subject B) ....

        1. (example) ....

        2. (explanation) ....

3 On a separate sheet of paper, write the first body paragraph about your point of comparison. Use the outline from page 241. Write a topic sentence that states the point of comparison. Discuss the point of comparison. Include supporting details, examples, and explanations for each product.

CONCLUDING PARAGRAPHS

The concluding paragraph of a comparison and contrast essay is brief, but it has three purposes:

- Restate the thesis statement in one sentence.

- Summarize the similarities and differences in one or two sentences.

- Give a comment that provides an insight or a discovery in a few sentences. The comment is the most important part of the concluding paragraph. This comment tells the reader what the writer has learned or realized about the subjects through comparing them. The comment may be:

Advice: *Going to school part-time and working can be a challenge. However, part-time students who work should not get discouraged. They should look forward to the freedom that they will have from less debt.*

A question: *Will fast-food restaurants' marketing efforts attract more Millennial consumers?*

A prediction: *Businesses that continue to offer both online and in-store options will attract more customers.*

 3.13 Notice Concluding Paragraphs

Read the concluding paragraph from the Student Model essay on pages 230–231. Then match the sentences to their purposes.

(1) In conclusion, studying full-time and studying part-time are different in many important ways. (2) Students enjoy school differently, do not complete school at the same time, and have different amounts of debt. (3) I chose to study part-time and work. (4) It is good for me because in the future I want a nice house for my family.

Sentence	Purpose
.... 1 Sentence 1	a end the essay with a comment
.... 2 Sentence 2	b restate the thesis statement
.... 3 Sentences 3 and 4	c summarize the comparison

Ⓐ Writing Skill: Hooks

A **hook** is usually the first one or two sentences in the introductory paragraph. Its purpose is to make the reader want to read the essay. A hook is not a thesis statement. A hook can be:

1 an interesting quotation

> *The journalist and author Malcolm Gladwell once wrote, "Any fool can spend money. But to earn it and save it and defer gratification – then you learn to value it differently."*

2 a relevant short story

> *The funniest place Donna Freedman ever found change was under a couch cushion. This may not seem unusual, except this sofa was sitting on the street with a "free" sign on it! Freedman, a writer for MSN Money, has a habit of saving coins that she finds on the street or in other places.*

3 an important or surprising statistic

> *Student loan debt is now larger than credit card debt in the United States. Americans' total student loan debt is over $1 trillion.*

4 a significant question or two

> *What makes a person a saver instead of a spender? Psychologists continue to debate about what shapes people.*

ACTIVITY 4.1 Examine Hooks

Work with a partner. Find the hook in the article on pages 228–229 and the Student Model essay on pages 230–231. Referring to the list above, write the number and type of hook used.

Writing in the Real World: ....

Student Model: ....

 **4.2** Use Hooks

Work with a partner. Read the introductory paragraph below.

"An iPod, a phone, an Internet mobile communicator … these are NOT three separate devices! And we are calling it iPhone!" With these words, Steve Jobs introduced the world to the iPhone in 2007. Now, consumers can purchase other multi-function devices besides smartphones. Some still prefer smartphones, such as the iPhone, but others argue that a tablet is more useful and, therefore, a smarter purchase. A tablet and a smartphone may appear very different, but the products actually share some interesting similarities.

A Complete the activities.

1 Underline the hook in the introductory paragraph.

2 This hook is an example of a:

   a short story   b statistic   c question   d quotation

3 Do you think this is an effective hook for this comparison and contrast essay? Why or why not?

B Write a hook for the introductory paragraph below. Share your idea with the class and discuss which hooks are the most effective way to start the essay.

....

....

Marketers create advertisements that target children. Two products that commonly have advertisements directed at children are fast-food restaurants and cereal companies. The advertisements for fast-food restaurants are similar to cereal advertisements because they use the same techniques to target children with toys, bright colors, and cartoon characters.

 4.3 Apply It to Your Writing

Look at your Venn diagram in Section 1 on page 225 and the thesis statement in Activity 3.9 on page 239. Is there a quotation, question, statistic, or short story that will make your reader want to read your essay? Write some ideas for hooks.

....

....

....

....

....

B Grammar for Writing: Comparative Adjectives

Writers often use **comparative adjectives** to show how two subjects are different. Follow these rules when using comparative adjectives.

COMPARATIVE ADJECTIVES	
1 Follow these spelling rules:	
a Add -er to one-syllable adjectives, such as *high, fast, long.*	A college graduate's income is usually **higher** than the income of someone who did not get a college degree.
b Change the -y to -ier for two-syllable adjectives ending in -y, such as *busy, easy, heavy.*	Students who work and go to school are **busier** than students who do not work.
c Use *more* with most adjectives that have more than one syllable, such as *convenient, expensive, important.*	Shopping online is **more convenient** than shopping in a store.
d Use *less* to talk about the opposite of *more.*	Gen X is **less dependent** on their family and friends than Gen Y.
2 *Less* is not usually used with one-syllable adjectives, except *clear, safe,* and *sure.* Use *not as* + adjective + *as* instead of *less* with one-syllable adjectives.	After college, Gen Y is **less sure than** Gen X was about getting married and having a family. My student loan debt is **not as high as** my husband's because I worked part-time while I went to college.
3 Some comparative adjectives are irregular: good → better bad → worse	In my brother's opinion, spending money is **better** than saving it. In my opinion, spending money is **worse** than saving it.
4 When using *than*, writers can:	
a Use a subject pronoun + verb after *than* if they do not want to repeat the noun.	My brother is a spender. I am better **than he is** at saving money.
b Omit the verb after *than* when both verbs are the same (or use an auxiliary verb).	I save money **better than my brother saves money.** I save money **better than my brother (does).**
c Omit *than* + the second part of the comparison when the meaning is clear.	Gen X has to do a lot of research before making a purchase. For this reason, when making a big purchase, Gen X **is** often **slower (than Gen Y).**
d Use a comparative adjective without *than* before a noun when the comparison is clear.	Some fast-food restaurants are offering **more creative products** in order to reach Millenials. (Their products are **more creative than** other fast-food restaurants' products.)

4.4 Use Comparatives

Work with a partner. Complete the sentences. Use the correct comparative forms of the adjectives in parentheses.

1 When comparing fast-food choices, Gen Y is .... (healthy) Gen X.

2 Buying a car online can be .... (fast) buying a car from a dealership because you do not have to visit different places to get information.

3 Online options from car dealerships are .... (common) in the past, since so many customers want to buy cars online.

4 Some people argue that smartphones are .... (good) tablets. For example, smartphones are much .... (small) tablets are.

5 Some experts argue that part-time students are .... (successful) full-time students at managing their time because part-time students are often too busy to waste time.

Avoiding Common Mistakes

Research tells us that these are the most common mistakes that students make when using comparative adjectives in academic writing.

1. **Do not use a comparative when you are not comparing two subjects.**

   It is ~~more~~ important to keep track of your credit score.

2. **Use *than*, not *that*, after a comparative.**

   than
   It is easy to spend more ~~that~~ you can afford.

3. **Do not use *-er* and *more* with the same adjective.**

   Their new house is ~~more~~ bigger than their old house.

 4.5 Editing Task

Find and correct five more mistakes in the paragraph below.

The most important difference between using a credit card and using cash is that cash is
harder
~~more harder~~ to spend than credit cards. For that reason, many financial advisors argue that
using cash is more better than using credit cards. Experts have found that shoppers make more
purchases when they use credit cards. There is a psychological reason for this. It is more easy
to swipe a credit card to buy something. This action does not make people feel like they are
spending money. On the other hand, studies show that people who use cash spend less. Cash
feels more real that credit cards, so people treat it differently. Most people try to keep cash.
They find cash more difficult to use that credit. People who are trying to save money may find
that using cash is helpful than using credit cards.

C Avoiding Plagiarism

Writing someone else's ideas in your own words can be hard.

When my instructor returned the draft of my essay about the differences in advertising between two companies, she said I was plagiarizing someone's work. I know I didn't! I changed words from my source's sentences, so I was not copying word for word. What did I do wrong?

Tenzin

Dear Tenzin,

This is a common problem. Your instructor knows your writing. She knows when the writing doesn't look like your own. Sometimes you need to do more than change a few words. You can also change the order of the words in the sentence, or you can change the forms of some of the words. You never want to change the meaning, though.

Hope this is helpful!

Professor Wright

STRATEGIES FOR PARAPHRASING

When writers paraphrase, they rewrite someone else's sentence or idea by using their own words. There are several ways to do this. Let's look at some of these ways.

First, read the original text:

Original text: Students spend more than $11 billion a year on snacks and beverages. Even students who live in the dorms and have meal plans spend a lot of money eating out.

Then use some of these strategies to help you paraphrase.

Paraphrase Strategies	Examples
Change words or phrases to synonyms.	Students **pay** more than $11 billion **each** year for snacks and **drinks**.
Change the order of words.	Many students **go out to eat** even if they **live in a dorm**.
Change the form of some words.	Student **spending** is more than $11 billion **yearly** on snacks and drinks. Students in dorms often **eat out**.
Change a quote to indirect speech. "Parents should absolutely make their college kids get a part-time job," says Kobliner.	**Kobliner states that** parents should be sure their children work part-time while they are in college.

4.6 Identify the Strategies

Work with a partner. Read the original text and the paraphrase. Write the three paraphrase strategies the writer used.

Original text: Millennials are drawn to more urban, walkable neighborhoods, unlike their suburban parents. They are more willing to use public transportation, bike sharing, and car sharing to get around.

Paraphrase: While their parents prefer the suburbs, people born between 1980 and 2000 prefer the city. They are comfortable getting around on public buses or subways, or sharing bicycles and cars.

1 ....

2 ....

3 ....

 4.7 Practice

Work with a partner. Read the original text. Then follow the steps to write a paraphrase.

Original text: The typical college student gets an average of $757 a month from jobs, parents, or other sources. Most money comes from work. Seventy-five percent of students maintain jobs while attending school, earning $645 per month on average.

Step 1. Tell your partner what you read. Don't look at the text. Use your own words.

Step 2. Read the text again. Circle the words that you can change to synonyms. Write a synonym above each circled word.

Step 3. Change the order of the words.

Step 4. Write a paraphrase.

....

....

....

....

....

In this section, you will follow the writing process to complete the final draft of your comparison and contrast essay.

STEP 1: BRAINSTORM

Work with a partner. Follow the steps below to brainstorm more ideas for your topic.

a Before you start, read the student's Venn diagram. He wrote ideas from the Venn diagram he used to reflect on this topic in Section 1 on page 224. Then he brainstormed more ideas. Finally, he crossed out the ideas that were the least strong, the least interesting, or not relevant.

STUDENT MODEL

Subject A:
Studying Full-Time

Subject B:
Studying Part-Time
while Working

DIFFERENCES
(Subject A)

- enjoy college life: take classes any time, meet other students, participate in campus activities, take vacations during school breaks
- can take many classes each term and graduate on time
- no income; may use loans or credit for school; have debt often in debt after graduating

SIMILARITIES
(Subjects A and B)
- students can study and earn a degree

DIFFERENCES
(Subject B)

- less time at school, busy with work, less time to socialize and participate in campus activities; have trouble making friends
- have to take fewer classes because of work; often has to go to school longer
- have an income; less debt after they graduate; can get married and buy house sooner

2 Now read your writing prompt again. Then review the ideas you brainstormed in Section 1 on page 225. Write the best ones in the diagram below. Include ideas from the Your Turns throughout the unit. Finally, brainstorm more ideas. You will probably not use every idea, but it is good to write as many ideas as possible.

Subject A: ....

Subject B: ....

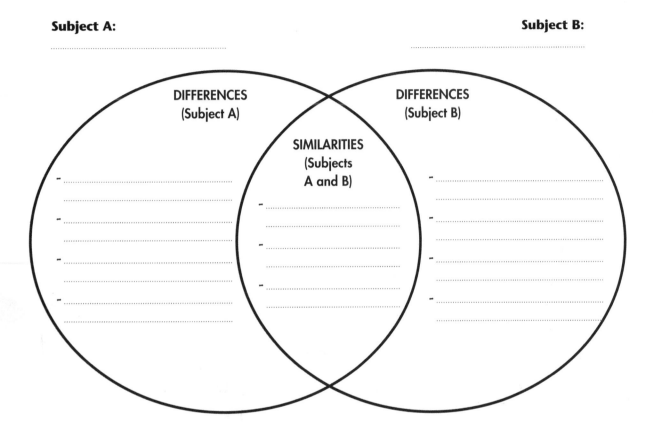

DIFFERENCES
(Subject A)

DIFFERENCES
(Subject B)

SIMILARITIES
(Subjects
A and B)

STEP 2: MAKE AN OUTLINE

Complete the outline below with the ideas from Step 1 on page 251.

ESSAY OUTLINE

I. Introductory paragraph ....

Thesis Statement ....

....

Body Paragraph 1   II. ....

Subject A   A. ....

Detail   1. ....

Sub-detail   a. ....

Sub-detail   b. ....

Subject B   B. ....

Detail   1. ....

Sub-detail   a. ....

Sub-detail   b. ....

Body Paragraph 2   III. ....

Sub-detail   A. ....

Detail   1. ....

Sub-detail   a. ....

Sub-detail   b. ....

Subject B	B. ....
Detail	1. ....
Sub-detail	a. ....
Sub-detail	b. ....
Body Paragraph 3	IV. ....
Sub-detail	A. ....
Detail	1. ....
Sub-detail	a. ....
Sub-detail	b. ....
Subject B	B. ....
Detail	1. ....
Sub-detail	a. ....
Sub-detail	b. ....
	V. Concluding paragraph ....
Concluding Sentence	....
	....

STEP 3: WRITE YOUR FIRST DRAFT

Now it is time to write your first draft. Here are some suggestions to help you get started.

1 Use your outline, notes, and the sentences you wrote in the Your Turns in this unit and in Step 2 on pages 252–253.

2 Focus on making your ideas as clear as possible.

3 Add a title.

After you finish, read your essay and check for basic errors.

1 Check that all sentences have subjects and verbs.

2 Check that you have used comparative adjectives correctly.

3 Check that you focus on one point of comparison in each body paragraph.

4 Check that your topic sentence and supporting sentences are clear.

STEP 4: WRITE YOUR FINAL DRAFT

1 After you receive feedback on your first draft, review it carefully. Fix any errors.

2 Make a note of errors that were most frequent. Try to avoid them as you write.

3 Review the Academic Words and Academic Phrases from this unit. Are there any that you can add to your essay?

4 Turn to page 262 and use the Self-Editing Review to check your work one more time.

5 Write your final draft and hand it in.

SELF-EDITING REVIEW

1 PARAGRAPHS EDUCATION: BRAINPOWER

Self-Editing: Review Your Work	Completed
1 Check your paragraph one last time. Include a topic sentence, three supporting sentences, specific details, and a concluding sentence.	
2 Make your paragraph appropriate for an academic audience.	
3 Use capitalization and punctuation correctly.	
4 Add a title.	
5 Underline the Academic Vocabulary words and collocations you used. Make sure you used at least two academic vocabulary words and one academic collocation.	
6 Underline your adverb clauses and make sure you avoided any mistakes.	
7 Review any feedback and think about mistakes that you typically make, such as using the wrong verb tense or form of the verb, using commas instead of periods, or missing *a/an* and *the*. Make a list of your common mistakes here: .... Look for these mistakes in your writing and correct them.	

Self-Editing: Review Your Work	Completed
1 Check your paragraph one last time. Read the writing prompt and your topic sentence again. Make sure your topic sentence addresses the writing topic.	
2 Check your paragraph for coherence and unity.	
3 Use transition words correctly to make the flow of ideas clear.	
4 Underline the Academic Vocabulary words and phrases. Make sure you use at least two academic vocabulary words and one academic phrase.	
6 Underline the subjects and verbs. Make sure they agree.	
7 Underline the quantifiers in your sentence and make sure you avoided any mistakes.	
8 Review any feedback and think about mistakes that you typically make, such as using the wrong verb tense or form of the verb, using commas instead of periods or missing *a/an* and *the*. Make a list of your common mistakes here: .... Look for these mistakes in your writing and correct them.	

Self-Editing: Review Your Work	Completed
1 Read the paragraph prompt again. Then read your topic sentence. Make sure your topic sentence addresses the writing topic.	
2 Reread your description. Make sure you used vivid language to describe your subject.	
3 Make sure that your sentences are complete. Check each sentence for fragments, run-ons, or comma splices.	
4 Check your paragraph for correct pronoun use.	
5 Underline the Academic Vocabulary words and collocations. Make sure you use at least two academic vocabulary words and one collocation.	
6 Use adjectives ending in -ed or -ing correctly.	
7 Check for proper adjectives.	
8 Review any feedback and think about mistakes that you typically make, such as using the wrong verb tense or form of the verb or missing a/an and the. Make a list of your common mistakes here: .... Look for these mistakes in your writing and correct them.	

Self-Editing: Review Your Work	Completed
1 Check your paragraph one last time. Read the writing prompt and your topic sentence again. Make sure your topic sentence addresses the writing topic.	
2 Reread your supporting sentences. Make sure that you used specific explanations and examples to support your ideas. Make sure you used facts to explain them.	
3 Make sure that your sentences are complete. Check each sentence for fragments, run-ons, or commas splices.	
4 Underline the Academic Vocabulary words and phrases that you used. Make sure you used at least two words and one academic phrase.	
5 Make sure that all of your verb forms are consistent.	
6 Check your count and noncount nouns. Make sure that you used determiners correctly.	
7 Check your sentences for *and, but, or*, and *so*. Add commas where necessary.	
8 Review any feedback and think about mistakes that you typically make, such as using the wrong verb tense or form or missing *a/an* and *the*. Make a list of your common mistakes here: .... Look for these mistakes in your writing and correct them.	

5 INTRODUCTION TO THE ESSAY: OPINION ESSAYS PSYCHOLOGY: CREATIVITY

Self-Editing: Review Your Work	Completed
1 Check your essay one last time. Make sure there is an introductory paragraph, three body paragraphs, and a concluding paragraph.	
2 Make sure your introductory paragraph includes background information and a thesis statement.	
3 Make sure your thesis statement includes your opinon and reasons for your opinion.	
4 Check that each body paragraph is about a different reason from your thesis statement.	
5 Underline the Academic Vocabulary words and collocations you used. Make sure you used at least two words and one collocation.	
6 Underline words with suffixes you used, and make sure you used the correct word form.	
7 Review any feedback and think about mistakes that you typically make, such as using the wrong verb tense or form of the verb, using commas instead of periods, or missing *a/an* and *the*. Make a list of your common mistakes here: .... Look for these mistakes in your writing and correct them.	

Self-Editing: Review Your Work	Completed
1 Check your essay one last time. Make sure there is an introductory paragraph, three body paragraphs, and a concluding paragraph.	
2 Make sure your introductory paragraph includes background information and a thesis statement.	
3 Make sure your thesis statement includes the topic and categories for your classification essay.	
4 Check the points of classification in each paragraph. Be sure they are relevant for the topic, and that you use the same points in each paragraph.	
5 Underline the Academic Vocabulary words and phrases you used. Make sure you used at least two words and one phrase.	
6 Underline verbs in the simple present and present progressive and make sure you have used them correctly.	
7 Review any feedback and think about mistakes that you typically make, such as using the wrong verb tense or form, using commas instead of periods, or missing *a/an* and *the*. Make a list of your common mistakes here: .... Look for these mistakes in your writing and correct them.	

Self-Editing: Review Your Work	Completed
1 Check your essay one last time. Make sure there is an introductory paragraph, appropriate body paragraphs, and a concluding paragraph.	
2 Reread your supporting sentences. Use transitions to show chronological order. Make sure they include enough details to help the reader understand your steps.	
3 Reread your concluding paragraph. Did you introduce it with a transition? Did you restate the main idea of your essay and conclude with a suggestion, opinion, or a prediction?	
4 Underline the Academic Vocabulary words and collocations you used. Make sure you used at least two words and one collocation.	
5 Underline any phrasal verbs and make sure you avoided any mistakes.	
6 Make sure your sentences and paragraphs are clear. Use specific adjectives. Make sure your pronoun references are accurate.	
7 Review any feedback and think about mistakes that you typically make, such as using the wrong verb form, using commas instead of periods, or missing *a/an* and *the*. Make a list of your common mistakes here: .... Look for these mistakes in your writing and correct them.	

Self-Editing: Review Your Work	Completed
1 Check your essay one last time. Make sure that your thesis statement is clear and answers the essay prompt.	
2 Make sure you started with a hook that makes your reader want to read your essay.	
3 Reread your body paragraphs. Check that there is one body paragraph for each point of comparison. Make sure each paragraph begins with a topic sentence that states the point of comparison.	
4 Reread your supporting sentences. Be sure they include details, examples, and explanations for the point of comparison.	
5 Underline the Academic Vocabulary words and phrases you used. Make sure you used at least two words and one phrase.	
6 Underline your comparative adjectives and make sure you avoided any mistakes.	
7 Review any feedback and think about the mistakes that you typically make, such as using the wrong verb tense or form of the verb, using commas instead of periods, or missing *a/an* and *the*. Make a list of your common mistakes here: .... Look for these mistakes in your writing and correct them.	

SOURCES

The following sources were consulted during the development of Final Draft *Student's Book 2.*

UNIT 1

"Lang Lang Talks Practising." News. *Classic FM*. This is Global Limited 2015, n.d. Web. 31 Mar. 2015.

Robinson, Lawrence, Jeanne Segal, and Melinda Smith. "How Exercise Benefits Depression, Anxiety, and Stress: Using Physical Activity to Improve Your Mental Health." *Helpguide.org*. Helpguide.org, Feb. 2015. Web. 31 Mar. 2015.

UNIT 2

Bjorseth, Lilllian D. "Business Body Language: Handshakes, Eye Contact, Posture, and Smiles." *The Sideroad*. Blue Boulder Internet Publishing, n.d. Web. 31 Mar. 2015.

"Eight Surprisingly Rude Gestures to Avoid When Travelling." Travel. *News.com.au*. News.com.au, 21 Nov. 2013. Web. 31 Mar. 2015.

"Kiss, Hug, or Shake Hands?" Online Posting. *PocketCultures*. PocketCultures, n.d. Web. 31 Mar. 2015.

Nakao Hones, Jenny. "The Asian Custom of Removing Shoes at the Door." *Asian Lifestyle Design: Food Culture, and Design*. Asian Lifestyle Designs, 11 Apr. 2010. Web. 31 Mar. 2015.

Singleton, Bonnie. "Proper Place Setting." *eHow*. Demand Media Inc., n.d. Web. 31 Mar. 2015.

UNIT 3

"Influenza (Flue)." Health Library. *Johns Hopkins Medicine*. Johns Hopkins University, n.d. Web. 31 Mar. 2015.

Taylor, Timothy. "Analogies for America: Beyond the Melting Pot." *StarTribune*. StarTribune, 29 June 2013. Web. 31 Mar. 2015.

"The U.S. Government and Global Malaria." Fact Sheet. *Global Health Policy*. Kaiser Family Foundation. 27 Mar. 2015. Web. 31 Mar. 2015.

UNIT 4

Brown, Anna. "Perceptions about Women Bosses Improve, but Gap Remains." *Pew Research Center*. Pew Research Center, 7 Aug. 2014. Web. 31 Mar. 2015.

Goldman, Alexandra. "Curbing the Google Bus." Opinion. *Aljazeera America*. Aljazeera America, 5 Feb. 2014. Web. 31 Mar. 2015.

New York. Dept. of Labor. "Minimum Wages." *Labor Standards*. N.Y. Dept. of Labor, n.d. Web. 31 Mar. 2015.

United States. Dept. of Labor. "How Are Vacation Pay, Sick Pay and Holiday Pay Computed and When Are They Due?" *elaws—Fair Labor Standards Act Advisor*. U.S. Dept. of Labor, n.d. Web. 31 Mar. 2015.

Wong, Venessa. "Ending the Tyranny of the Open-Plan Office." *Bloomberg Business*. Bloomberg LP, 1 July 2013. Web. 31 Mar. 2015.

UNIT 5

Bartel, Marvin. *Eleven Classroom Creativity Killers*. Goshen College, 4 Dec. 2014. Web. 31 Mar. 2015.

Collins, Glenn. "Exploring the Past: Creativity in Old Age." Style. *New York Times*. New York Times, 2 Mar. 1981. Web. 31 Mar. 2015.

Department of European Paintings. "Vincent van Gogh (1853–1890)" *Heilbrunn Timeline of Art History*. Metropolitan Museum of Art. Mar. 2010. Web. 31 Mar. 2015.

"*Fountain* (Duchamp)." *Wikipedia*. Wikipedia, n.d. Web. 31 Mar. 2015.

"Interview with Mr. Harold Secord, Sr.": *The Oral History of the Principalship*. Virgina Tech New Media Center, 11 Feb. 1989. Web. 31 Mar. 2015.

Graham, Kathy. "In Their Words: Mihaly Csikszentmihalyi and the Creative Personality." *Happy + Well*. Happy + Well, 31 Mar. 2014. Web. 31 Mar. 2015.

Johnson, Christopher M., and Jenny E. Memmott. "Examination of Relationships between Participation in School Music Programs of Differing Quality and Standardized Test Results." *Journal of Research in Music Education* 54.4 (2006), 293–307. Print.

"Jonathan Ive." Designers. *Design and Designers*. Design Museum, n.d. Web. 31 Mar. 2015.

"*My Bed*." *Wikipedia*. Wikipedia, n.d. Web. 31 Mar. 2015.

"National Endowment for the Arts to Award More Than $74 Million to U.S. Nonprofits." News. *National Endowment for the Arts*. National Endowment for the Arts, 16 Apr. 2014. Web. 31 Mar. 2015.

Pierce, Stacia. "Why Writing Lists Is Still Relevant and Important." *LifeCoach2Women.com*. Ultimate Lifestyle Enterprise, n.d. Web. 31 Mar. 2015.

Root-Berstein, Michele, and Robert Root-Bernstein. "Can Creativity Be Taught? Creative Outcomes in the Classroom Can't Be Mandated." *Psychology Today*. Sussex Publishers, 2011. Web. 31 Mar. 2015.

Schellenberg, E. Glenn. "Music Lessons Enhance IQ." *Psychological Science* 15.8 (2004), 511–14. Web. 31 Mar. 2015.

Smith, Fran. "Why Arts Education Is Crucial, and Who's Doing It Best." *Edutopia*. George Lucas Educational Foundation, 28 Jan. 2009. Web. 31 Mar. 2015.

Zielinski, Sarah. "5 Ways to Spark Your Creativity." *Joe's Big Idea*. Natl. Public Radio, 21 June 2012. Web. 31 Mar. 2015.

UNIT 6

Barclay, Laurie. "Fighting Depression and Improving Cognition with Omega-3 Fatty Acids." *Life Extension Magazine*. Life Extension, Oct. 2007. Web. 31 Mar. 2015.

Lappé, Frances Moore. *Diet for a Small Planet*. New York: Ballantine, 1971. Print.

"Myths and Facts about Caffeine." *Food Today*. European Food Information Council, Sept. 2002. Web. 31 Mar. 2015.

Rodale, Maria. "Kids Can Make Healthy Food Choices: Education Is Key." *Huff Post Food*. TheHuffingtonPost.com, Inc., 18 Aug. 2014. Web. 31 Mar. 2015.

UNIT 7

"About Us." *Medecins Sans Frontieres/Doctors without Borders*. MSF USA, n.d. Web. 31 Mar. 2015.

"Beading Program." Our Work. *Bead for Life*. BeadforLife, n.d. Web. 31 Mar. 2015.

"Hosting a Blood Drive." *American Red Cross*. American National Red Cross, n.d. Web. 31 Mar. 2015.

"Safe Water in Fiji and Zambia." *Habitat World*. Habitat for Humanity Intl., n.d. Web. 31 Mar. 2015.

TOMS. "How We Give Shoes: Step-by-Step." *Stories*. TOMS Shoes. 2 July 2013. Web. 31 Mar. 2015.

Tully, Kathy Shiels. "Volunteers Gleaning Fresh Produce for Those in Need." North. *Boston Globe*. Boston Globe Media Partners, 10 July 2014. Web. 31 Mar. 2015.

UNIT 8

"A Look at the Spending Habits of College Students." *StateUniversity.com*. StateUniversity.com, n.d. Web. 31 Mar. 2015.

Chopra, Rohit. "Student Debt Swells, Federal Loans Now Top a Trillion." *CFPB*. Consumer Financial Protection Bureau. 17 July 2013. Web. 31 Mar. 2015.

Gladwell, Malcolm. *David and Goliath: Underdogs, Misfits, and the Art of Battling Giants*. New York: Little, 2013. Print.

Jobs, Steve. "IPhone Keynote 2007." Tech. *Genius*. Genius Media Group, 2007. Web. 31 Mar. 2015.

Van Hoven, Matt. "A.1. Updates for the Facebook Generation." *Digiday*. Digiday, 14 May 2014. Web. 31 Mar. 2015.

INDEX

Words that are part of the Academic Word List are noted with an Ⓐ in this index.

TEXT CREDITS

The authors and publishers acknowledge the following sources of copyright material and are grateful for the permissions granted. While every effort has been made, it has not always been possible to identify the sources of all the material used, or to trace all copyright holders. If any omissions are brought to our notice, we will be happy to include the appropriate acknowledgements on reprinting.

Corpus

Development of this publication has made use of the Cambridge English Corpus (CEC). The CEC is a multi-billion word computer database of contemporary spoken and written English. It includes British English, American English and other varieties of English. It also includes the Cambridge Learner Corpus, developed in collaboration with the University of Cambridge ESOL Examinations. Cambridge University Press has built up the CEC to provide evidence about language use that helps to produce better language teaching materials.

ART CREDITS

NOTES